W9-BID-553

The Family Meal

Home cooking with Ferran Adrià

Φ

From elBulli to your kitchen

What is the family meal?

The family meal is the dinner eaten every day by the 75 members of staff at elBulli restaurant. We call it that because the staff members are like a family, and the family meal is an important moment when everyone sits down together to eat. You might assume that the staff would eat the same food as the guests, but they don't. In fact, people are often surprised when we tell them that we eat ordinary food.

Why is the family meal so important at elBulli? The answer is very simple: we believe that if we eat well, we cook well.

WHY THIS BOOK?

This book is the result of three years' work by Eugeni de Diego (one of the head chefs, and responsible for the family meal) and Ferran Adrià, who created and planned the recipes together. We thought it would be a shame for all this work to end up gathering dust in a drawer. Once we knew that elBulli would close on July 30, 2011, we decided to collect all the family meal recipes into a book. At first we thought only professionals would be interested. Restaurants around the world feed their staff every day, and we hoped we could contribute to our profession by offering varied and nutritionally balanced menus for large numbers.

But then we thought, why not offer our philosophy to home cooks too? Domestic cooks can learn many tips from how things are organized in a professional kitchen, and *The Family Meal* aims to show people how easy it can be to cook in an organized way by adapting our recipes for home cooks.

It was never our intention to invent brand-new recipes; this is simply a collection of everyday varied and inexpensive meals. It is a book about simple cooking. We wanted to showcase ordinary recipes for dishes that people might imagine are difficult to make, such as vichyssoise or chocolate cookies. The food we like to eat at elBulli is the same as what most people like to eat.

You don't need experience to follow the recipes, because each recipe is explained step by step. In fact, what is presented here is more a way of thinking about food than a way of cooking. We truly believe that if you don't eat well, it's because you haven't tried.

RECIPES OR MEALS?

There are many recipe books, but very few based on meals. People often pick up a cookbook at home, but have no idea how to combine the recipes into a sensible meal. This book aims to help by providing meals that have been thought out in their entirety. They have been organized into thirty-one balanced menus, each one containing three courses. You can also make your own menus by combining the recipes using the list on page 65.

WHAT WAS THE THINKING BEHIND EACH MEAL?

It is a myth that good food has to be expensive, and all the recipes in this book were designed to feed people very well on a low budget. Of course, the price will not be the same everywhere in the world.

Shopping in a supermarket is not the same as shopping in a market, just as shopping in Barcelona is different from in Birmingham, New York, or Melbourne. However, the principle is still the same: it's about planning and cooking reasonably priced meals with locally available ingredients. Second, each meal contains an appetizer, main course, and dessert. Third, the menus are practical. In general, the thirty-one meals offer a healthy, balanced diet with an interesting variety of ingredients and cooking methods.

The ingredients are, for the most part, everyday ones that can be found anywhere in the world, and are not expensive. To make sure of this, one of the chefs at elBulli spent thirty-one days cooking all the meals for two people, buying all the necessary ingredients at the market or supermarket. If he couldn't get hold of them easily, that particular menu was rejected. And whenever possible, we have suggested substitute ingredients.

The elBulli staff eat the same food as in many Spanish homes. However, given that we have staff members of many nationalities, other dishes and methods of preparation have been introduced, for example, from Mexico and Japan. But the ingredients required for these recipes can still be found nearly everywhere.

Although most of the recipes use only fresh ingredients, we don't object to using frozen foods when it makes sense, for example, in the case of peas, which are more expensive when fresh, have a short season, and are almost the same quality when frozen. It's also important to make good use of the freezer when preparing large quantities of basic recipes, such as stocks or sauces, in advance (see page 40).

–

The elBulli system

–

PRODUCTION SHEETS

Planning a different meal every day for 75 people can't be left to chance. At elBulli, we have a system of procedures to make the task easier, which has been perfected over time. First, the recipe is recorded and the details are updated on a production sheet. This means that the dish is always made the same way, regardless of who is in the kitchen and how many people need to be fed. Twice or three times a year, we prepare large batches of the basic recipes (such as sauces or stocks) to freeze and use when needed, dividing them into convenient portions.

MONTHLY AND WEEKLY SHEETS

Each month we make up a menu sheet, showing what is going to be eaten every day of the following month, with special attention paid to variety, rotation, season, and availability of ingredients. On the last day of each week, the monthly sheet is used to confirm the sheet for the following week. This is only changed if something out-of-the-ordinary happens, such as when a supplier brings us an unexpected ingredient. All of this monthly and weekly planning is done by Eugeni and Ferran.

QUARTZ

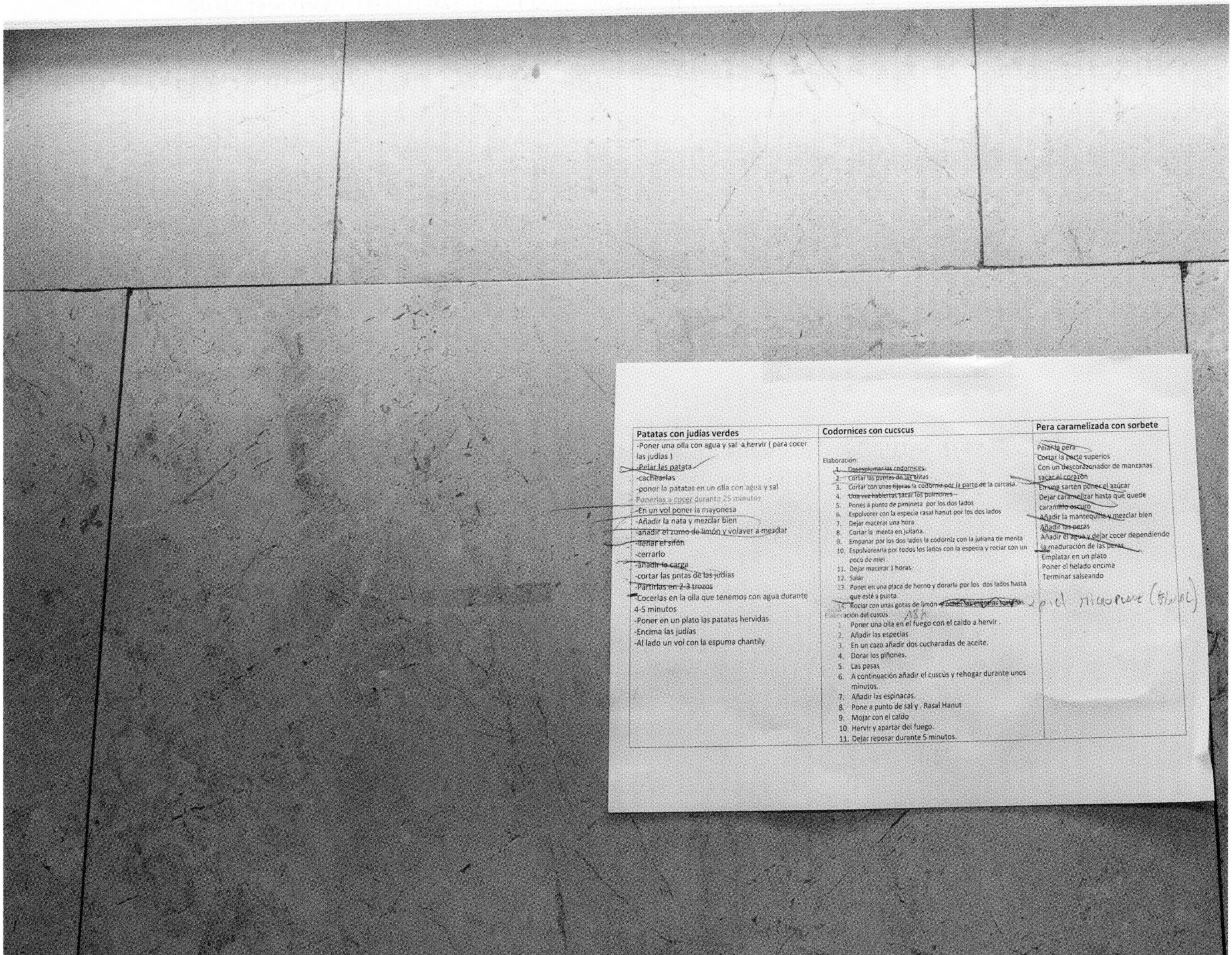
Patatas con judías verdes
-Poner una olla con agua y sal a hervir (para cocer las judías)
-Pelar las patata
-cachearlas
-poner la patatas en un olla con agua y sal
Ponerlas a cocer durante 25 minutos
-En un vol poner la mayonesa
-Añadir la nata y mezclar bien
-añadir el zumo de limón y volaver a mezclar
-llenar el sifón
-cerrarlo
-añadir la carga
-cortar las pntas de las judías
-Partirlas en 2-3 trozos
-Cocerlas en la olla que tenemos con agua durante 4-5 minutos
-Poner en un plato las patatas hervidas
-Encima las judías
-Al lado un vol con la espuma chantily
Codornices con cucscus
Elaboración:
1. Desesplumar las codornices.
2. Cortar las puntas de las alitas
3. Cortar con unas tijeras la codorniz por la parte de la carcasa.
4. Una vez habiertas sacar los pulmones
5. Pones a punto de pimineta por los dos lados
6. Espolvorer con la especia rasal hanut por los dos lados
7. Dejar macerar una hora
8. Cortar la menta en juliana.
9. Empanar por los dos lados la codorniz con la juliana de menta
10. Espolvorearla por todos los lados con la especia y rociar con un poco de miel .
11. Dejar macerar 1 horas.
12. Salar
13. Poner en una placa de horno y dorarla por los dos lados hasta que esté a punto.
14. Rociar con unas gotas de limón
Elaboración del cuscús
1. Poner una olla en el fuego con el caldo a hervir .
2. Añadir las especias
3. En un cazo añadir dos cucharadas de aceite.
4. Dorar los piñones.
5. Las pasas
6. A continuación añadir el cuscús y rehogar durante unos minutos.
7. Añadir las espinacas.
8. Pone a punto de sal y . Rasal Hanut
9. Mojar con el caldo
10. Hervir y apartar del fuego.
11. Dejar reposar durante 5 minutos.
Pera caramelizada con sorbete
Pelar la pera
Cortar la parte superios
Con un descorazonador de manzanas sacar el corazón
En una sartén poner el azúcar
Dejar caramelizar hasta que quede caramelo oscuro
Añadir la mantequilla y mezclar bien
Añadir las peras
Añadir el agua y dejar cocer dependiendo la maduración de las peras
Emplatar en un plato
Poner el helado encima
Terminar salseando

DAY TO DAY

The night before each meal is to be prepared, we check our ingredients are on hand, unless they must be bought fresh on the day, which is the case with fish. On the day itself, between 2:00 p.m. and 6:25 p.m., the work of the *mise en place* (or preparation for that night's service) is alternated with preparing the family meal. It is rare for something to be prepared the day before; this would only apply to a dish such as a special stew.

The *mise en place* for the restaurant dishes is complete by 6:25 p.m. At this point we clear the work surfaces, arrange the chairs, and put out bottles of water, glasses, and bread ready for the family meal. In the meantime, the rest of the chefs and waiting staff line up to collect the first course, which is served in the kitchen. The main course is usually placed on the table on big platters that we call *violines* ("violins"). The dessert is usually served separately (in individual servings or on platters) and it can be collected before or after the main course. Bread is always served with the meal. After trying several different varieties, we decided to serve sliced country loaves, because there is less wastage than with rolls or baguettes. Any unused bread is kept for the following day or used in a dish.

QUANTITIES, PLATTERS, AND BOWLS

The recipes in this book are given for 2, 6, 20, and 75 people. The quantities have been carefully calculated to yield the correct amount for each number of people; it's not as simple as straightforward multiplying or dividing. We don't plate each dish individually when cooking for 75 people, but often serve food on platters instead, allowing for the staff to take the amount they want. Over time we have worked out how much food is really needed, adjusting the production sheets as we repeated the recipes. Leftover food can be recycled or reused. Side dishes and salads are served in small bowls for the same reason, enabling us to cook more accurate quantities. Of course, when cooking at home for two or six, this is less of a concern, and it is easier to calculate quantities precisely.

STAFF PREFERENCES

The staff have their favorite dishes; in fact, they aren't all that different from the preferences of people who don't work in a cutting-edge restaurant. We noticed, for instance, that staff members took more second helpings of fresh pasta than of other dishes. So we started to make it in larger quantities, allowing for everyone to have a second serving. Another staff favorite is rice in any form: black rice, risotto, rice stew. Among the main courses, hamburgers are always high on the list of favorites.

COFFEE AND CLEAR UP

When the staff have finished their meal, they clear away their plates, glasses, and cutlery, and have a coffee. Every day, a member of the waiting staff takes a turn at making coffee for everybody. In the end, only Ferran is left at the table. He has a brief meeting with Eugeni to deal with anything that has cropped up during the meal. The chairs are cleared away at 7:00 p.m. After a few minutes' rest, it's time to get back to work.

TRICKS TO MAKE THE MOST OF INGREDIENTS OR PREPARATIONS

One of the most useful resources of professional kitchens are the ingredients or preparations left over from the *mise en place*, which can be used when making the staff meal. Here are some tips that we have developed at elBulli. Naturally, the individual character and style of each restaurant means it will have its own ingredients and preparations that it can use in different ways.

* After making almond milk, the almond pulp can be saved for use in *ajo blanco* (a traditional Spanish garlic and almond soup), or ice cream.

* After making cheese water, especially with Parmesan, the leftover fat can be used in a risotto.

* If we need the loin of a mackerel (or any other specific part of a fish) for the restaurant, the rest can go to make soup, tartare, or fishcakes.

* After using asparagus tips, the stalks can be boiled and served with mayonnaise, or made into a soup, purée or crème.

* Fruit that is too ripe to be served, and leftover pieces of fruit, can be used in sorbets and fruit sauces.

* After making olive water, the olive pulp can be used in soup or for vinaigrette.

* The leftover pulp from making coconut milk can be used in desserts, such as macaroons and coconut crème caramel.

* After making tomato water (for water ice, for example), the leftover pulp can be used for *sofrito* or tomato sauce. This operation can also be reversed; if the pulp is needed, the leftover water can be made into a refreshing drink.

* When making stock, the remaining solids can be simmered again with fresh water. The resulting liquid (which we call the "second stock") is used instead of water the next time we make stock, making it tastier.

* When making chicken stock, the chicken meat can be shredded for use in a salad.

* When making ham stock, the leftover scraps of ham can be made into a dish with peas.

* When using egg yolks, the whites can be saved for another dish (a mousse or meringue, for instance). When using egg whites, the yolks can go into an egg yolk and caramel pudding.

These are some of the many options that can provide tasty and interesting dishes, as well as helping you use leftover food more efficiently and save money.

THE MAGIC THICKENER

For many years, it has been common practice for restaurant professionals to use xanthan gum, a hydrocolloid with great thickening power, for binding and thickening sauces, among other things. It's a very effective product; just the tiniest amount can be used to replace traditional thickeners such as cornstarch. This is also significant for flavor; because so little xanthan gum is used, it doesn't affect the taste of the dish at all. For these reasons, it makes sense to use xanthan gum in professional kitchens. However, the quantities needed at home would be very small and difficult to measure. If you are cooking for a few people at home, it's easier to thicken a sauce or vinaigrette with cornstarch by making a paste with a liquid and stirring it into the sauce, heating until it thickens. If you are cooking for 75 people this operation would be difficult to do with cornstarch. In this case, a tiny and very precise quantity of xanthan gum gives a perfect result.

THE CRU TECHNIQUE

The technique we call "CRU" at elBulli consists of vacuum sealing an ingredient that contains a good proportion of liquid (a fruit or vegetable, for instance) along with a liquid with another flavor and aroma. The liquid from the outside penetrates the ingredient, replacing its own liquid and flavoring it. Some examples of this are apple with Calvados, pineapple with fennel, apple with basil, artichoke with vinaigrette, and asparagus with Parmesan water.

–

Cooking at home

–

ORGANIZATION COMES FIRST

While we were adapting the family meals to be made easily at home, we realized how important the *mise en place* (or advance preparation) is for restaurants. At home, of course, people don't usually prepare in advance. But *mise en place* can be very helpful, even at home. There are always things that need to be done on the same day, but there are other things, such as stocks and sauces, that can be made in advance. Practical concerns will dictate what you can do in advance—the most important thing is to make efficient use of your time. First, it's useful to plan your meals for the week and make a list of everything you can buy in advance (the freshest ingredients will have to wait until the actual day). Following the "Organizing the Menu" instructions at the beginning of each of our thirty-one meals will enable you to prepare the three courses in very little time. Leave the more complex menus or the ones requiring longer preparation times for the weekend.

SHOPPING

Is it better to shop at a market or a supermarket? Both have their critics and fans, and their advantages and disadvantages. Markets and small private stores let you become familiar with the suppliers, so that direct contact and confidence can build up. Many people place great value on knowing their butcher and fish supplier. When buying meat or seafood, they take advantage of these professionals' experience and leave the preparation to them, including the most tiresome operations, such as scaling, boning, gutting, chopping, and so on. They can also offer good advice on the most suitable meat cuts or types of fish for a specific recipe. Supermarkets, on the other hand, often offer lower prices because they buy in bulk. Don't forget that you can also do your shopping on the Internet. Some large supermarkets offer this service, which helps you to shop efficiently, especially for items to fill the pantry. In the end, the best idea is to combine all the options, and to shop however it suits you.

FRUIT AND VEGETABLES

It's always best to give priority to fruit and vegetables that are in season. Keep in mind that the price of fruit and vegetables is always higher at the start of the season than at its height. Compare prices and always choose the most reasonably priced ones. You can buy them in small quantities and use them as you need.

DAIRY PRODUCTS Buy products made with whole milk, because the percentage of fat in them makes them more suitable for many of the dishes in this book. When buying cream, it's important to know if it's for whipping or cooking. The different kinds have a different fat content, so always read the information on the package. Yogurt is an excellent product because it has so many possibilities. There are many varieties with different characteristics, such as flavor, creaminess, sweetness, and fat content. When it comes to choosing yogurt for cooking, it's best not to complicate matters: good-quality whole-milk plain yogurt is the best option.

BREAD Bakeries nowadays sell fresh bread in all shapes and sizes. You can also find ready-to-bake or partially baked baguettes and different kinds of packaged loaves. Follow your preferences, but keep in mind how it can be bought and stored. Remember that you can freeze bread and defrost it quickly in the oven or toaster.

OIL You can buy oil of many different qualities and at varying price levels. The menus in this book require three basic types of oil: ordinary olive oil for cooking, extra-virgin olive oil for dressings, and sunflower oil for frying.

FISH Try to develop a personal contact at a local fish supplier. It's helpful to talk to someone you can trust and who knows the characteristics of the different species of fish to help you make the best choices.

The quickest way to test whether fish is fresh is to look at its eyes and skin. The eyes should be black, shiny, and convex; if they are gray or look flat or sunken, the fish is past its best. The skin should be shiny and firm; if it's dull or wrinkled, it isn't fresh. Smell can also help you to determine whether fish is fresh. It shouldn't smell; if it does, it should smell more of the sea than of fish. A strong fishy smell means it isn't as fresh as it should be. When storing fish in the fridge, use a plastic container with a lattice tray to separate the fish from the liquid it releases.

When buying fish for home use, ask the fish supplier to gut and scale it for you. You can also ask for the fish to be skinned and filleted, if you prefer.

Pages 16–17 contain photographs of the fish used in the book. Unlike vegetables or meat, one fish can look quite similar to another, so it is helpful to know what you are looking for before you go shopping. If you can't find the fish specified in the recipe, ask your fish supplier to suggest a suitable alternative.

75cl
Jerez

MEAGRE

Lime-marinated fish
(see page 152)

COD

Salt cod & vegetable stew
(see page 104)
Cod & green pepper sandwich
(see page 292)

HORSE MACKEREL

Mackerel with vinaigrette
(see page 164)

WHITING

Whiting in salsa verde
(see page 233)

SEA BASS

Lime-marinated fish
(see page 152)
Japanese-style bream
(see page 194)
and *Baked sea bass*
(see page 332)

–

SARDINE

–

Sesame sardines with carrot salad
(see page 114)

–

MEGRIM

–

Fried fish with garlic
(see page 252)

–

MACKEREL

–

Mackerel & potato stew
(see page 84)

–

BLUE WHITING

–

Whiting in salsa verde
(see page 233)

–

GILTHEAD BREAM

–

Japanese-style bream
(see page 194)

MEAT Price is an essential consideration when buying meat, since it can be a very expensive ingredient. However, there is fantastic scope for making high-quality and varied meat dishes using cheaper cuts. Some meats, such as free-range chicken, turkey, duck, pork, and certain veal and beef cuts, are quite affordable. Remember that it's always better to buy a good-quality cheap cut than a poor example of an expensive one. You can always make an exception and choose a good sirloin steak every now and again. When it comes to buying meat, you can buy it already cut and packaged, or ask the butcher to cut it up in front of you, in which case the meat will be fresher. The same is true of ground meat: you can buy it packaged (even as ready-to-cook hamburgers) or ask the butcher to grind it for you on the spot, allowing you to specify how fine you would like it.

HOW TO COOK MEAT Every kind of meat needs its own cooking technique and temperature. However, as a general guideline, follow the four principles of what we call the "heat equation":

1. the intensity of the heat should be high
2. the amount of oil should be minimal
3. the pan should be thick: the thicker the pan, the better the heat will be distributed over the surface, as the entire surface does not come into direct contact with the heating element or gas flame
4. the quantity of meat should be proportionate to the pan surface area. If you put too much meat in a small frying pan, it will lose a lot of heat. For the same reason, it's best to take the meat out of the fridge 30 minutes before you start cooking.

SIDE DISHES There are many different side dishes that can accompany meat, including the following:

* broiled vegetables, such as zucchini, potatoes, or bell peppers
* boiled vegetables, such as cauliflower, potatoes, or cabbage
* baked or roasted vegetables, such as potatoes, or zucchini
* fried vegetables, such as onion rings, or eggplant slices
* beans or garbanzo beans (chickpeas)
* salads, which could include vegetables, nuts, meat or cheese, such as Waldorf salad (page 370) or Caesar salad (page 72)
* rice, such as plain boiled rice or Mexican rice (page 242)
* other dishes that appear as appetizers in this book, such as Roasted vegetables with olive oil (page 350), Polenta and Parmesan gratin (page 112), Grilled lettuce hearts (page 360), Creamed potatoes (page 362), or Cauliflower with béchamel (page 260)

HOW TO MAKE FRENCH FRIES

We have not included French fries in any of the menus in this book, but many people consider them the perfect accompaniment to meat dishes. To make the best fries, cut, wash, and dry the potatoes, then blanch them quickly in plenty of hot oil (285°F) in a deep-fat fryer. They shouldn't change color at this stage. You can do this in advance, then set the fries aside on paper towels to drain, keeping them at room temperature. Just before serving, fry them in very hot oil (360°F) until golden and crisp.

HOW TO COOK EGGS

Some of the dishes in this book can be accompanied with an egg. There are many ways to cook this versatile ingredient, and there are many ways to use it: by itself, in a hot or cold soup, in a salad, or to accompany cooked garbanzo beans (chickpeas), to name just a few.

To check whether an egg is fresh, immerse it in water. If it stays horizontal at the bottom of the receptacle, it's fresh. If the larger end rises, it's not fresh, and the higher it rises the less fresh it is. If it floats, you should throw it away.

The simplest and most popular way of cooking eggs is to fry them and add to salads, soups, or other dishes. You can also use soft-boiled eggs for the same purpose, cooking them in boiling water for 3 minutes so that the inside is still runny.

Another classic method is poaching, which involves immersing an egg in very hot water until the white surrounding the yolk is set.

Finally, there is a wonderful way to cook eggs known in Japan as *onsen tamago*. This originally meant cooking eggs in hot springs with a temperature of 140–160°F. The same technique can be used in restaurant kitchens using a Roner (a low-temperature water bath) or a steam oven set to 145°F, and cooking the eggs for 40 minutes.

The following page shows the most common techniques for cooking eggs.

1. Frying
   Crack the egg into a small bowl before pouring it carefully into the frying pan. Make sure the frying pan is very hot before adding the egg. If you are serving the eggs in a salad or soup, you can trim off most of the white with a cookie cutter for a neater presentation.

2. Boiling
   Make sure the water is fully boiling and have a timer handy when you immerse the egg. Boil for 3–4 minutes for a soft-boiled egg and 7 minutes for a hard-boiled egg. Place immediately in iced water, then peel carefully.

3. Poaching
   Crack the egg into a small bowl before pouring it carefully into the water. Make sure the water is just below boiling point and gently slide the egg in. Cook for 3–4 minutes, then remove with a slotted spoon. The yolk should be runny inside.

Frying →
Boiling →
Poaching →

HERBS, SPICES, AND CONDIMENTS

Herbs are a very useful ingredient in any kitchen, because a relatively small amount lets you modify the flavor of a dish. If you only need small quantities, you can grow a few pots of the most commonly used herbs in or near your kitchen. This requires basic care, including watering, careful pruning, and so on, but it's economical and the best way to have ready access to the goodness of fresh herbs. It's like having a living pantry. Alternatively, you can buy fresh herbs at the supermarket. You can also generally find large bunches of fresh herbs in markets, which is especially useful when you need larger quantities.

FRESH HERBS

The fresh herbs used in the recipes in this book are:

* parsley
* cilantro
* mint
* basil
* thyme
* rosemary
* chives

DRIED HERBS

Another way to add flavor and aroma is to use dried herbs, a practical option available all year round. There is also a long tradition of using dried herbs. The following dried herbs are used in our recipes:

* oregano
* bay leaves
* thyme
* rosemary

SPICES, SAUCES, AND CONDIMENTS

No other ingredient has as much power to enhance flavor and aroma as spices. For many centuries, they were considered precious commodities for precisely this reason. Spices are also easy to store in a pantry. Even so, it's best to buy them only in small quantities; if you keep them in the cupboard for months or even years, they lose their aroma and freshness. Like spices, condiments can have an important influence on flavor, and can give preparations and dishes an unmistakable quality.

The following spices and condiments appear in this book:

* cinnamon
* cloves
* saffron
* black pepper
* white pepper
* sweet paprika
* nutmeg
* fresh ginger
* red miso paste
* soy sauce
* dashi
* yellow curry paste
* achiote paste
* red *mole* paste
* vanilla beans
* green anise
* cumin
* five-spice powder
* *ras el hanout* (a Moroccan spice mix)
* *sichimi togarashi* (a Japanese spice mix)
* chile
* Dijon mustard
* Worcestershire sauce
* oyster sauce
* whole-grain mustard

Using spices and condiments is a very appealing way to experiment with your cooking. If you dare to invent, change, and modify, each spice will impart a distinctive flavor to your cooking.

STORING FOOD AT HOME

Ground meat can spoil more quickly than whole meat cuts, because it has a larger surface area in contact with the air. When storing meat in the fridge, discard the bags or paper wrapping from the store and transfer to plastic containers with lids in order not to mix smells and to prevent the cold air from drying out the meat. Once the packaging of a product is opened, the period for its safe use varies depending on the type of food and the temperature at which it is stored. As a general rule, an opened fresh product can safely be stored for two or three days at the correct temperature. Always transfer the contents of open cans to other (nonmetallic) containers.

Fruit and vegetables can lose their nutritional properties once they have been cut or sliced, so use them quickly after preparing them. Don't store vegetables in plastic bags or other wrapping that can shorten their life.

The recipe quantities have been carefully calculated to avoid wastage. If there are any leftovers, however, they can be stored in the fridge for a few days.

FREEZING FOOD

Label everything you want to freeze, and include the date of freezing. Frozen food should be well packed to preserve its properties and to prevent it from taking on other smells. Freeze ingredients and preparations in small portions, keeping in mind the quantities you are likely to need for the recipes. Defrost and clean your freezer regularly to make sure it is working efficiently. Every type of food has a different freezer life, but it is generally unwise to keep food in the freezer for longer than 6 months. Not all ingredients can withstand freezing in the same way. For example, peas and beans barely experience any reduction in quality, but the same is not true of artichokes and zucchini. Remember to take things out of the freezer the day before you want to use them. Thaw meat or fish by leaving it on a plate, covered, in the fridge.

KITCHEN EQUIPMENT

To make the meals, in this book you will need only basic kitchen utensils and equipment. The most essential equipment is listed on pages 24–25, and additional useful, but not essential, equipment is listed on pages 26–27.

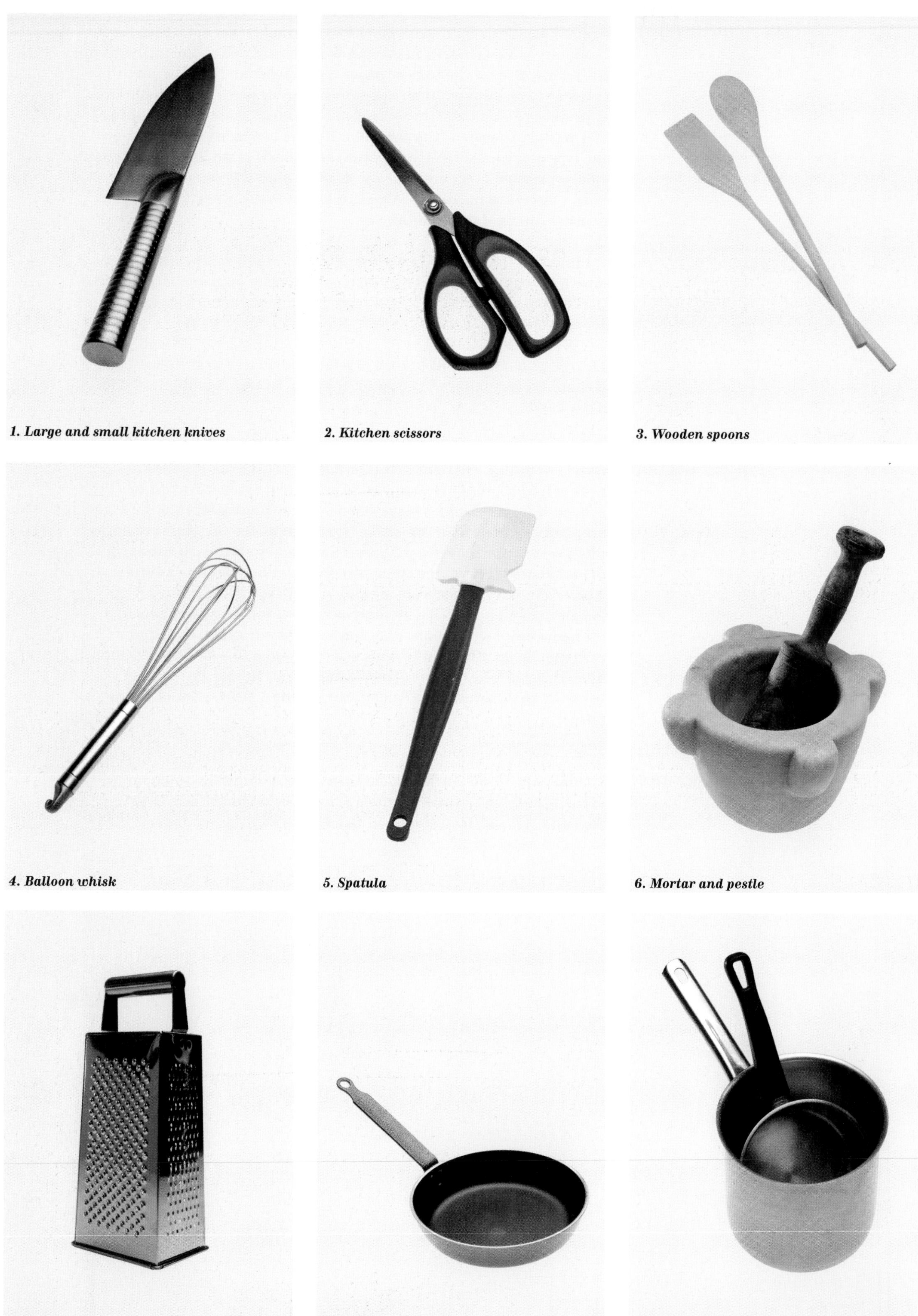
1. Large and small kitchen knives
2. Kitchen scissors
3. Wooden spoons
4. Balloon whisk
5. Spatula
6. Mortar and pestle
7. Grater
8. Nonstick frying pan
9. Large, medium, and small saucepans

10. Ovenproof dishes

11. Measuring cup

12. Fine-mesh sieves

13. Pepper mill

14. Paper towels

15. Aluminum foil

16. Plastic wrap

17. Parchment paper or wax paper

18. Molds of different sizes

19. *Squeeze bottles*

20. *Citrus juicer*

21. *Pasta machine*

22. *Nonstick baking mat*

23. *Mandoline*

24. *Microplane grater*

25. *Flat griddle*

26. *Casserole dish*

27. *Pressure cooker*

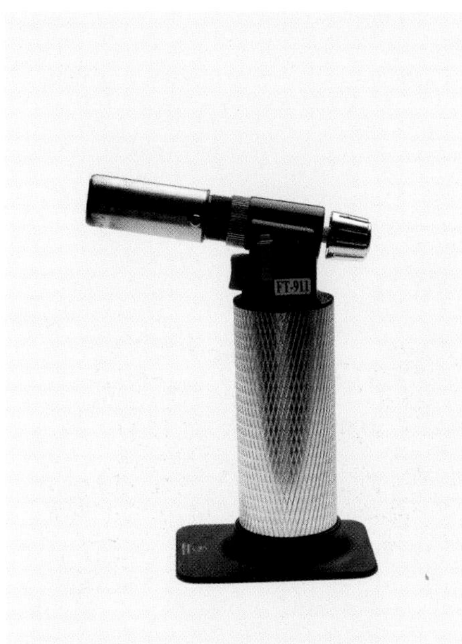

28. Kitchen blowtorch

29. Whipped cream siphon and cartridges

30. Soda siphon

31. Electric scale

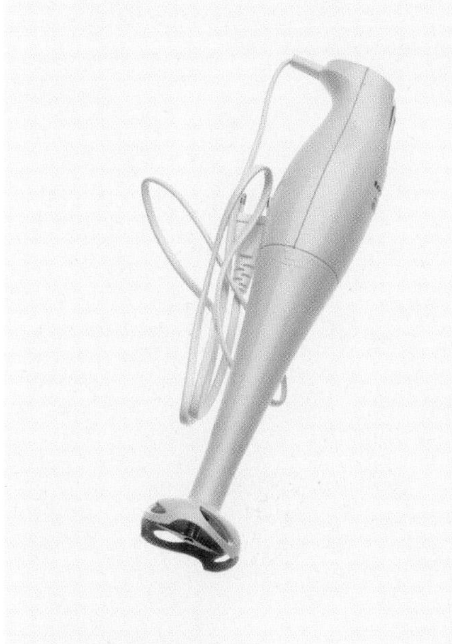

32. Hand-held blender

33. Electric citrus juicer

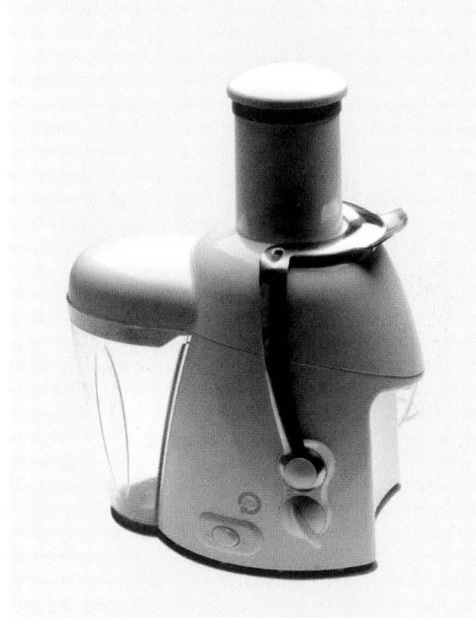

34. Electric fruit and vegetable juicer

35. Blender

36. Food processor

POLPA DE
INTEGRAL

The essentials

A good pantry should be well stocked with ingredients with a relatively long shelf life. Start by buying a few of these basic ingredients now, and complete the list as you prepare the menus. By the time you have cooked all the recipes, you will have built up a very good basic pantry.

Store all fresh ingredients in the fridge. The freezer is an ideal place to store freshly made preparations, such as stocks and sauces, for use in different menus over a period of several months.

FRIDGE

* eggs
* butter
* whole milk
* whipping cream (35% fat)
* Parmesan cheese
* cheese slices
* plain yogurt
* smoked bacon
* Frankfurters
* limes
* lemons
* other citrus fruits
* apples
* oranges

FREEZER

* fish stock (see page 56)
* chicken stock (see page 57)
* beef stock (see page 58)
* ham stock (see page 59)
* picada (see page 41)
* tomato sauce (see page 42)
* sofrito (see page 43)
* bolognese sauce (see page 44)
* romesco sauce (see page 45)
* pesto sauce (see page 46)
* peas
* spinach
* nougat ice cream
* vanilla ice cream
* squid ink

PANTRY

HERBS, SPICES, AND FLAVORINGS

* five-spice powder
* green anise seeds
* saffron
* ground cinnamon
* cloves
* ground cumin
* dried chiles
* ground nutmeg
* achiote paste
* dashi powder
* *ras el hanout*
* *sichimi togarashi* spice mix
* sweet paprika
* table salt
* sea salt flakes
* white pepper
* black pepper
* vanilla beans
* dried bay leaves
* dried oregano
* dried rosemary
* dried thyme

VEGETABLES

* garlic
* onions
* potatoes

OILS AND VINEGARS

* sunflower oil
* ordinary olive oil
* extra-virgin olive oil
* toasted sesame seed oil
* sherry vinegar
* white wine vinegar
* red wine vinegar

PRESERVED INGREDIENTS

* pickled capers
* canned coconut milk
* pickles
* canned cooked beans
* canned cooked lentils
* canned anchovy fillets
* canned tomato sauce
* canned corn kernels
* canned chopped tomatoes
* dried shiitake mushrooms

STARCH

* rice
* couscous
* polenta or cornmeal
* tagliatelle
* spaghetti
* short egg noodles
* farfalle
* macaroni
* egg noodles
* white superfine sugar
* confectioners' sugar
* brown sugar
* honey
* molasses
* cornstarch
* ground almonds
* all-purpose white flour
* corn tortillas
* croutons (see page 52)
* potato flakes

SAUCES AND CONDIMENTS

* mayonnaise
* red miso paste
* black olive paste (tapenade)
* red *mole* paste
* whole-grain mustard
* Dijon mustard
* barbecue sauce (see page 48)
* oyster sauce
* soy sauce
* teriyaki sauce (see page 50)
* Worcestershire sauce

ALCOHOL

* brandy
* Cointreau
* Cognac
* kirsch
* anisette liqueur
* white rum
* white wine
* Chinese Shaoxing rice wine
* *vino rancio* (or dry sherry)
* red wine

NUTS AND SEEDS

* caramelized almonds
* whole toasted Marcona almonds
* caramelized hazelnuts
* dried plums (prunes)
* crushed almonds
* peeled walnuts
* raisins
* pine nuts
* peeled green pistachio nuts
* white sesame seeds
* toasted white sesame seeds

OTHER PRODUCTS

* potato chips
* potato straws
* dark chocolate
* white chocolate
* unsweetened cocoa
* instant coffee
* grated coconut
* menthol candies or throat lozenges
* honey-flavored hard candies

luengo
Precinto de Garantía
GOURMET
Produce of Mauritius

–

A look behind the scenes at the family meal

–

The following pages provide a glimpse of the restaurant before it opens its doors. These are the precious minutes between preparation and service: a time to sit down, talk, enjoy a coffee, and, of course, to eat.

First, the work surface is cleared and the plates are set out; then the staff line up to get their meal from the kitchen. Platters of food are set out along the table and everyone sits down together in the kitchen to eat.

Finally, the tables are cleared and the work surfaces are made ready for the beginning of the restaurant service.

Basic recipes

Basic recipes

The basic recipes are for base preparations, such as sauces and stocks, that are used in the meals that follow, and preparing them in advance will make it easier for you to cook in a more organized way. In fact, the main difference between cooking at home and cooking professionally lies in the level of advance preparation (or *mise en place*) that happens in restaurants. Restaurant chefs make large batches of basic stocks, sauces, and garnishes ahead of time to make cooking both staff meals and restaurant dishes simpler and quicker. These preparations are sometimes vacuum packed before freezing, but at home it's fine just to freeze them.

Think of the basic recipes as your *mise en place* on a domestic scale. We recommend that you set aside time to prepare your basic recipes, and to make the largest possible quantities (depending on the size of your pans and freezer), to make it worth your while. By having these preparations on hand at any time, you can greatly expand your repertoire of delicious everyday dishes.

The amounts that the basic recipes will yield are given in ounces, pounds, or cups, instead of serving numbers, because different recipes will require different quantities. It is simple to multiply the recipes up or down to prepare the quantity you need. When making stocks, it's best to make as much as you can, then store in smaller quantities in the freezer to use as you need. Ice-cube trays and small plastic cups or resealable food storage bags are excellent for storing small portions of preparations, such as *picada, sofrito,* or pesto, and plastic bottles or airtight containers are ideal for storing stock. Remember that liquids expand as they freeze, so always leave a little room in the top of the bottle or container. Always label the preparation clearly with the name, quantity, and date of freezing.

Of course, good alternatives to these stocks and sauces can be bought from any good supermarket or delicatessen. What you choose to use will depend on the time you have available and the amount you want to spend. When buying prepared stocks and sauces, always look for the best quality you can afford. There are a number of alternatives to making your own stock, as explained in the following pages, and another good option is to buy stock from a restaurant that you trust.

To make this way of cooking work for you, it's important to remember to take whatever you need from the freezer the day before.

Picada

Picada is an aromatic sauce traditionally used in Catalan cuisine as a base flavoring for many dishes. It is also often added toward the end of cooking.

•

Picada will keep for 1 week in the fridge or 6 months in the freezer.

•

This sauce appears in:
Beans with clams (page 102)
Crab & rice stew (page 204)
Black rice with squid (page 272)
Fish soup (page 320)
Rice with duck (page 342)
Salmon stewed with lentils (page 352)
Noodle soup with mussels (page 372)

	for ½ cup	for 2½ cups
Saffron threads	1 tsp	5¼ tsp
Garlic cloves	1	6
Fresh parsley leaves	⅔ cup	3⅓ cups
Extra-virgin olive oil	2½ tbsp	scant 1 cup
Toasted blanched hazelnuts	¼ cup	1 cup

Start →

Tomato sauce

The sauce will keep for 5 days in the fridge or 6 months in the freezer.

•

<u>This sauce appears in</u>:
Sausages with tomato sauce (page 144)
Osso buco (page 154)
Spaghetti with tomato & basil (page 250)

	for scant 1 cup	for 8⅔ cups	for 1¾ gallons
Extra-virgin olive oil	½ cup	5 cups	1 gallon
Garlic cloves	½	5	15
Onions, finely chopped	1 tsp	¾ cup	2¼ cups
Canned chopped tomatoes	12½ oz	7¾ lb	26½ lb
Salt	1 pinch	2½ tbsp	scant ½ cup
Pepper	1 pinch	1 tsp	1½ tbsp
Sugar	1 pinch	2½ tsp	scant ½ cup

Start →

Sofrito

Sofrito is a basic preparation of tomatoes, garlic, oil, and onions that forms the base of many traditional Spanish dishes.

•

The sauce will keep for 5 days in the fridge or 6 months in the freezer.

•

This sauce appears in:
Beans with clams (page 102)
Crab & rice stew (page 204)
Black rice with squid (page 272)
Fish soup (page 320)
Rice with duck (page 342)
Salmon stewed with lentils (page 352)
Noodle soup with mussels (page 372)

	for ¾ cup	for 2⅓ cups	for 7¼ cups
Garlic cloves	1	8½	30
Extra-virgin olive oil	2 tsp	½ cup	1¾ cups
Onions, finely chopped	1⅓ cups	4⅓ cups	14 cups
Dried thyme	1 pinch	¾ tsp	2½ tsp
Dried rosemary	1 pinch	¾ tsp	2¾ tsp
Dried bay leaf	⅙ leaf	½ leaf	10 leaves
Pureed fresh tomatoes or canned tomato puree	1½ tbsp	8 oz	1 lb 12 oz
Salt	1 pinch	½ tsp	1⅔ tsp

Start →

Bologneese sauce

The sauce will keep for 5 days in the fridge or 6 months in the freezer.

•

If you prefer to cook it in the oven, cover the sauce with a lid or foil and cook for 1½ hours at 365°F.

•

This sauce appears in:
Pasta bolognese (page 82)

	for 10 cups	for 2 gallons
Butter	1 cup	3½ cups
Ground beef	2¼ lb	8¾ lb
Pork sausage meat	12 oz	scant 3 lb
Onions, finely chopped	2 cups	7⅔ cups
Celery, finely chopped	1⅓ cups	4½ cups
Carrots, finely chopped	2 cups	8¼ cups
Extra-virgin olive oil	5 fl oz	2¼ cups
Canned chopped tomatoes	3½ lb	11½ lb
Tomato paste	4 tsp	4½ tbsp
Sugar	1 pinch	½ tsp

Start →

Romesco sauce

Romesco is a traditional Catalan sauce made with nuts and peppers pounded with oil and sherry vinegar. It is usually served with seafood, chicken or vegetables. *Choricero* pepper paste is available from specialist Spanish food shops and delicatessens.

•

The sauce will keep for 5 days in the fridge or 6 months in the freezer.

•

This sauce appears in:
Baked potatoes with romesco sauce (page 232)

	for 1½ gallons	for 4¼ gallons
Ripe tomatoes	¾ lb	1⅔ lb
Garlic, whole heads	5¼ oz	14 oz
Extra-virgin olive oil	1¼ cups	4 cups
Toasted blanched hazelnuts	2½ cups	6¾ cups
White country-style loaf, sliced	2 lb	3¾ lb
Sherry vinegar	10½ cups	2 gallons
Choricero pepper paste	5 cups	4¼ gallons

Start →

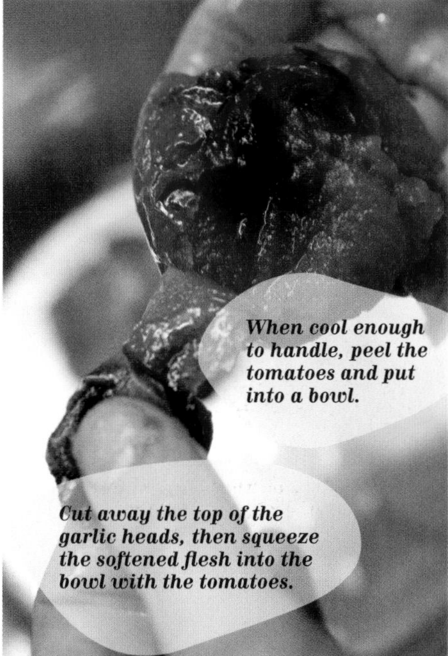

Pesto sauce

Pesto will keep for 2 days in the fridge or 6 months in the freezer.

•

This sauce appears in:
Farfalle with pesto (page 192)

	for 7 cups	for 1⅔ gallons
Fresh basil	15 oz	3½ lb
Garlic cloves	1 oz	3½ oz
Pine nuts	1 cup	3¾ cups
Extra-virgin olive oil	scant ¾ cup	3 cups
Olive oil	1¾ cups plus 1 tbsp	6½ cups
Pecorino romano cheese, finely grated	½ cup	2⅓ cups
Parmesan cheese, finely grated	2⅔ cups	10¼ cups

Start →

Pick the basil leaves from the stems, discarding any that are damaged.

Bring a saucepan of water to a boil, then add the basil leaves.

Let stand in the water for 5 seconds, until wilted.

Drain in a sieve, then when cool enough to handle, squeeze dry and set aside.

Cut each garlic clove in half. Fill a small saucepan with cold water, then add the garlic. Bring the water to a boil.

Lift the garlic out of the water and transfer to a bowl of iced water to cool.

Continue →

Coarsely chop the basil.
Put the basil, pine nuts, blanched garlic and both types of olive oil into a large bowl.
Process with a hand-held blender to make a coarse and grainy sauce.
Stir the cheeses into the sauce. Season with salt.
Transfer into small containers for storage.

Barbecue sauce

The sauce will keep for 1 week in the fridge or 6 months in the freezer.

•

This sauce appears in:
Pork ribs with barbecue sauce (page 262)

	for 8½ cups	for 1¾ gallons
Red onions, coarsely chopped	6 cups	8¾ lb
Garlic cloves, finely chopped	1 tbsp	¼ cup
Lemongrass, finely chopped	2 tbsp	½ cup
Fresh ginger, finely chopped	⅓ cup	1¼ cups
Oranges	1 lb	3⅓ lb
Granulated sugar	1⅓ cups	4½ cups
Honey	½ cup	1¾ cups
Molasses	⅓ cup	1 cup
Sherry vinegar	⅔ cup	2¼ cups
Dijon mustard	¼ cup	scant 1 cup
Worcestershire sauce	1 tbsp	3½ tbsp
Ketchup	2¾ cups	10½ cups
Canned chopped tomatoes	2½ lb	8¾ lb

Start →

Coarsely chop the onions.

Using a rolling pin or other heavy utensil, crush the garlic cloves, lemongrass, and ginger, then finely chop them.

Squeeze the oranges and reserve the juice.

Put a large saucepan over medium heat, then add the oil. Add the onion and cook for 5 minutes, until dark golden.

Add the garlic and cook for 3 minutes.

Add the sugar, orange juice, and molasses and let the mixture cook for 3 minutes.

Continue →

Pour in the honey.

*Add the ginger
and lemongrass.*

*Add the mustard,
Worcestershire
sauce, and ketchup.*

*Add the tomatoes
and simmer
for 30 minutes.*

Season with salt.

*Strain through a fine sieve
and let cool.*

Teriyaki sauce

The sauce will keep for 15 days in the fridge or 6 months in the freezer.

•

This sauce appears in:
Glazed teriyaki pork belly (page 302)

	for 4⅓ cups	for 3½ quarts
Lemongrass, chopped	⅓ cup	¾ cup
Fresh ginger, chopped	2 tbsp	½ cup
Chicken stock (see page 57)	1¾ cups	6¼ cups
Soy sauce	1¾ cups	6¼ cups
Sugar	3 cups	10 cups
Honey	1¾ cups	5¼ cups

Start →

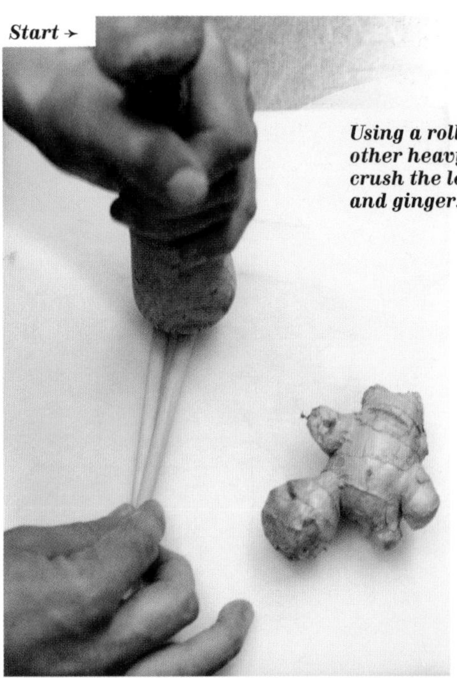

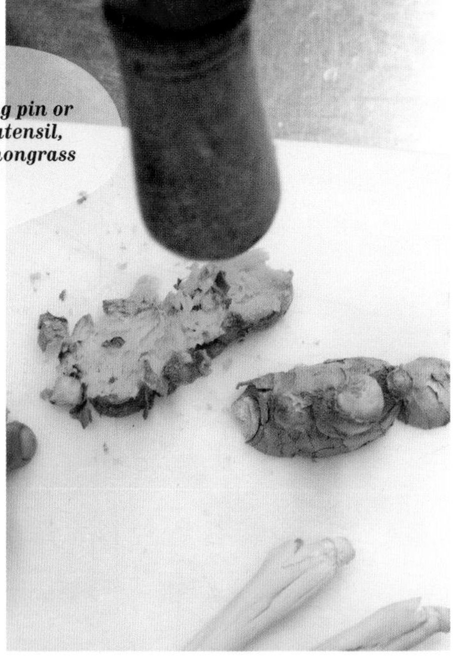

Using a rolling pin or other heavy utensil, crush the lemongrass and ginger.

Put the chicken stock, sugar, and soy sauce into a large saucepan.

Add the honey.

Add the crushed lemongrass and ginger. Put the pan over medium heat, bring to a boil, then boil for 15 minutes.

Strain and reserve.

Chimichurri sauce

Chimichurri is a sauce made from parsley, garlic, spices, olive oil, and vinegar. It comes from South America, where it is often served with steak, but it can accompany all types of roasted or grilled meat.

•

The sauce will keep for 15 days in the fridge and 6 months in the freezer.

•

This sauce appears in:
Duck with chimichurri sauce (page 226)

	for 14 cups	for 1¾ gallons
Onions	13 oz	1 lb 10 oz
Garlic cloves	21	42
Fresh parsley, finely chopped	4 cups	8 cups
Ripe tomatoes	3¼ lb	6½ lb
Small chiles	2	4
Dried thyme	4 tsp	8½ tsp
Dried oregano	⅔ cup	1⅓ cups
Ground cumin	1 tsp	2½ tsp
Sweet paprika	5 tsp	3½ tsp
Coarse salt	2 tbsp	¼ cup
Lemons	1	2
Sherry vinegar	½ cup	1 cup
Chardonnay vinegar	1 cup	2 cups
Olive oil	3 cups plus 2 tbsp	6¼ cups
Sunflower oil	2 cups	4⅓ cups
Water	3 cups plus 2 tbsp	6¼ cups

Start →

Chop the onions and garlic very finely, then put into a large bowl. Pick the parsley leaves from the stems and chop finely. Add to the bowl.

Deseed and cut the tomatoes into small cubes. Deseed and finely chop the chillies. Mix both into the onions and garlic and stir in the herbs and spices. Finely grate in the zest of the lemons.

Finish by pouring in the vinegars, oil, and the water.

Croutons

This recipe is for fried croutons, but if you prefer to toast the croutons, preheat the oven to 375°F. Spread the croutons out on a baking sheet and bake for 8–10 minutes.

•

<u>This recipe appears in</u>:

Caesar salad (page 72)
Vichyssoise (page 92)
Gazpacho (page 270)
Fish soup (page 320)

	for ¼ lb	for 14 oz
Slices from a white country-style loaf	3	20
Extra-virgin olive oil	2¼ cups	4¼ cups

Start →

Aioli

Aioli is a thick mayonnaise-like sauce from southern France made with garlic, eggs, and oil.

•

This sauce appears in:
Mackerel & potato stew (page 84)
Crab & rice stew (page 204)
Black rice with squid (page 272)

	for 6 cups
Garlic cloves	5
Eggs	8
Extra-virgin olive oil	5 cups

Start →

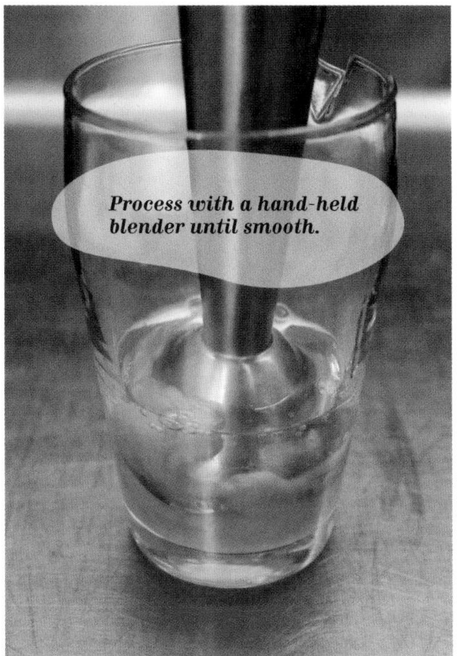

Stock

Wherever stock appears in a recipe, you can use store-bought concentrated or fresh liquid stock, or homemade stock. A concentrated bouillon cube produces an instant stock when dissolved in boiling water. Many chefs prefer not to use this kind of stock, but it is a valid option for the home cook, with the advantages of being cheap and easy to use. The flavor of the stock can sometimes be enhanced with meat or yeast concentrates, if needed. Prepared liquid stock is available in the form of a concentrated liquid for diluting, or a fully diluted stock that has been prepared naturally, then packed. The latter is the better choice, although it is also more expensive. The third option—making the stock at home following the recipes we provide—involves the most effort, but will give you the best quality results.

The quantity of stock you can make at home will be limited by the size of pans in your kitchen: the largest domestic pans usually have a capacity of around 2½ gallons. Filled with plenty of good ingredients, that pot will yield approximately 1½ gallons of stock, which can later be frozen in 2-cup portions, ready for use. The idea that stock needs a lot of time and attention is unfounded; it takes just 20 minutes to cook fish stock, and up to 2½ hours will be long enough for most meat stocks. Once a stock is simmering, it can be left to cook while you do something else. After straining a meat stock, don't throw the bones and other ingredients away. They can be reboiled for 45 minutes, and the liquid from this second boiling (which we call the "second stock"), can be used instead of water when making the next batch of stock to give it a deeper flavor. Fish bones cannot be reboiled, because they become bitter.

Fresh stock will keep in the fridge for up to 2 days, or in the freezer for up to 3 months.

Fish stock

Fish stock can be made with a mixture of any white fish and crustaceans, and crabs are a very good addition.

•

This stock is used in the following recipes:
Mackerel & potato stew (page 84)
Beans with clams (page 102)
Crab & rice stew (page 204)
Black rice with squid (page 272)
Salmon stewed with lentils (page 352)
Noodle soup with mussels (page 372)

	for 12½ cups
Olive oil	5 tsp
Crabs	14 oz
Fish	3¾ lb
Water	1 gallon

Start →

Chicken stock

This stock is used in the following recipes:
Vichyssoise (page 92)
Saffron risotto with mushrooms (page 132)
Bread & garlic soup (page 212)
Garbanzo beans with spinach & egg (page 300)
Rice with duck (page 342)

	for 8½ cups
Onions	1 small
Carrots	1
Celery	1
Whole, cleaned, raw chicken carcasses	2¾ lb (4 carcasses)
Water	1⅓ gallons

Start →

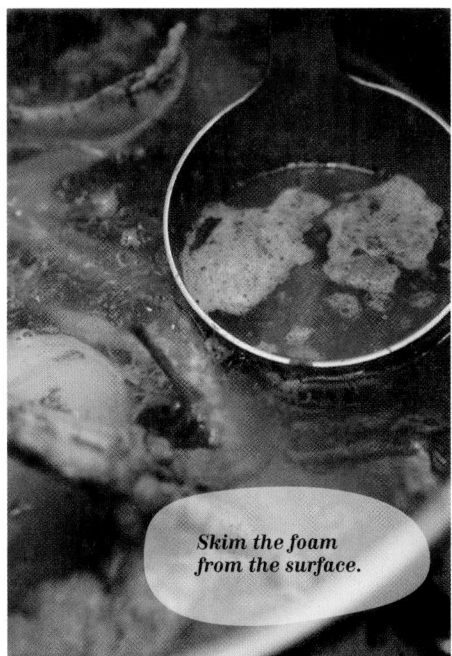

Beef stock

This stock is used in the following recipes:
Osso buco (page 154)

	for 8½ cups
Onion	1 small
Beef scraps or cheap pieces of meat, such as shank	4½ oz
Beef bones, raw	1½ oz
Carrots	2¼ lb
Celery	6 lb
Water	1⅓ gallons

Start →

Ham stock

This recipe requires the bones from a cured ham. Ask your butcher to supply them. Remove any meat from the bones and use in another recipe.

•

This stock is used in the following recipes:
Peas & ham (page 280)

	for 8½ cups
Ham bones	3 lb
Water	1 gallon

Start →

The meals

-

Meals & Recipes

-

Meal 1

-

Caesar salad

-

Cheeseburger & potato chips

-

Santiago cake

-

Meal 2

-

Pasta bolognese

-

Mackerel & potato stew

-

Chocolate cookies

-

Meal 3

-

Vichyssoise

-

Lamb with mustard & mint

-

Chocolate truffles

-

Meal 4

-

Beans with clams

-

Salt cod & vegetable stew

-

Baked apples

-

Meal 5

-

Polenta & Parmesan gratin

-

Sesame sardines with carrot salad

-

Mango with white chocolate yogurt

-

Meal 6

-

Potato chip omelet

-

Pork loin with peppers

-

Coconut macaroons

-

Meal 7

-

Saffron risotto with mushrooms

-

Catalan-style turkey

-

Yogurt foam with strawberries

-

Meal 8

-

Roasted eggplant with miso dressing

-

Sausages with tomato sauce

-

Crème Catalane

-

Meal 9

-

Lime-marinated fish

-

Osso buco

-

Piña colada

-

Meal 10

-

Miso soup with clams

-

Mackerel with vinaigrette

-

Almond cookies

-

Meal 11

-

Fried egg with asparagus

-

Chicken wings with mushrooms

-

Sangria with fruit

-

Meal 12

-

Potato salad

-

Thai beef curry

-

Strawberries in vinegar

-

Meal 13

-

Farfalle with pesto

-

Japanese-style bream

-

Mandarin oranges with Cointreau

-

Meal 14

-

Tomato & basil salad

-

Crab & rice stew

-

Coconut flan

-

Meal 15

-

Bread & garlic soup

-

Mexican-style slow-cooked pork

-

Figs with cream & kirsch

-

Meal 16

-

Noodles with shiitake & ginger

-

Duck with chimichurri sauce

-

Pistachio custard

-

Meal 17

-

Baked potatoes with romesco sauce

-

Whiting in salsa verde

-

Rice pudding

-

Meal 18

-

Guacamole with tortilla chips

-

Mexican-style chicken with rice

-

Watermelon with menthol candies

-

Meal 19

-

Spaghetti with tomato & basil

-

Fried fish with garlic

-

Caramel foam

-

Meal 20

-

Cauliflower with béchamel

-

Pork ribs with barbecue sauce

-

Banana with lime

-

Meal 21

-

Gazpacho

-

Black rice with squid

-

Bread with chocolate & olive oil

-

Meal 22

-

Peas & ham

-

Roasted chicken with potato straws

-

Pineapple with molasses & lime

-

Meal 23

-

Tagliatelle carbonara

-

Cod & green pepper sandwich

-

Almond soup with ice cream

-

Meal 24

-

Garbanzo beans with spinach & egg

-

Glazed teriyaki pork belly

-

Sweet potato with honey & cream

-

Meal 25

-

Potatoes & green beans with Chantilly

-

Quail with couscous

-

Caramelized pears

-

Meal 26

-

Fish soup

-

Sausages with mushrooms

-

Oranges with honey, olive oil & salt

-

Meal 27

-

Mussels with paprika

-

Baked sea bass

-

Caramel pudding

-

Meal 28

-

Melon with cured ham

-

Rice with duck

-

Chocolate cake

-

Meal 29

-

Roasted vegetables with olive oil

-

Salmon stewed with lentils

-

White chocolate cream

-

Meal 30

-

Grilled lettuce hearts

-

Veal with red wine & mustard

-

Chocolate mousse

-

Meal 31

-

Waldorf salad

-

Noodle soup with mussels

-

Melon & mint soup with pink grapefruit

-

—

How to choose and prepare for the meals

—

1. **Choose a menu, considering factors such as the amount of time you have available and the preferences of your guests. Check the Organizing the Menu time line first. Most of the meals take between 30 minutes and 2 hours to make all three dishes. The most time-consuming recipe is usually the dessert. If you leave out dessert, preparation times rarely exceed 30 minutes.**

2. **Read the recipes, ingredients lists, and the Organizing the Menu time line carefully.**

3. **Study the shopping lists to check which ingredients you already have.**

4. **Buy the ingredients you need.**

5. **Follow the recipe carefully.**

Create your own menu

Although the recipes have been carefully designed to form complete meals, you can combine the recipes in different ways to create new meals or to avoid certain dishes that you or your guests may not like. Use this list to help you choose recipes for different types of dish and compile your own menu, resulting in a more varied and balanced meal.

COURSE	TYPE OF DISH	RECIPE	PAGE	MEAL
Cold appetizers	*Salads*	*Lime-marinated fish*	*152*	*9*
		Potato salad	*182*	*12*
		Caesar salad	*72*	*1*
		Tomato & basil salad	*202*	*14*
		Melon with cured ham	*340*	*28*
		Waldorf salad	*370*	*31*
	Soups	*Gazpacho*	*270*	*21*
		Vichyssoise	*92*	*3*
	Vegetables	*Guacamole with tortilla chips*	*240*	*18*
Warm appetizers	*Rice & pasta*	*Tagliatelle carbonara*	*290*	*23*
		Spaghetti with tomato & basil	*250*	*19*
		Farfalle with pesto	*192*	*13*
		Pasta bolognese	*82*	*2*
		Noodles with shiitake & ginger	*222*	*16*
		Polenta & Parmesan gratin	*112*	*5*
		Saffron risotto with mushrooms	*132*	*7*
	Eggs	*Fried eggs with asparagus*	*172*	*11*
		Potato chip omelet	*122*	*6*
	Beans	*Garbanzo beans with spinach & egg*	*300*	*24*
		Beans with clams	*102*	*4*
	Soups	*Miso soup with clams*	*162*	*10*
		Bread & garlic soup	*212*	*15*
		Fish soup	*320*	*26*
	Shellfish	*Mussels with paprika*	*330*	*27*
	Vegetables	*Roasted eggplant with miso dressing*	*142*	*8*
		Grilled lettuce hearts	*360*	*30*
		Cauliflower with béchamel	*260*	*20*
		Roasted vegetables with olive oil	*350*	*29*
		Peas & ham	*280*	*22*
		Baked potatoes with romesco sauce	*232*	*17*
		Potatoes & green beans with Chantilly	*310*	*25*

COURSE	TYPE OF DISH	RECIPE	PAGE	MEAL
Main courses	*Rice & pasta*	*Crab & rice stew*	*204*	*14*
		Rice with duck	*342*	*28*
		Black rice with squid	*272*	*21*
		Noodle soup with mussels	*372*	*31*
	Chicken	*Chicken wings with mushrooms*	*174*	*11*
		Roasted chicken with potato straws	*282*	*22*
		Mexican-style chicken with rice	*242*	*18*
	Turkey	*Catalan-style turkey*	*134*	*7*
	Duck	*Duck with chimichurri sauce*	*226*	*16*
	Quail	*Quail with couscous*	*312*	*25*
	Pork	*Mexican-style slow-cooked pork*	*214*	*15*
		Sausages with mushrooms	*322*	*26*
		Pork loin with roasted peppers	*124*	*6*
		Pork ribs with barbecue sauce	*262*	*20*
		Glazed teriyaki pork belly	*302*	*24*
		Sausages with tomato sauce	*144*	*8*
	Lamb	*Lamb with mustard & mint*	*94*	*3*
	Beef	*Cheeseburger & potato chips*	*74*	*1*
		Thai beef curry	*184*	*12*
	Veal	*Veal with red wine & mustard*	*362*	*30*
		Osso buco	*154*	*9*
	Fish	*Salmon stewed with lentils*	*352*	*29*
		Mackerel & potato stew	*84*	*2*
		Japanese-style bream	*194*	*13*
		Mackerel with vinaigrette	*164*	*10*
		Baked sea bass	*332*	*27*
		Cod & green pepper sandwich	*292*	*23*
		Whiting in salsa verde	*233*	*17*
		Fried fish with garlic	*252*	*19*
		Salt cod & vegetable stew	*104*	*4*
		Sesame sardines with carrot salad	*114*	*5*
Desserts	*Creamy desserts*	*Crème Catalane*	*146*	*8*
		Caramel foam	*254*	*19*
		Coconut flan	*206*	*14*
		Pistachio custard	*227*	*16*
		Almond soup with ice cream	*294*	*23*
	Chocolate	*Chocolate cookies*	*86*	*2*
		White chocolate cream	*354*	*29*
		Chocolate mousse	*364*	*30*
		Bread with chocolate & olive oil	*274*	*21*
		Chocolate cake	*344*	*28*
		Chocolate truffles	*96*	*3*
	Fruit	*Strawberries in vinegar*	*186*	*12*
		Figs with cream & kirsch	*217*	*15*

COURSE	TYPE OF DISH	RECIPE	PAGE	MEAL
Desserts	*Fruit*	*Mandarin oranges with Cointreau*	*197*	*13*
		Mango with white chocolate yogurt	*116*	*5*
		Baked apples	*106*	*4*
		Oranges with honey, olive oil & salt	*324*	*26*
		Caramelized pears	*314*	*25*
		Piña colada	*157*	*9*
		Pineapple with molasses & lime	*284*	*22*
		Banana with lime	*264*	*20*
		Watermelon with menthol candies	*245*	*18*
		Sangría with fruit	*176*	*11*
		Melon & mint soup with pink grapefruit	*374*	*31*
	Others	*Rice pudding*	*235*	*17*
		Yogurt foam with strawberries	*136*	*7*
		Almond cookies	*166*	*10*
		Coconut macaroons	*126*	*6*
		Santiago cake	*76*	*1*
		Caramel pudding	*334*	*27*
		Sweet potato with honey & cream	*304*	*24*

–

Meal 1

–

Caesar salad

–

Cheeseburger & potato chips

–

Santiago cake

INGREDIENTS

BUY FRESH
* Romaine
  or iceberg lettuce
* ground beef
* burger buns
* fresh burger toppings,
  such as onions
  or tomatoes
* lemons

IN THE PANTRY
* garlic
* anchovy fillets
  in olive oil
* sherry vinegar
* sunflower oil
* salt
* white peppercorns
* olive oil
* croutons (see page 52)
* potato chips
* pickles or condiments
  to go with the burgers
* flour
* sugar
* ground almonds
* ground cinnamon
* confectioners' sugar

IN THE FRIDGE
* Parmesan cheese
* whole milk
* eggs
* cheese slices
* butter

–

Caesar salad

–

–

Cheeseburger & potato chips

–

Santiago cake

ORGANIZING THE MENU

	Hours before the meal
	4
	3½
	3
	2½
2 hours before Make the Santiago cake and let cool	2
Make the burgers and keep in the fridge	1½
	1
30 minutes before Make the Caesar dressing and wash the lettuce Turn the cake out of the pan, slice, and dust with confectioners' sugar	½
5 minutes before Cook the burgers	
Just before eating Finish the Caesar salad and put in a serving dish Toast the burger buns and make up the cheeseburgers to your taste	
	Start of the meal

Caesar salad

To make your own croutons, see page 52.

•

Mild olive oil can be used instead of sunflower oil, and iceberg lettuce can be used instead of romaine.

•

The secret of a good Caesar salad is to use good ingredients and to dress the salad at the last minute.

	for 2	for 6	for 20	for 75
For the dressing:				
Garlic cloves	½	1½	4	12
Anchovy fillets packed in olive oil, drained	2	6	1½ oz	4¾ oz
Egg yolks	1	2	3	12
Sunflower oil	3 tbsp plus 1 tsp	scant ½ cup	1¾ cups	6¼ cups
Sherry vinegar	2 tsp	2 tbsp	⅛ cup	scant 1¾ cups
Finely grated Parmesan cheese	¼ cup	½ cup	scant 1½ cups	3 cups
For the salad:				
Romaine lettuce	1 small head	1½ heads	3 heads	12 heads
Finely grated Parmesan cheese	¼ cup	⅔ cup	1¾ cups	6 cups
Croutons	1 cup	3 cups	10 cups	2¼ lb

Start →

Put the garlic, anchovies, and egg yolks into a tall jar or pitcher.

Process with a hand-held blender until smooth.

Very gradually pour in the sunflower oil while blending to make a smooth, thickened sauce that looks similar to mayonnaise. Blend in the vinegar.

Stir in the grated Parmesan.

Continue →

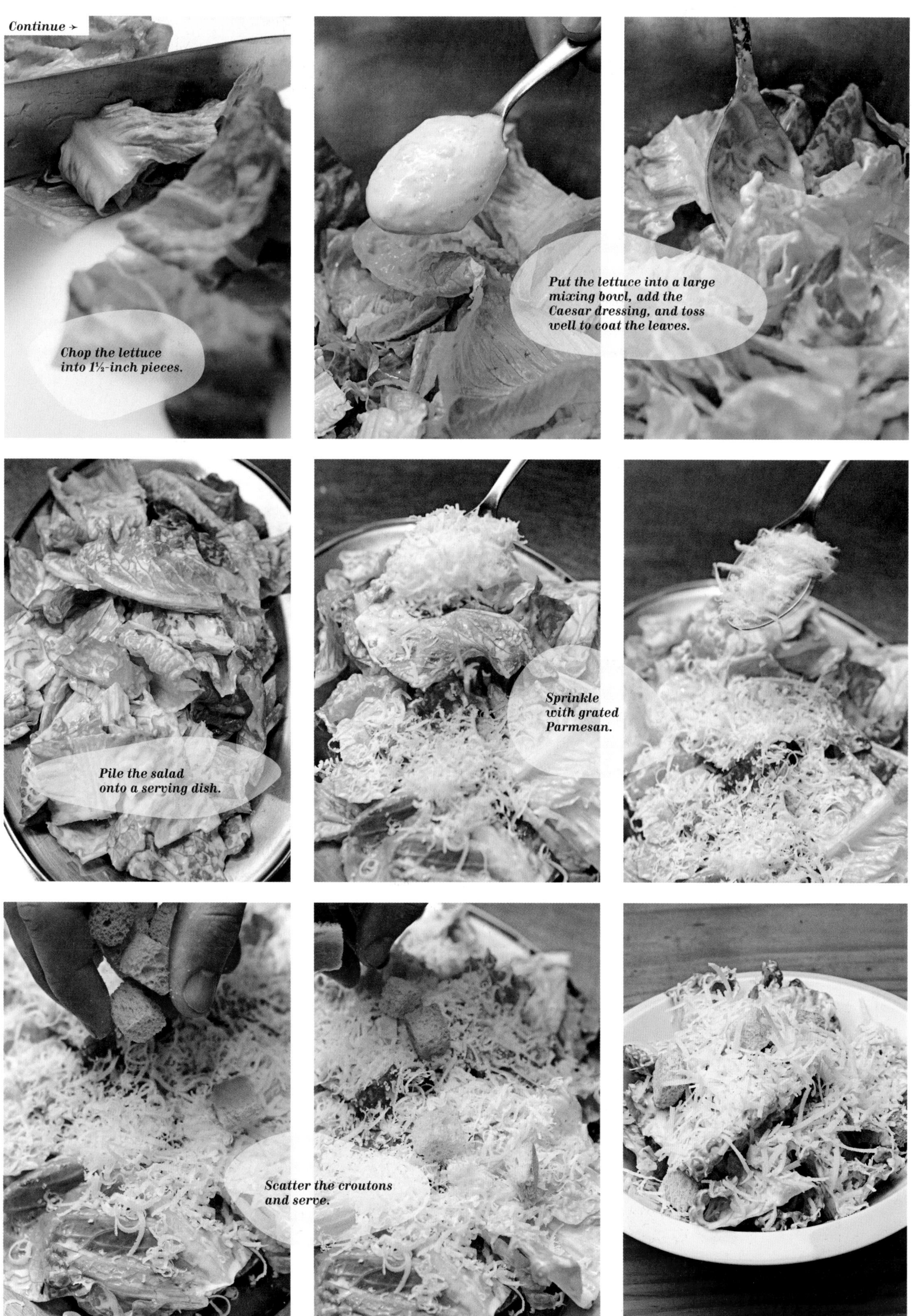
Chop the lettuce
into 1½-inch pieces.
Put the lettuce into a large
mixing bowl, add the
Caesar dressing, and toss
well to coat the leaves.
Pile the salad
onto a serving dish.
Sprinkle
with grated
Parmesan.
Scatter the croutons
and serve.

Cheeseburger & potato chips

To make it even easier, you could use good-quality store-bought burger patties. If making your own, look for good-quality beef chuck with about 10% fat.

•

You can add any other toppings you like, such as onion, tomato, pickles, mustard, ketchup, and mayonnaise. To make a caramelized onion topping, thinly slice some onions and cook very gently with a little oil for about 1 hour, until soft and golden.

	for 2	for 6	for 20	for 75
White bread (crusts removed)	¼ slice	¾ slice	2½ slices	9 slices
Whole milk	1½ tsp	4 tsp	¼ cup	1 cup
Ground beef	9 oz	1½ lb	5 lb	17½ lb
Eggs	½	1	4	15
Salt	¼ tsp	1 tsp	2 tbsp	6 tbsp
Freshly ground white pepper	1 pinch	¼ tsp	2½ tsp	2⅔ tbsp
Olive oil	2 tbsp	6 tbsp	1¾ cups	6¼ cups
Burger buns	2	6	20	75
Cheddar cheese slices	2	6	20	75
Potato chips	2 oz	6 oz	1 lb 2 oz	4½ lb

Start →

To make the burgers, tear the bread into pieces and soak in the milk for 5 minutes.

Combine the meat, eggs, soaked bread, salt, and pepper in a large bowl.

Stir together with your hands until you have an even mixture.

Divide into the appropriate number of portions and shape into patties.

Continue →

Cook the burgers with the oil in a frying pan over medium heat, or under a hot broiler, turning once during cooking.

Cook for 3 minutes for rare, 5 minutes for medium, and 8 minutes for well done.

Cut the buns in half and toast them lightly in a dry pan or under the broiler.

Top each burger with a slice of cheese.

Using a spatula, lift each burger onto a bun.

Sandwich with the top half of the bun.

Add your choice of toppings.

Serve the burgers with potato chips on the side.

Santiago cake

This traditional almond cake originated in the Spanish city of Santiago de Compostela in the sixteenth century.

•

The cake can be flavored with dessert wine or port. Add 2 tbsp when you fold in the ground almonds.

•

We do not recommend making less than the quantity given for one cake, which will serve 12 people. Any leftover cake will keep in an airtight container for up to 4 days.

	for 2	for 12 (one cake)	for 20	for 75
Butter	-	1 tbsp	¼ oz	2½ tbsp
Flour	-	1 tbsp	¼ oz	¼ cup
Extra-large eggs	-	3	6	22
Sugar	-	¾ cup	1½ cups	5 cups
Ground almonds	-	2½ cups	3¼ cups	10¾ cups
Ground cinnamon	-	1 pinch	¼ tsp	2 tsp
Lemons	-	½	1	2
Confectioners' sugar	-	1 tbsp	¼ cup	¾ cup

Start →

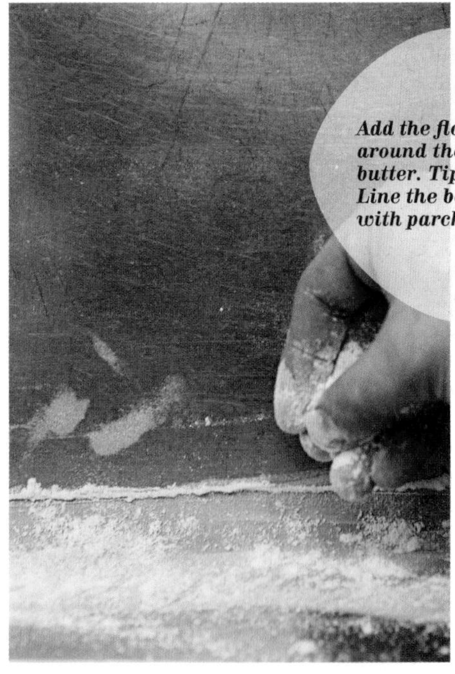

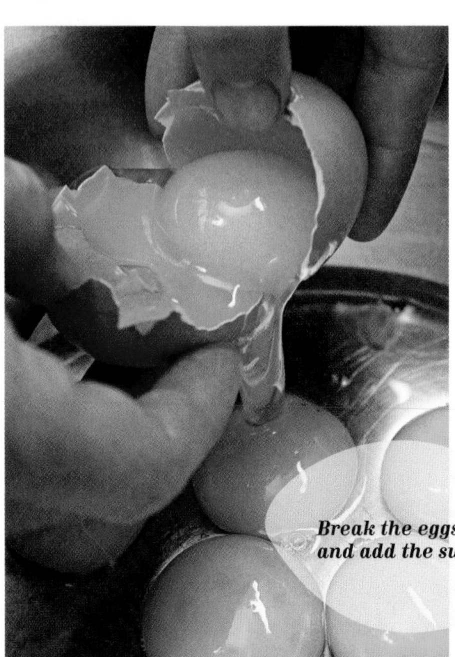

Continue →

Mix the ground almonds with the cinnamon.

Finely grate in lemon zest, then stir until evenly mixed.

Add the ground almond mixture to the eggs and sugar. Fold in carefully with a spatula to retain as much air as possible.

Pour the mixture into the prepared pan.

The cake batter should be about ⅝ inch deep.

Bake in the oven for 17 minutes, or until evenly risen, golden, and shrinking away from the sides of the pan. Remove from the oven and let cool in the pan.

Remove the cake from the pan and cut into portions.

Sprinkle confectioners' sugar over the top using a fine-mesh strainer before serving.

–

Meal 2

–

Pasta bolognese

–

Mackerel & potato stew

–

Chocolate cookies

Pasta bolognese

Mackerel & potato stew

INGREDIENTS

BUY FRESH
* mackerel
* ripe tomatoes
* fresh parsley
* new potatoes

IN THE PANTRY
* garlic
* salt
* pasta
* extra-virgin olive oil
* olive oil
* mild paprika
* black peppercorns
* cornstarch
* vanilla beans
* sugar
* dark chocolate, 75% cocoa
* white chocolate
* flour
* five-spice powder
* instant coffee

IN THE FRIDGE
* Parmesan cheese
* aioli (see page 53)
* eggs
* butter

IN THE FREEZER
* bolognese sauce (see page 44)
* fish stock (see page 56)

Chocolate cookies

ORGANIZING THE MENU

	Hours before the meal
	4
	3½
	3
	2½
	2
At least 1 hour before Make and freeze the cookie dough	1½
1 hour before Prepare the fish, potatoes, garlic, herbs, and tomatoes for the stew	1
30 minutes before Start the sauce for the stew	½
20 minutes before Add the potatoes to the stew Preheat the oven for baking the cookies Heat the bolognese sauce	
10 minutes before Cook the pasta	
Just before eating Cut the cookies and bake Drain the pasta and toss with the oil Add the mackerel to the stew and cook while eating the pasta	
	Start of the meal
Just before main course Thicken the stew sauce and add the mayonnaise and parsley	
	Main course

Pasta bolognese

Bolognese sauce (see page 44) can be made ahead and frozen. Do not forget to defrost it in advance.

•

You can use any kind of pasta for this dish. In Italy, bolognese sauce is traditionally eaten with tagliatelle.

	for 2	for 6	for 20	for 75
Bolognese sauce (see page 44)	⅔ cup	2¼ cups	scant 6 cups	1¼ gallons
Water	6¼ cups	12 cups	1½ gallons	5¾ gallons
Salt	3 tsp	2½ tbsp	5 tbsp	scant 1 cup
Penne pasta	6¼ oz	1 lb 3 oz	4 lb	15½ lb
Extra-virgin olive oil	3 tbsp	½ cup	1¾ cups	6¼ cups
Parmesan cheese, finely grated	⅔ cup	2⅛ cups	7 cups	4½ lb

Start →

Continue →

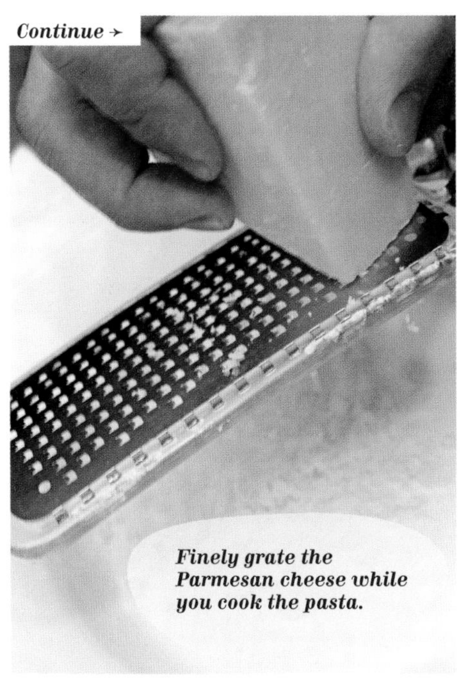
Finely grate the
Parmesan cheese while
you cook the pasta.

Drain the pasta.

Transfer it back into
the pan and stir in the
olive oil to prevent
it from sticking
together.

Serve the pasta topped
with a large spoonful
of bolognese sauce.

Serve the Parmesan
cheese separately
for everyone to sprinkle
their own.

Mackerel & potato stew

This dish is a *suquet*, a traditional Catalan fish stew with a simple sauce of tomatoes, paprika, and parsley.

•

Ask your fish supplier to clean and gut the fish for you if you prefer.

•

You can use picada (see page 41), or mayonnaise instead of the aioli if you like.

•

The combination of garlic, oil, parsley, and tomato makes a kind of instant sofrito.

	for 2	for 6	for 20	for 75
Mackerel, 12 oz each	1	3	10	38
New potatoes	9 oz	1 lb 10 oz	5½ lb	19¾ lb
Garlic cloves	2	5	10½	32
Coarsely grated tomatoes	1½ tbsp	¼ cup	2¼ lb	8¾ lb
Finely chopped fresh parsley	1½ tbsp	3 tbsp	1½ cups	5¾ cups
Olive oil	1½ tbsp	3 tbsp	1 cup	3 cups
Sweet paprika	1 tsp	3 tsp	⅓ cup	1⅔ cups
Fish stock (see page 56)	¾ cups	5 cups	1 gallon	3 gallons
Cornstarch	1 tsp	2 tsp	¾ cup	2¼ cups
Aioli (see page 53)	½ tsp	1 tsp	scant ½ cup	1⅓ cups

Start →

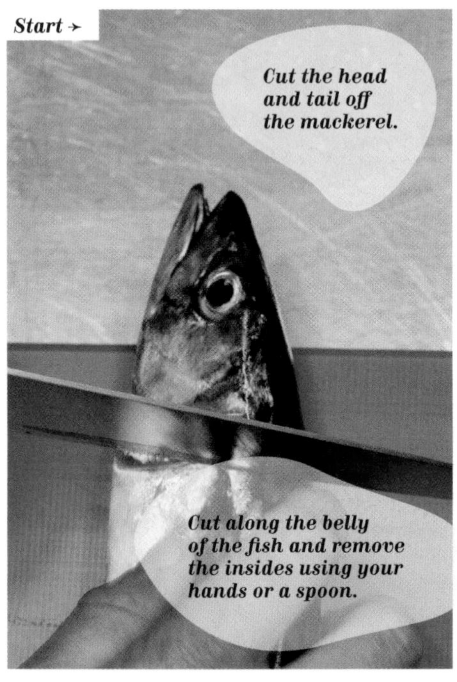

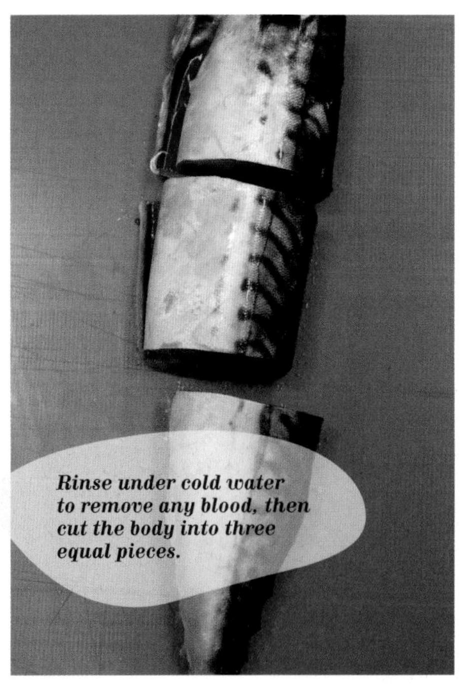

Continue →

As soon as the garlic starts to turn golden, add most of the chopped parsley and all of the grated tomato.

Cook for 5 minutes, then stir in the paprika.

Add the potatoes and stir until well coated in the garlic, tomato, and paprika mix.

Pour in half of the stock and simmer for 20 minutes, or until the potatoes are just tender.

Season the mackerel with salt and pepper and add to the pan. Cook the fish gently for 5 minutes.

Mix the cornstarch with a little cold water until smooth. Stir into the pan until the sauce thickens slightly. Stir carefully so that the potato and mackerel do not break up.

Cook gently for another 5 minutes, or until the fish is opaque and flakes easily away from the back bone. Meanwhile, loosen the aioli with a little of the sauce. Add to the pan.

Finish the dish by sprinkling with the remaining chopped parsley and seasoning with salt.

Serve the stew in shallow bowls.

Chocolate cookies

We do not recommend making less than the quantity given for 20 cookies. If you want to bake just a few at a time, simply cut as many slices as you need and return the dough to the freezer.

•

Five-spice is a Chinese spice mix, usually containing ground fennel, cardamom, star anise, Sichuan pepper, and cinnamon. You can find it at any Asian supermarkets.

•

If you do not have a microwave, melt the chocolate in a heatproof bowl set over a pan of barely simmering water.

	For 20 cookies	For 100 cookies
Vanilla bean	¼	1
Eggs	1	5
Sugar	scant ½ cup	2 cups
Butter	2 tsp	6 tbsp
Dark chocolate, 75% cocoa	2½ oz	1 lb 2 oz
White and dark chocolate pieces	1 oz	8 oz
Flour	2 tsp	¾ cup
Five-spice powder	½ tsp	1 tsp
Instant coffee, ground	½ tsp	1 tsp

Start →

Split the vanilla bean lengthwise and scrape out the seeds with a knife.

Put the eggs into a large mixing bowl. Add the sugar.

Using a free-standing mixer or an electric hand-held whisk, beat the eggs and sugar until combined. Add the vanilla seeds.

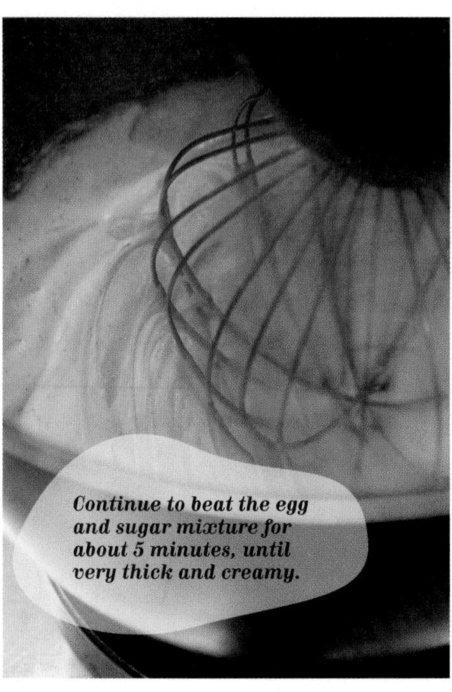

Continue to beat the egg and sugar mixture for about 5 minutes, until very thick and creamy.

Meanwhile, put the butter and two-thirds of the dark chocolate into a microwave-safe bowl. Heat on full power for 1–2 minutes, stirring every 30 seconds, until melted and smooth.

Coarsely chop the white chocolate pieces and remaining dark chocolate. Set aside.

Continue →

Pour the melted chocolate and butter into the egg and sugar mixture, then beat or fold together until smooth.

Mix together the flour, five spice, and coffee.

Fold into the cookie mixture.

Now fold in the chopped chocolate.

Spread the cookie dough over a large sheet of parchment paper, then roll into a cylinder about 1½ inches across.

Freeze the dough until solid (about 1 hour). Unwrap, then cut the cylinder into disks ½-inch thick.
Preheat the oven to 350°F.

Line baking sheets with parchment paper, arrange the disks on the the sheets, and bake for 10 minutes.

Cool on a wire rack and serve.

–

Meal 3

–

Vichyssoise

–

Lamb with mustard & mint

–

Chocolate truffles

Vichyssoise

Lamb with mustard & mint

INGREDIENTS

BUY FRESH
* small red onions
* leeks
* whole lamb necks, cut in half
* fresh mint

IN THE PANTRY
* potatoes
* salt
* black peppercorns
* croutons
* extra-virgin olive oil
* olive oil
* wholegrain mustard
* soy sauce
* Worcestershire sauce
* dark chocolate, 60% cocoa
* brandy
* cocoa powder

IN THE FRIDGE
* whole milk
* eggs
* butter
* whipping cream, 35% fat

IN THE FREEZER
* chicken stock (see page 57)

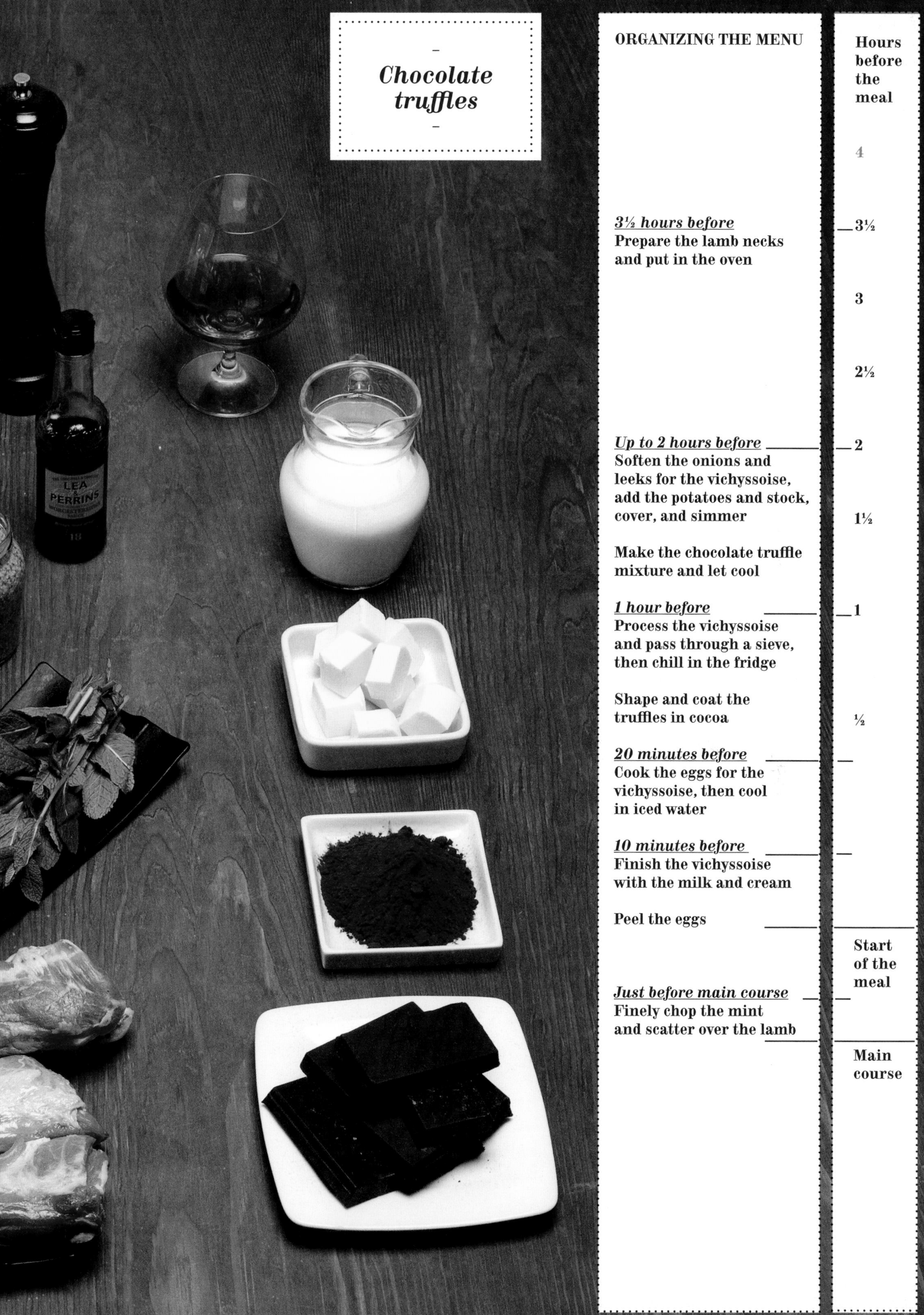

Chocolate truffles

ORGANIZING THE MENU	Hours before the meal
	4
3½ hours before **Prepare the lamb necks and put in the oven**	3½
	3
	2½
Up to 2 hours before **Soften the onions and leeks for the vichyssoise, add the potatoes and stock, cover, and simmer**	2
	1½
Make the chocolate truffle mixture and let cool	
1 hour before **Process the vichyssoise and pass through a sieve, then chill in the fridge**	1
Shape and coat the truffles in cocoa	½
20 minutes before **Cook the eggs for the vichyssoise, then cool in iced water**	
10 minutes before **Finish the vichyssoise with the milk and cream**	
Peel the eggs	
	Start of the meal
Just before main course **Finely chop the mint and scatter over the lamb**	
	Main course

Vichyssoise

Vichyssoise is a classic leek and potato soup from France.

•

We sometimes cook the eggs in a low-temperature water bath called a Roner at 145°F for 40 minutes. This gives a soft and silky result.

•

Store-bought croutons are ideal for this recipe and will save you time. However, to make your own, see page 52.

	for 2	for 6	for 20	for 75
Potatoes	½	2	7	23
Red onions	½	1	3	9
Leeks	1	2	2½ lb	7½ lb
Butter	1½ tbsp	scant ½ cup	1¾ cup	2⅔ cups
Chicken stock (see page 57)	¾ cup	4¼ cups	10½ cups	8½ quarts
Eggs	2	6	20	75
Whipping cream, 35% fat	2¾ tbsp	1 cup	3¼ cups	12 cups
Croutons (see page 52)	2 tbsp	¼ cup	10 cups	2¼ lb
Extra-virgin olive oil	1 tsp	1 tbsp	¼ cup	¾ cup

Start →

Cut the potatoes into small pieces and drop into a bowl of cold water until needed.

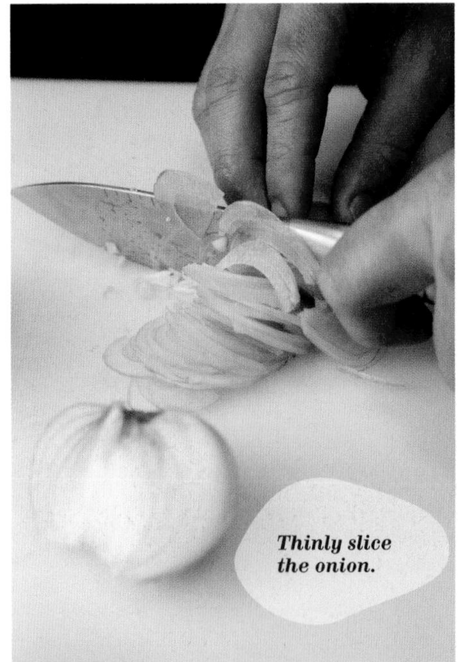

Thinly slice the onion.

Trim the dark green leaves from the leeks and cut the leeks in half lengthwise. Rinse under running water to remove any dirt or grit.

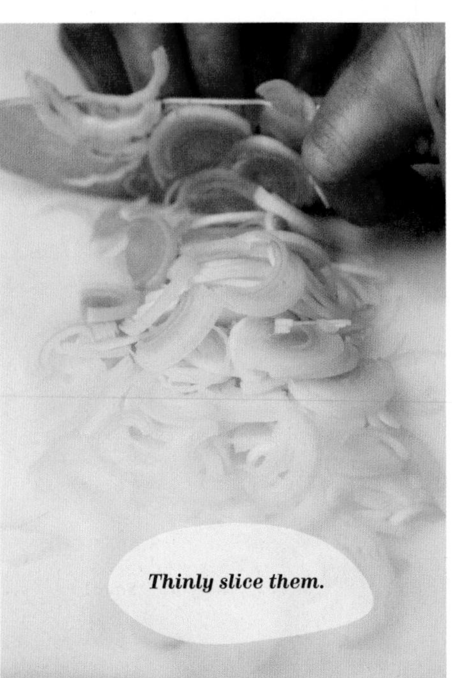

Thinly slice them.

Melt the butter in a large saucepan over low heat, and add the onions. Cook for 5 minutes, until softened but not browned.

Add the leeks and cook for another 10 minutes, stirring often, until the leeks and onions are very soft.

Meanwhile, pour the chicken stock into a large pot and bring to a boil.

Continue →

Add the potatoes
to the onions and leeks.

Add the hot stock,
cover, and simmer
for 30 minutes.

Bring a pot of
water to a boil.
Add the eggs and
boil for 3 minutes.

Cool the eggs in a bowl
of ice water, then peel
off the shells. Keep them
in a bowl of warm water
until ready to serve.

After 30 minutes of cooking,
process the soup, using a
hand-held blender, until
smooth and creamy.

Pass the soup through
a fine-mesh strainer and
let cool in the pan. Chill in
the fridge until very cold.

Whisk the cream into the
soup, then season with
salt and pepper.

Place an egg in the middle
of each serving bowl and
pour in the vichyssoise.

Scatter the croutons
and drizzle with the
extra-virgin olive oil.

Lamb with mustard & mint

Ask your butcher to prepare the lamb necks. The excess fat should be removed, then the necks cut in half lengthwise to create two large, meaty chops.

	for 2	for 6	for 20	for 75
Fresh mint	8 sprigs	1 small bunch	2 bunches	5 bunches
Whole lamb necks, cut in half	1	3	10	38
Olive oil	2 tbsp	⅓ cup	1⅛ cup	3⅓ cup
Wholegrain mustard	1 tbsp	3 tbsp	1 cup	3¼ cups
Soy sauce	1 tbsp	3 tbsp	½ cup	1½ cups
Worcestershire sauce	1 tbsp	3 tbsp	⅔ cup	2 cups
Water	4¼ cups	6¼ cups	4½ quarts	4¼ gallons

Start →

Continue →

Add the soy sauce,
Worcestershire sauce,
and water.

Cover the lamb with half of the
mint and cover with foil.

Roast for 3 hours, turning the
lamb occasionally, until golden
and very tender.

Finely chop
the remaining
mint leaves.

Sprinkle the chopped
mint over the lamb.

Pour the sauce from the pan
over the lamb and serve.

Chocolate truffles

To make chocolate hazelnut truffles, add some Nutella at the same time as the butter.

•

You can replace the brandy with another distilled spirit or liqueur, if you like.

•

You can also pipe the truffles using a pastry bag. In this case, you will need to remove them from the fridge to soften before piping.

	for 2 (makes 8 truffles)	for 6	for 20	for 75
Dark chocolate, 60% cocoa	2⅛ oz	4 oz	14 oz	2¼ lb
Whipping cream, 35% fat	¼ cup	½ cup	¾ cup	5 cups
Butter, cut into small pieces	1 tsp	2 tsp	2½ tbsp	7 tbsp
Brandy	½ tsp	2 tsp	1 tbsp	¼ cup
Unsweetened cocoa powder	2 tbsp	4 tbsp	½ cup	scant 1 cup

Start →

Chop the chocolate into small pieces and place in a large bowl. Pour the cream into a saucepan, then bring to a boil.

Pour the hot cream over the chocolate.

Leave the chocolate to melt for 3 minutes, then stir well with a balloon whisk, until smooth and creamy.

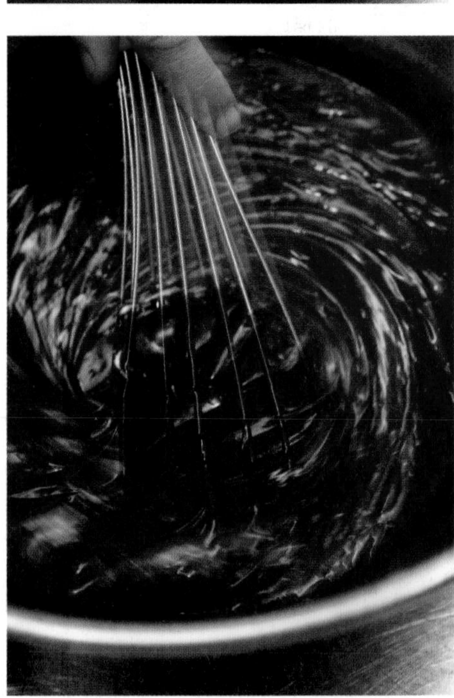

Continue →

Whisk in the butter.

Pour in the brandy and
stir until smooth.

Cover the surface of the mixture
with plastic wrap to prevent
a skin from forming, then set
aside to cool until firm.

Use two teaspoons to shape
the mix into walnut-size.
irregular-shape pieces.

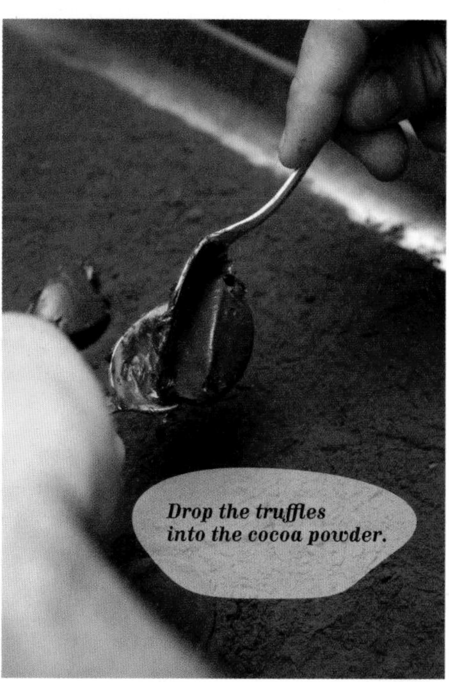
Drop the truffles
into the cocoa powder.

Carefully roll them to coat.

Serve the truffles
at room temperature.

–

Meal 4

–

Beans with clams

–

Salt cod & vegetable stew

–

Baked apples

Beans with clams

Salt cod & vegetable stew

INGREDIENTS

BUY FRESH
* small round clams
* long, sweet red peppers
* long, sweet green peppers
* eggplants
* zucchini
* large ripe tomatoes
* Golden Delicious apples
* salt cod

IN THE PANTRY
* canned white beans
* salt
* black peppercorns
* onions
* garlic
* sunflower oil
* extra-virgin olive oil
* brandy
* honey
* ground cinnamon
* sugar

IN THE FRIDGE
* butter
* whipping cream, 35% fat

IN THE FREEZER
* fish stock (see page 56)
* sofrito (see page 43)
* picada (see page 41)

Baked apples

ORGANIZING THE MENU

	Hours before the meal
24 hours before Put the salt cod into a container, cover with cold water, and let soak in the fridge, changing water regularly	
	4
	3½
	3
	2½
	2
1½ hours before Cover the clams with water and leave to soak	1½
1 hour before Prepare the apples and put into the oven	1
Make the salt cod stew and let simmer	
	½
25 minutes before Cook the beans	
10 minutes before Whip the cream for the apples	
Just before eating Add the clams to the beans	
	Start of the meal
Just before main course Add the salt cod to the vegetables	
	Main course

Beans with clams

We use a variety of white bean known as *planchada*, which give a creamy result. Cannellini or lima beans make a good substitute.

•

If round clams are not available, use mussels or small razor clams instead.

•

The dish should be soupy. You may need to add a little more stock if you are using a wide pan. When cooking it for large numbers, add the stock before the beans so that they do not break up too much.

	for 2	for 6	for 20	for 75
Small round clams	5½ oz	1 lb 2 oz	3½ lb	13¼ lb
Sofrito (see page 43)	2 tsp	2 tbsp	2¼ cups	7¼ cups
Canned white beans, drained	1 cup	3½ cups	4¼ cups	22 lb
Fish stock (see page 56)	¾ cup	6¼ cups	12 cups	1⅞ gallons
Picada (see page 41)	2 tsp	2 tbsp	½ cup	1¾ cups

Start →

Pick over the clams, discarding any that are damaged.

Put the clams in a large bowl and cover with salted water.

Let soak for 1 hour. This will help the clams to purge themselves of any sand.

Heat the sofrito in a large pan over medium heat.

Stir in the beans, followed by the fish stock.

Continue →

Simmer the beans
for 15 minutes.
Add the picada.
Lift the clams out
of the water, leaving
any sand behind
in the bowl, and add
to the pan.
Cook for 3 minutes, until
the clams open. Discard
any clams that stay shut.
Season to taste with
salt and pepper.
Serve in soup dishes.

Salt cod & vegetable stew

This traditional dish of vegetables cooked in olive oil is called *samfaina* in Catalonia.

•

You can serve the stew on toast as an open-faced sandwich.

•

Salt cod can vary in its saltiness, so ask your fish supplier how long they would recommend to soak yours for before use. Change the water regularly.

	for 2	for 6	for 20	for 75
Onions	2¾ oz	7 oz	1 lb 8½ oz	5 lb
Garlic cloves	½	2	¼ oz	1 oz
Long, sweet red peppers	2 oz	5 oz	1 lb 2 oz	4½ lb
Long, sweet green peppers	2 oz	5 oz	1 lb 2 oz	4½ lb
Eggplants	4 oz	12 oz	2½ lb	8¾ lb
Zucchini	4 oz	12 oz	2½ lb	8¾ lb
Ripe tomatoes	3½ oz	11 oz	2¼ lb	7¾ lb
Sunflower oil	scant 1 cup	2¼ cups	4¼ cups	12½ cups
Extra-virgin olive oil	1½ tbsp	3 tbsp	⅔ cup	2½ cups
Salt cod, soaked	5 oz	1 lb	2¼ lb	11 lb

For 2, you will need to buy 1 of each vegetable, and for 6, you will need to buy 2 of each vegetable. In both cases, choose small ones.

Start →

Continue →

Pour the sunflower oil into a large, deep pan and place over medium heat.
Once the oil is hot, carefully add the eggplant and zucchini in small batches and fry until golden.

Drain in a colander to remove the excess oil.

Pour the olive oil into a large saucepan and place over medium heat. Add the garlic and fry for 1 minute. Add the onion and cook for 5 minutes, until golden.

Add the peppers and cook until they start to soften.

Add the fried and drained eggplant and zucchini, then add the grated tomato. Simmer for 1 hour.

When the vegetables are very soft and the tomatoes have thickened, season with salt and pepper and add enough water to give a creamy texture.

Tear the cod into pieces about ¾-inch wide and 2 inches long. Add to the stew and simmer for 2 minutes. Do not overcook.

Remove from the heat and serve on plates, or on top of toasted bread.

Baked apples

You can use cognac, armagnac, calvados, or any other similar distilled spirit instead of the brandy.

•

You can use any type of apple, but we like Golden Delicious.

•

When preparing the dish for 2 people, you may prefer to use thick heavy cream instead, because it is difficult to whip small quantities of cream.

	for 2	for 6	for 20	for 75
Apples	2	6	20	75
Brandy	2 tsp	2 tbsp	½ cup	1⅔ cups
Honey	2 tsp	2 tbsp	scant 1 cup	3 cups
Ground cinnamon	1 pinch	2 pinches	4 tsp	¼ cup
Butter, cut into small pieces	2 tsp	2 tbsp	5½ tbsp	1⅜ cups
Whipping cream, 35% fat	5 tbsp	¾ cup	2½ cups	8 cups
Sugar	½ tsp	2 tsp	scant ½ cup	1½ cups

Start →

Continue →

Pour the honey over top.

Dust the apples with cinnamon.

Put some butter inside each apple.

Top each apple with a lid and cover the pan with foil.

Bake for 1 hour, until the apples are tender.

Pour the cream into a large bowl, and add the sugar.

Whip until soft peaks form.

Lift the warm apples out from the pan and onto serving plates. Spoon over the pan juices and serve with the cream.

–

Meal 5

–

Polenta & Parmesan gratin

–

Sesame sardines with carrot salad

–

Mango with white chocolate yogurt

Polenta & Parmesan gratin

Sesame sardines with carrot salad

INGREDIENTS

BUY FRESH
* sardines
* lemons
* carrots
* fresh mint
* mangoes

IN THE PANTRY
* salt
* sesame seeds
* extra-virgin olive oil
* olive oil
* Dijon mustard
* sherry vinegar
* caramelized hazelnuts
* instant polenta
* white chocolate

IN THE FRIDGE
* Parmesan cheese
* butter
* plain yogurt
* whipping cream, 35% fat

Mango with white chocolate yogurt

ORGANIZING THE MENU

Hours before the meal

4

3½

3

2½

2

1½

1

1 hour before
Make the white chocolate yogurt and let cool

½

Break up the caramelized hazelnuts and set aside

Clean the sardines and coat in sesame seeds. Chill until needed

Peel and slice the carrots. Make the vinaigrette

20 minutes before
Peel and cut the mango and chill

Grate the cheese and boil the water for the polenta

15 minutes before
Make the polenta and set aside

Just before eating
Sprinkle Parmesan over the polenta and broil it

Start of the meal

Just before main course
Fry the sardines. Dress the carrot with the vinaigrette

Main course

Just before dessert
Spoon the yogurt over the mango and sprinkle with the nuts

Dessert

Polenta & Parmesan gratin

For the creamiest polenta, make it just before you want to serve it.

•

Look for the instant type of polenta, which cooks in 5–10 minutes. Otherwise, substitute with cornmeal.

	for 2	for 6	for 20	for 75
Water	1¼ cups	4 cups	1 gallon	3 gallons
Polenta	6½ tbsp	1 cup	4 cups	4¾ lb
Whipping cream, 35% fat	scant ½ cup	1¼ cups	6¼ cups	1 gallon
Parmesan cheese, finely grated	½ cup	1⅓ cups	6 cups	3½ lb
Butter	1 tsp	2 tsp	¾ cup	2⅔ cups
For the gratin:				
Parmesan cheese, finely grated	1½ tbsp	4 tbsp	7⅓ cups	4½ lb

Start →

Pour the water into a saucepan and bring to a boil. Sprinkle in the polenta a little at a time, whisking continuously.

When all the polenta has been added, cook for 2 minutes over medium heat, whisking continuously.

Pour in the cream and cook for another 2 minutes.

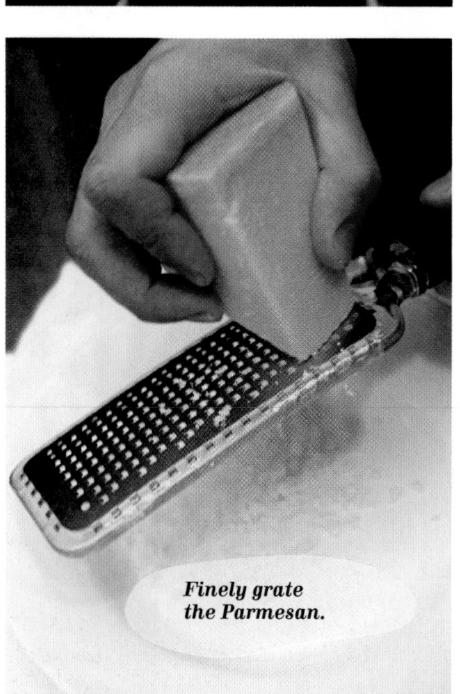

Finely grate the Parmesan.

Gradually add the first quantity of Parmesan cheese.

Add the butter.

Continue →

Keep whisking
until the polenta
has thickened.
Season with salt.

Pour the polenta
into a large baking
pan or heatproof dish.
The polenta should
be about ½ inch deep.

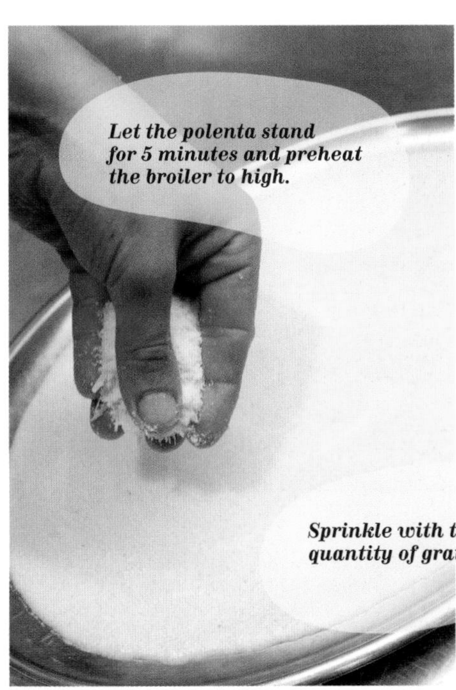
Let the polenta stand
for 5 minutes and preheat
the broiler to high.

Sprinkle with the second
quantity of grated Parmesan.

Broil until the cheese
is golden and bubbling.

Serve immediately.

Sesame sardines with carrot salad

Ask your fish supplier to clean and gut the fish for you if you prefer.

	for 2	for 6	for 20	for 75
Medium sardines	10	30	100	375
Sesame seeds	3 tbsp	½ cup	2¼ cups	7 cups
Olive oil	2 tsp	2 tbsp	scant ½ cup	1¼ cups
Lemons, halved	½	2	4	10
For the carrot salad:				
Carrots	2	6	4½ lb	13¼ lb
Dijon mustard	2 tsp	2 tbsp	¾ cup	2¼ cups
Extra-virgin olive oil	2 tbsp	6 tbsp	¾ cup	5 cups
Sherry vinegar	2 tsp	2 tbsp	½ cup	¾ cup
Fresh mint	1 sprig	3 sprigs	1 bunch	2 bunches

Start →

Continue →

Finely chop the mint leaves.

Stir them into the vinaigrette.

Place a nonstick frying pan over medium heat, then add the oil. Season the sardines with salt.

Fry on both sides for 1 minute, or until golden brown and juicy.

Transfer the sardines to a plate, then squeeze over the juice of the lemon.

Toss the carrot slices with the vinaigrette.

Season with salt.

Serve the sardines with the carrot salad.

Mango with white chocolate yogurt

If you prefer, toasted or caramelized almonds, walnuts, or pine nuts can be substituted for the hazelnuts.

•

Take the yogurt out of the fridge before you start, so that it is not too cold when the white chocolate is added.

	for 2	for 6	for 20	for 75
White chocolate	2 oz	5 oz	14 oz	2¾ lb
Plain yogurt	½ cup	¾ cup	2⅔ cups	8 cups
Caramelized hazelnuts	8	24	1¾ cups	4⅜ cups
Ripe mangoes	1	3	8	30

Start →

Continue →

Gradually whisk the melted chocolate into the yogurt to make a smooth sauce. Cool at room temperature.

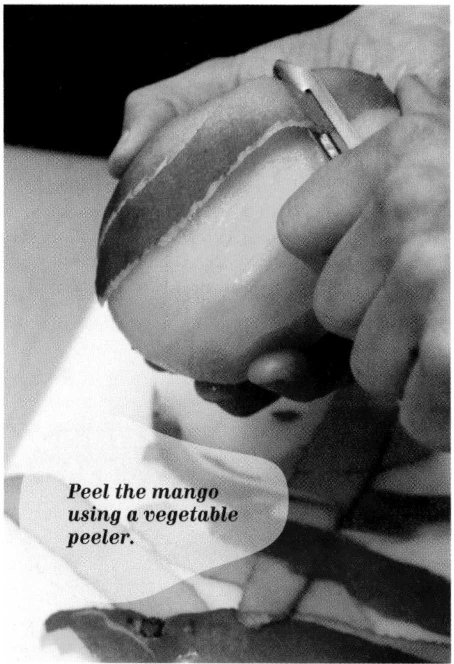

Peel the mango using a vegetable peeler.

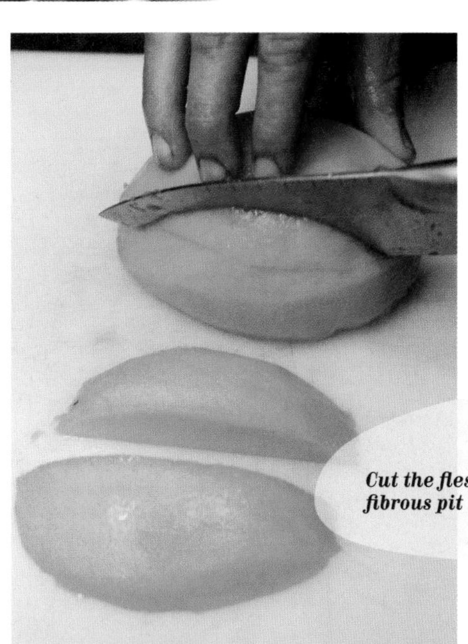

Cut the flesh away from the fibrous pit in the middle.

Cut the mango flesh into ½-inch cubes or slices, then chill until needed.

Transfer the mango to serving plates and spoon over the yogurt. Sprinkle with hazelnuts and serve.

–

Meal 6

–

Potato chip omelet

–

Pork loin with peppers

–

Coconut macaroons

Potato chip omelet

INGREDIENTS

BUY FRESH
* large red bell peppers
* fresh parsley
* thin-cut pork loin steaks
* unsweetened dried coconut

IN THE PANTRY
* olive oil
* salted potato chips
* garlic
* salt
* black peppercorns
* sugar

IN THE FRIDGE
* eggs

Pork loin with peppers

Coconut macaroons

ORGANIZING THE MENU

	Hours before the meal
	4
	3½
	3
	2½
	2
1½ hours before **Roast the bell peppers, then cool and slice them**	1½
1 hour before **Make and bake the coconut macaroons, then cool**	1
Prepare the garlic and parsley oil for the pork and finish cooking the bell peppers in their juices	½
5 minutes before **Soak the potato chips in the egg, then cook the potato omelet**	
	Start of the meal
Just before main course **Fry the pork and serve with the peppers and the garlic and parsley oil**	
	Main course

Potato chip omelet

It is essential to use good-quality chips and eggs.

•

Because the chips are salted, there is no need to season with salt.

•

For large quantities, we make large omelets to serve 4–6 people each and placethem on the table for people to help themselves.

	for 2	for 6	for 20	for 75
Eggs	6	18	60	225
Salted potato chips	2¾ oz	7½ oz	1 lb 7 oz	9 lb
Olive oil	1½ tbsp	4 tbsp	scant ½ cup	scant 1 cup

Start →

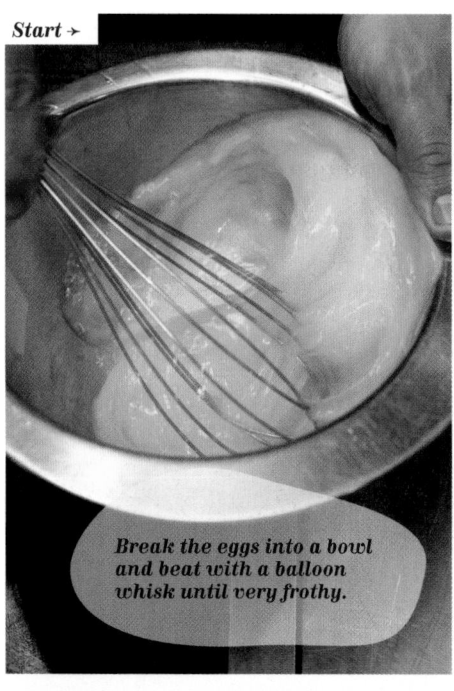

Break the eggs into a bowl and beat with a balloon whisk until very frothy.

Add the chips, being careful not to break them, then let soak in the egg for for 1 minute.

Place a 10-inch nonstick frying pan over medium heat, then add 2 teaspoons of oil.

Continue →

Pour the mixture into the pan and stir gently with a rubber spatula.

Use the spatula to loosen the omelet from the edge of the pan.

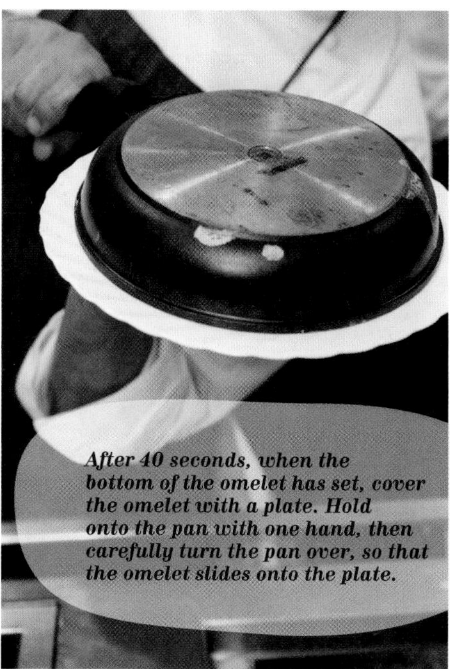

After 40 seconds, when the bottom of the omelet has set, cover the omelet with a plate. Hold onto the pan with one hand, then carefully turn the pan over, so that the omelet slides onto the plate.

Remove the pan and return it to the heat. Add another 2 teaspoons oil.

Slide the omelet from the plate and into the pan, so that the uncooked side is in contact with the heat. Cook for another 20 seconds.

Serve the omelet on a plate.

Pork loin with roasted peppers

This recipe also works well with beef.

	for 2	for 6	for 20	for 75
Large red bell peppers	1	2	8	30
Olive oil, plus extra for frying	3½ tbsp	scant ½ cup	⅔ cup	1¾ cup
Garlic cloves	1	3	18	48
Fresh parsley	1 sprig	3 sprigs	½ bunch	1 bunch
Thin-cut pork loin steaks	6	18	60	225

Start →

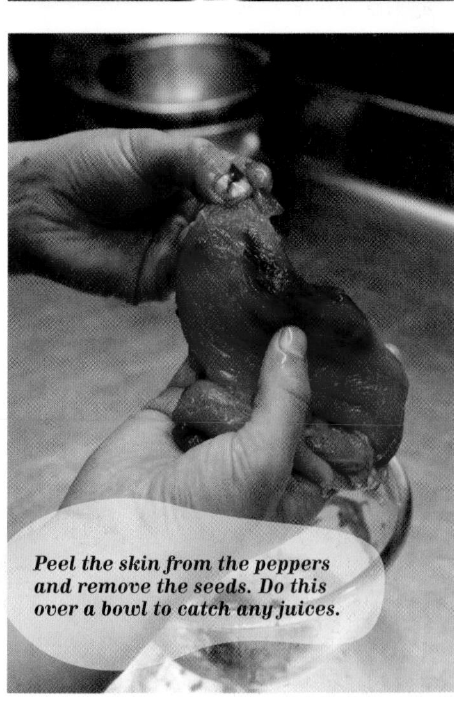

Continue →

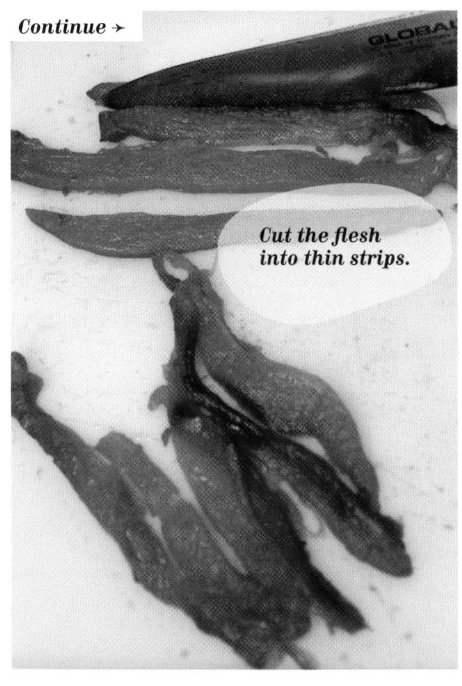

Cut the flesh into thin strips.

Put the peppers and the reserved juices into a pan and simmer over a low heat for 5 minutes.

Pick the leaves from the parsley stems.

Put the drained, blanched garlic, parsley leaves, and remaining oil into a tall jar or pitcher.

Process with a hand-held blender until finely chopped.

Place a large frying pan over high heat and add a little olive oil. Fry the pork for 1½ minutes, until golden on both sides and juicy in the middle.

Season the pork with salt and pepper, and serve with the roasted peppers. Finish with a tablespoon of the garlic and parsley oil.

Coconut macaroons

We do not recommend making less than the amount given for 15 macaroons to ensure a good result. Any leftover macaroons will keep for a few days in an airtight container.

	for 2 (makes 15)	for 6 (makes 30)	for 20	for 75
Unsweetened dried coconut	1 cup	2 cups	6 cups	3⅓ lb
Sugar	scant ½ cup	1 cup	3 cups	7½ cups
Eggs	1	2	5	15

Start →

Continue →

Using your hands or two teaspoons, shape the mixture into walnut-size balls.

Place on the baking sheet.

Bake for 13 minutes, or until slightly golden.

Let cool before serving.

–

Meal 7

–

Saffron risotto with mushrooms

–

Catalan-style turkey

–

Yogurt foam with strawberries

INGREDIENTS

BUY FRESH
* white mushrooms
* lemons
* red onions
* turkey drumsticks
* strawberries

IN THE PANTRY
* saffron
* olive oil
* onions
* white wine
* risotto rice
* salt
* black peppercorns
* raisins
* dried plums (prunes)
* *vino rancio* or dry sherry
* canned chopped tomatoes
* pine nuts
* sugar, optional
* N_2O cartridges for the siphon

IN THE FRIDGE
* butter
* Parmesan cheese
* plain yogurt
* whipping cream, 35% fat

IN THE FREEZER
* chicken stock (see page 57)

Saffron risotto with mushrooms

Catalan-style turkey

Yogurt foam with strawberries

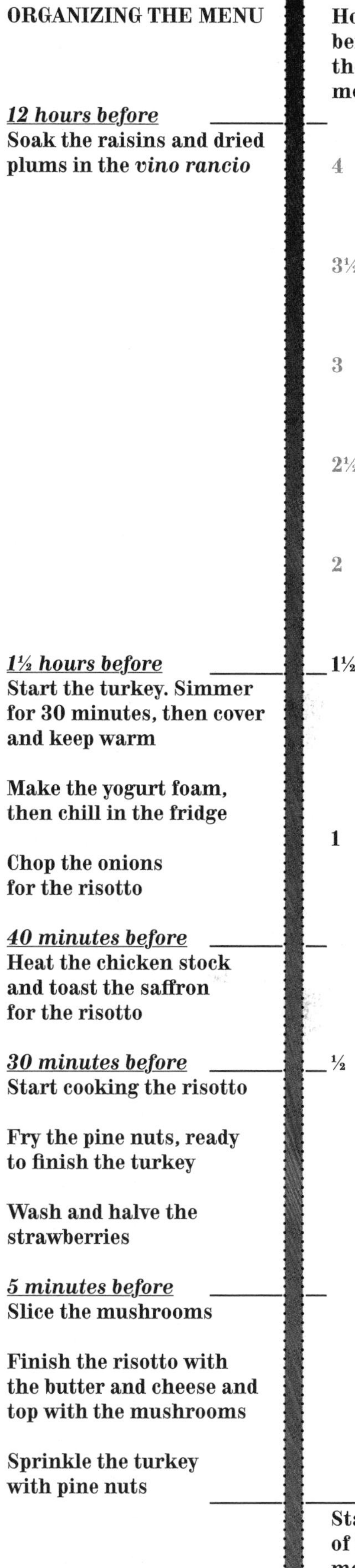

ORGANIZING THE MENU	Hours before the meal
12 hours before Soak the raisins and dried plums in the *vino rancio*	
	4
	3½
	3
	2½
	2
1½ hours before Start the turkey. Simmer for 30 minutes, then cover and keep warm Make the yogurt foam, then chill in the fridge	1½
Chop the onions for the risotto	1
40 minutes before Heat the chicken stock and toast the saffron for the risotto	
30 minutes before Start cooking the risotto Fry the pine nuts, ready to finish the turkey Wash and halve the strawberries	½
5 minutes before Slice the mushrooms Finish the risotto with the butter and cheese and top with the mushrooms Sprinkle the turkey with pine nuts	
	Start of the meal
Just before dessert Dispense the yogurt foam into bowls, then finish with the strawberries	
	Dessert

Saffron risotto with mushrooms

It is essential to choose the right rice for your risotto. Types of risotto rice such as arborio, carnaroli, and vialone nano, are commonly used in Italy. If risotto rice is not available, you can substitute it with a short-grain rice that has a high starch content.

	for 2	for 6	for 20	for 75
Chicken stock (see page 57)	2½ cups	7¾ cups	1¾ gallons	5¾ gallons
Saffron strands	1 pinch	2 pinches	2½ tsp	2¾ tbsp
Olive oil	1½ tbsp	¼ cup	½ cup	1¾ cups
Finely chopped onion	1 tsp	2 tsp	½ cup	1¾ cups
White wine	2 tbsp	¼ cup	1 cup	3 cups
Risotto rice	1 cup	3 cups	10½ cups	15½ lb
Medium white mushrooms	2	6	1¾ lb	6½ lb
Butter	1 tsp	1 tbsp	4½ tbsp	scant 2 cups
Finely grated Parmesan cheese	6⅔ tbsp	1⅓ cups	3⅔ cups	12 cups
Lemon juice	1 tsp	2 tsp	7 tsp	½ cup

Start →

Continue →

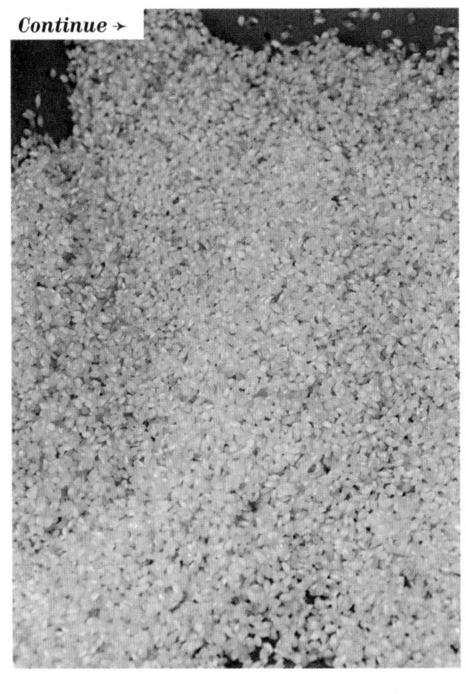

Add a ladle of hot stock.
Stir the rice frequently
for 2–3 minutes to prevent
it from sticking.

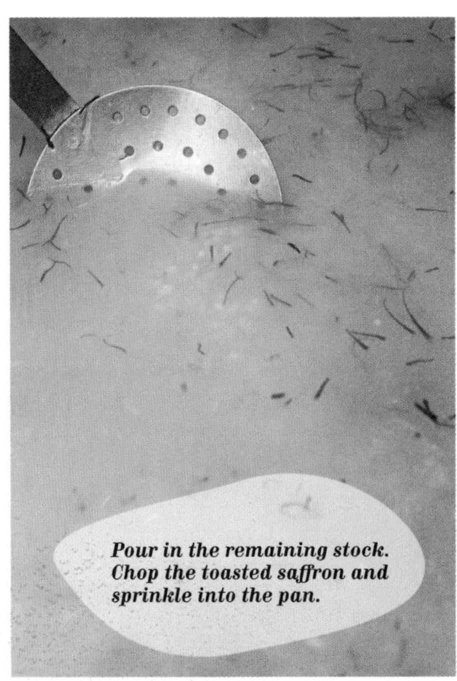
Pour in the remaining stock.
Chop the toasted saffron and
sprinkle into the pan.

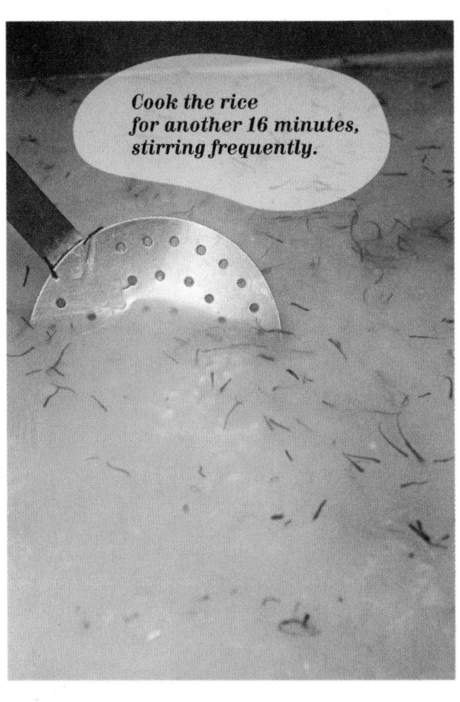
Cook the rice
for another 16 minutes,
stirring frequently.

Meanwhile, quickly wipe
clean the mushrooms
with a paper towel, then
finely slice using a
mandoline or sharp knife.

When the rice has absorbed
most of the liquid and is just
firm to the bite, add the butter.

Add the Parmesan cheese.
Stir well until the rice becomes
creamy. Season with salt,
pepper, and lemon juice. Spoon
the risotto onto serving plates.

Scatter the mushroom slices over
the risotto. The heat from the rice
will lightly "cook" the mushrooms.

Catalan-style turkey

Vino rancio **is a Catalan fortified oxidized wine. If you cannot find it, use dry sherry instead.**

	for 2	for 6	for 20	for 75
Raisins	¼ cup	scant ⅔ cup	2¼ cups	7 cups
Pitted dried plums (prunes)	3 tbsp	½ cup	1¾ cups	6½ cups
Vino rancio	6 tbsp	1 cup	scant 3½ cups	12⅝ cups
Red onions, thinly sliced	7 oz	1 lb 5 oz	5¼ lb	17½ lb
Turkey drumsticks	2	6	20	75
Olive oil	1½ tbsp	3 tbsp	⅔ cup	¾ cups
Chopped tomatoes	⅓ cup	1 cup	4¾ cups	11 lb
Water	1 cup	3 cups	10 cups	2 gallons
Pine nuts	2 tsp	2 tbsp	scant 1 cup	2¾ cups

For 2 people you will need 1 onion, and for 6 people you will need 3.

Start →

Put the raisins and dried plums in a bowl and pour over the vino rancio.

Let soak for 12 hours.

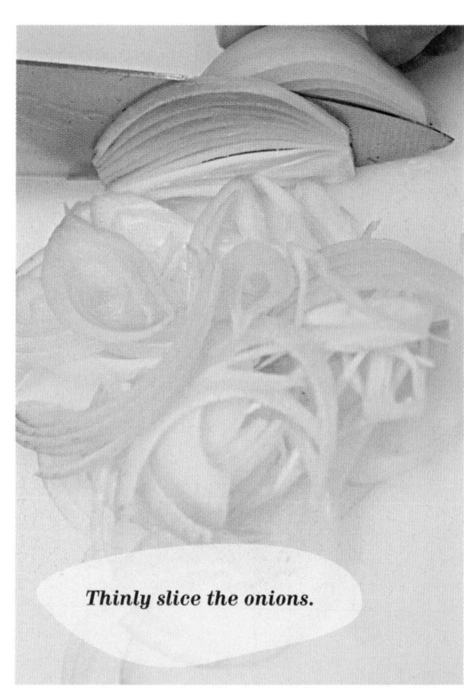

Thinly slice the onions.

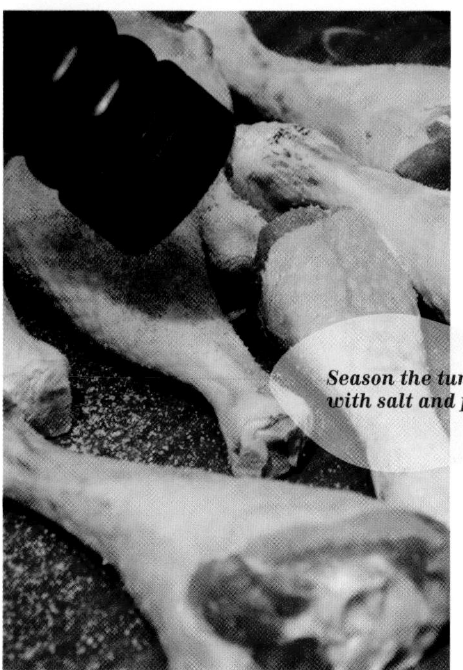

Season the turkey with salt and pepper.

Put a wide pan over medium heat, then add most of the oil. Brown the turkey for 10 minutes, until golden all over.

Continue →

Add the onions.

Fry the onions and turkey for about 10 minutes, stirring often, until the onions are caramelized and dark golden brown.

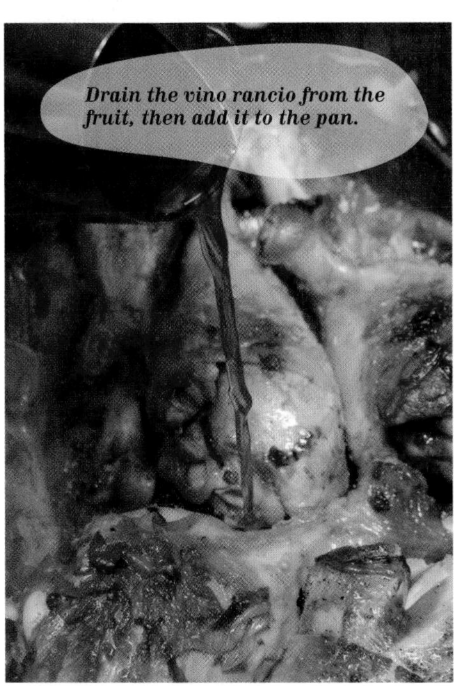
Drain the vino rancio from the fruit, then add it to the pan.

When most of the vino rancio has evaporated, add the chopped tomatoes and continue to cook until everything is well caramelized.

Pour in the water, reduce the heat and simmer for 30 minutes.

Add the raisins and plums. Cover the pan and let cook for another hour, or until the turkey is very tender and the sauce is thick and tasty.

Meanwhile, heat the remaining oil in a frying pan, then add the pine nuts. Cook over low heat for about 5 minutes, stirring often, until golden.

Put the turkey onto a serving dish, cover with the sauce, raisins, and plums. Finish by sprinkling with pine nuts.

Yogurt foam with strawberries

If you prefer a sweeter dessert, add 2 tsp sugar for every 1⅔ cups yogurt.

•

You can substitute any seasonal fruit for the strawberries, such as peach, apricot, banana, or pineapple.

•

Look for small strawberries that weigh around ½ oz. Allow 3 per person.

	for 2	for 4–6	for 20	for 75
Plain yogurt	-	1⅔ cups	4½ cups	7¾ cups
Whipping cream, 35% fat	-	½ cup	1 cup	4 cups
N_2O cartridges for the siphon	-	1	6	12
Strawberries	-	6–9½ oz	2 lb	7½ lb

The minimum quantity of foam you can make in a whipped-cream siphon is 4–6 portions. If you do not have a siphon, you can whip the cream and yogurt with a whisk, although the texture will not be as airy.

Use a pint-size siphon for 4–6 people, and quart-size siphons for 20 or 75.

Start →

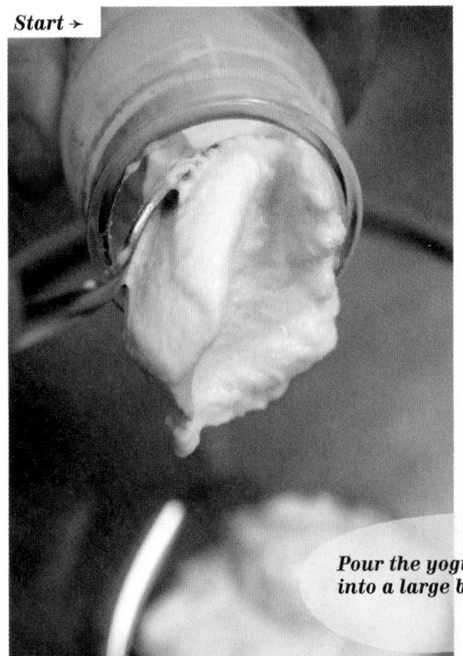
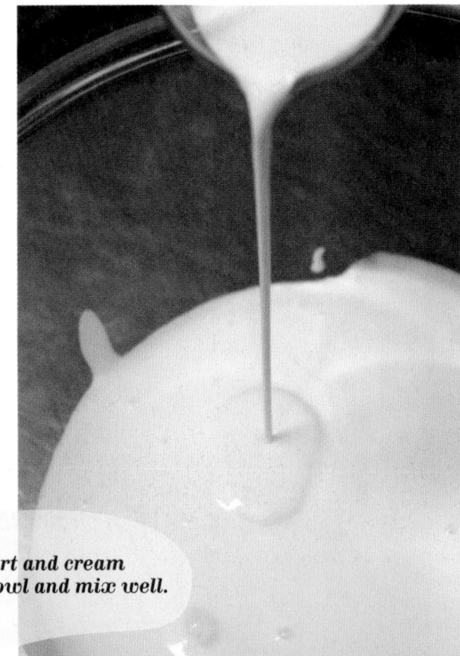

Pour the yogurt and cream into a large bowl and mix well.

Sweeten with sugar, if you like.

Pass the mixture through a fine-mesh strainer into the siphon.

Continue →

Charge the siphon with the cartridge. Let cool in the fridge.

Wash and hull the strawberries, then halve them.

Shake the siphon vigorously just before serving.

Dispense the foam into small bowls or glasses, then top with the strawberries.

–

Meal 8

–

Roasted eggplant with miso dressing

–

Sausages with tomato sauce

–

Crème Catalane

Roasted eggplant with miso dressing

Sausages with tomato sauce

INGREDIENTS

BUY FRESH
* eggplants
* pork sausages
* fresh thyme
* lemons
* oranges

IN THE PANTRY
* sesame seeds
* dashi powder
* red miso paste
* soy sauce
* toasted sesame oil
* sunflower oil
* olive oil
* garlic
* *vino rancio* or dry sherry
* cinnamon sticks
* green anise, star anise, or fennel seeds
* vanilla beans
* sugar
* cornstarch

IN THE FRIDGE
* whipping cream, 35% fat
* whole milk
* eggs

IN THE FREEZER
* tomato sauce (see page 42)

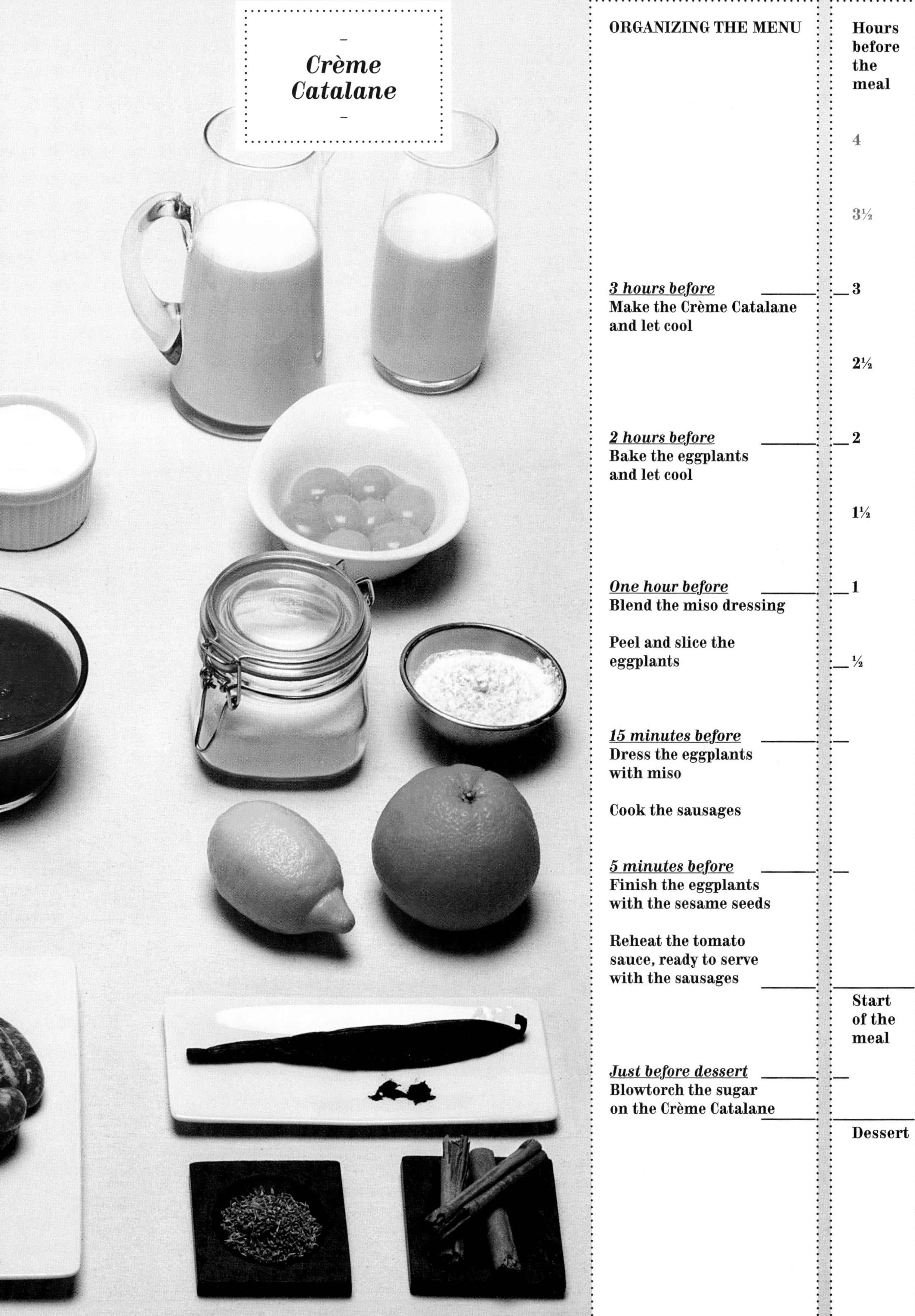

Crème Catalane

ORGANIZING THE MENU	Hours before the meal
	4
	3½
3 hours before Make the Crème Catalane and let cool	3
	2½
2 hours before Bake the eggplants and let cool	2
	1½
One hour before Blend the miso dressing	1
Peel and slice the eggplants	½
15 minutes before Dress the eggplants with miso Cook the sausages	
5 minutes before Finish the eggplants with the sesame seeds Reheat the tomato sauce, ready to serve with the sausages	
	Start of the meal
Just before dessert Blowtorch the sugar on the Crème Catalane	
	Dessert

Roasted eggplant with miso dressing

Dashi is a traditional Japanese stock made with kombu seaweed and *katsuobushi* (dried bonito or tuna), and adds a unique savoriness to soups, dressings, and other dishes.

•

Also important in Japanese cuisine, miso is a paste made from fermented soybeans. Both ingredients can be bought from Asian food stores and some larger supermarkets.

•

The miso dressing also goes well with other roasted vegetables, such as zucchini or potatoes.

	for 2	for 6	for 20	for 75
Eggplants	2	6	20	75
Sesame seeds	2 tbsp	⅓ cup	⅔ cup	2¼ cups
Water	¼ cup	⅔ cup	2¼ cups	6¾ cups
Dashi powder	2 tsp	2 tbsp	⅓ cup	¾ cup plus 2 tbsp
Red miso paste	½ tsp	1 tbsp	2½ tbsp	½ cup
Soy sauce	2 tsp	2 tbsp	scant ⅓ cup	scant 1 cup
Toasted sesame oil	1 tsp	1 tbsp	2 tbsp	scant ½ cup
Sunflower oil	2 tbsp	⅓ cup	⅔ cup	2¼ cups

Start →

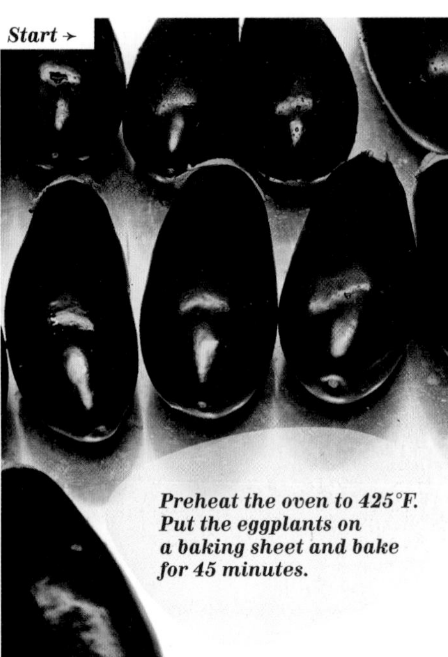

Preheat the oven to 425°F. Put the eggplants on a baking sheet and bake for 45 minutes.

Put the sesame seeds in a frying pan and heat gently for 5 minutes, stirring often, until golden.

For the miso dressing, put the water into a tall jar or pitcher.

Add the dashi powder, miso paste, soy sauce, sesame oil, and sunflower oil.

Process with a hand-held blender until slightly thickened.

Continue →

After 45 minutes, remove the softened eggplants from the oven. Let stand until cool enough to handle.

Peel the skins off the eggplants.

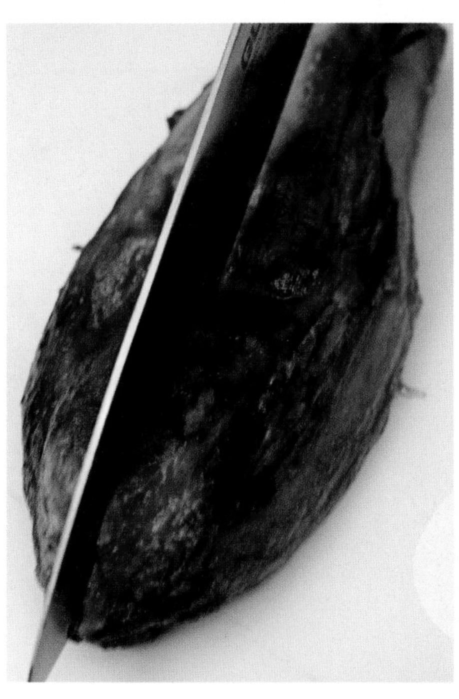

Cut the flesh into ½-inch strips.

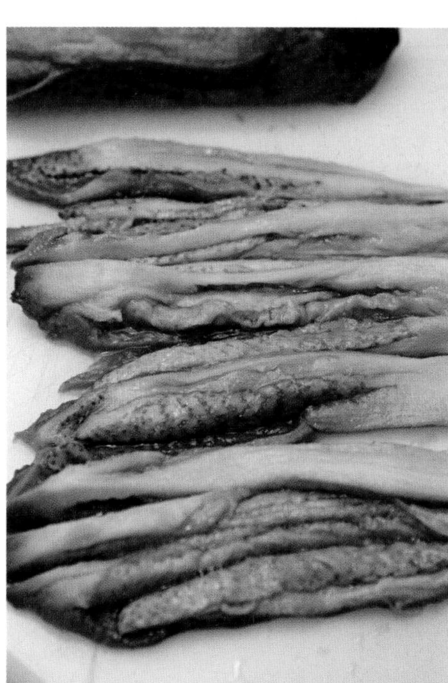

Process the miso dressing again to make sure it has not separated. Arrange the eggplants in a serving dish and spoon over the dressing.

Let the eggplants cool completely, then sprinkle with the sesame seeds and serve.

Sausages with tomato sauce

If you prefer, use store-bought tomato sauce, flavored with a little extra-virgin olive oil (1 tsp per ½ cup).

•

Vino rancio is a Catalan fortified oxidized wine. If you cannot find it, use dry sherry instead.

•

You could serve the sausages with simple, roasted vegetables, such as potatoes or zucchini.

	for 2	for 6	for 20	for 75
Olive oil	3 tbsp	½ cup	⅔ cup	2¼ cups
Pork sausages	5 oz	2 lb	6½ lb	24¼ lb
Garlic cloves	2	6	9	26
Sprigs fresh thyme	1	2	⅕ bunch	¾ bunch
Vino rancio or dry sherry	2 tbsp	scant ½ cup	scant 1½ cups	5½ cups
Tomato sauce (see page 42)	⅓ cup	scant 2 cups	7 cups	11 lb

Start →

Heat the oil in a large frying pan.

Add the sausages and cook for 5 minutes, or until golden underneath.

Tuck the whole garlic cloves and thyme between the sausages.

Continue →

Turn the sausages over.

When the sausages are well browned and cooked through, remove the pan from the heat.

Add the vino rancio and loosen any sediment from the bottom of the pan with a wooden spoon.

Heat the tomato sauce in a saucepan.

Put the sausages in a serving dish.

Spoon over some of the cooking juices and garlic.

Pour the tomato sauce over the sausages to serve.

Crème Catalane

Crème Catalane (or Crema Catalana), is one of the oldest desserts in Europe and appears in medieval Catalan literature.

•

Instead of caramelizing the surface of the crème with a blowtorch, you can scatter it with crushed pieces of dark caramel.

•

We do not recommend making a smaller quantity than given for 4 people. The crème can be set in individual ramekins and stored in the fridge for a few days.

	for 2	for 4	for 20	for 75
Whole milk	-	1 cup	5 cups	1 gallon
Whipping cream, 35% fat	-	¼ cup	1½ cups	4¼ cups
Cinnamon sticks	-	¼	2	4
Lemon zest	-	1 strip	2 strips	4 strips
Orange zest	-	1 strip	2 strips	4 strips
Green anise, star anise, or fennel seeds	-	1 pinch	1⅛ tsp	4⅛ tsp
Vanilla beans, split	-	½	1½	4
Egg yolks	-	3	13	45
Sugar, plus extra for sprinkling	-	¼ cup	1 cup	3⅔ cups
Cornstarch	-	2 tsp	½ cup	1½ cups

Start →

Pour the milk and cream into a large saucepan.

Add the cinnamon, strips of lemon and orange zest, anise or fennel seeds, and vanilla beans.

Bring the milk and cream mixture to a boil over a gentle heat.

Put the egg yolks, sugar, and cornstarch into a large bowl.

Continue →

Whisk until smooth.

Strain the hot milk and cream into the egg yolk mixture, whisking continuously.

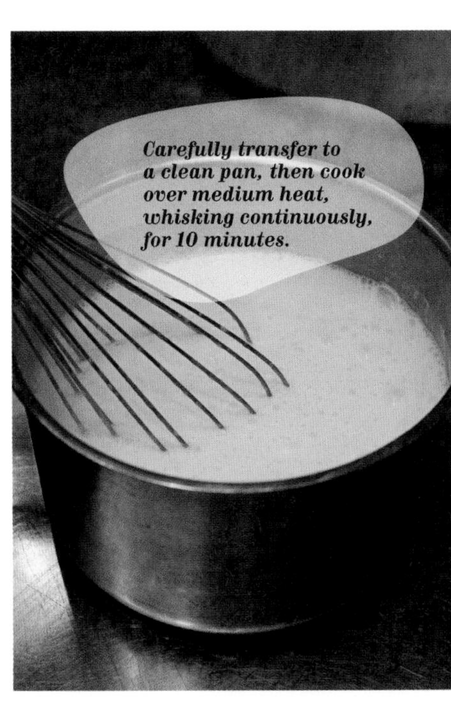
Carefully transfer to a clean pan, then cook over medium heat, whisking continuously, for 10 minutes.

When the mix is thickened and smooth, ladle into a heatproof dish and let cool.

Cover the top of the crème with an even layer of sugar.

Use a blowtorch to caramelize the sugar. Let the sugar set hard before serving.

–

Meal 9

–

Lime-marinated fish

–

Osso buco

–

Piña colada

Lime-marinated fish

Osso buco

INGREDIENTS

BUY FRESH
* fresh meagre, sea bass, or drum fillet
* limes
* scallions
* cilantro
* veal shanks
* carrots
* celery
* fresh parsley
* lemons
* oranges
* pineapples

IN THE PANTRY
* garlic
* onions
* olive oil
* salt
* black peppercorns
* flour
* white wine
* bay leaves
* coconut milk
* white rum

IN THE FRIDGE
* butter

IN THE FREEZER
* tomato sauce (see page 42)
* beef stock (see page 58)

Piña colada

ORGANIZING THE MENU

	Hours before the meal
	4
	3½
	3
2½ hours before Make the osso buco and let cook in the oven	2½
2 hours before Make the piña colada mix and chill	2
	1½
	1
30 minutes before Slice the fish and chill until needed. Slice the onions and prepare the dressing Make the gremolata	½
Just before eating Season the fish and finish with the onion, dressing, and cilantro	
	Start of the meal
Just before main course Sprinkle the gremolata over the osso buco	
	Main course
Just before dessert Pour the piña colada into small glasses or bowls with your choice of topping	
	Dessert

Lime-marinated fish

This dish is a *tiradito,* a Peruvian dish similar to ceviche, which consists of thinly sliced fish with lime juice.

•

We make this dish with meagre, a large, white fish with firm flesh popular in Spain and the Mediterranean. If you cannot find meagre, use another white fish, such as sea bass or drum.

•

Ask your fish supplier to remove the skin and any bones from the fish, or refer to the instructions for skinning salmon on page 352.

	for 2	for 6	for 20	for 75
Fresh fish fillet	5 oz	1 lb 2 oz	4½ lb	17¼ lb
Lime juice	1 tbsp	⅓ cup	scant 1 cup	2¾ cups
Small green onions (or use the white parts from a bunch of scallions)	½	1	11 oz	2 lb
Cilantro	4 sprigs	12 sprigs	1 bunch	3 bunches
Olive oil	¼ cup	⅔ cup	2¼ cups	7¾ cups

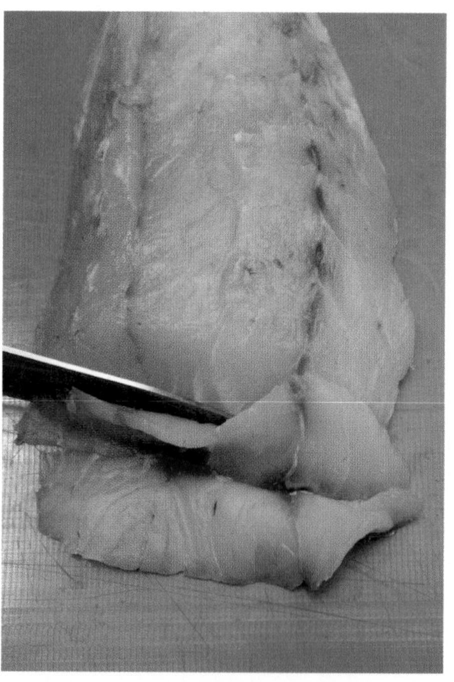

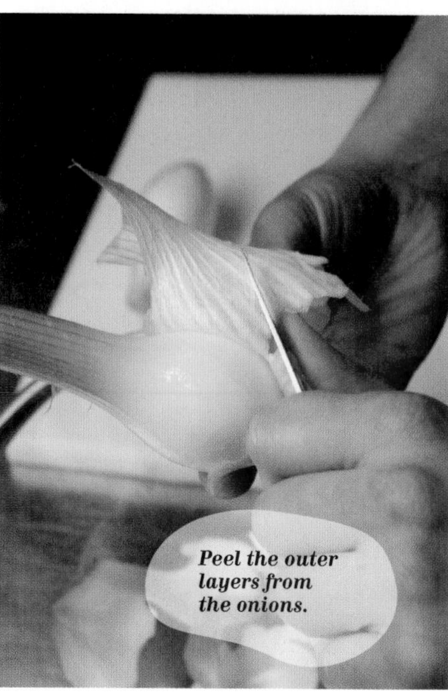

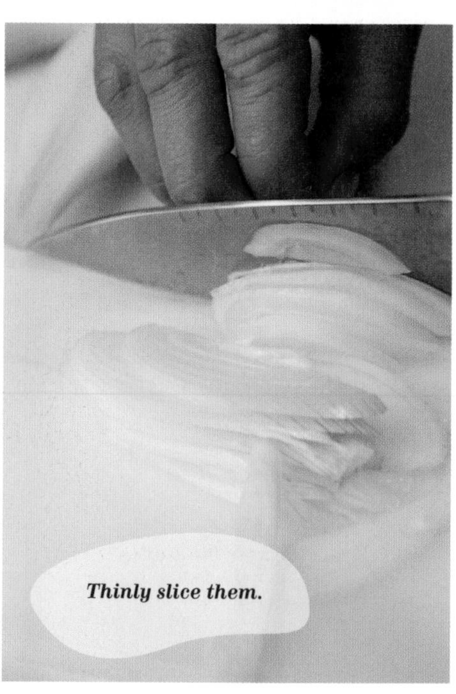

Continue →

Pick the cilantro leaves from the stems and chop finely.

Slowly pour the oil into the lime juice, whisking continuously with a balloon whisk (or using a hand-held blender) to make a slightly thickened and cloudy dressing.

Mix the onions with the lime juice and oil.

Scatter the scallions over the fish and season with salt.

Pour the dressing over the fish and sprinkle with the chopped cilantro.

Osso buco

The term *osso buco* is Italian for "bone with a hole," and refers to the cut of veal used in this famous dish. The meat surrounds a thick piece of bone, which is full of marrow. The marrow enriches the sauce and should be eaten as part of the dish.

•

The gremolata (a mixture of chopped parsley and garlic with orange and lemon zest) is sprinkled over just before serving, so that the fresh citrus oils in the skin are still fragrant.

	for 2	for 6	for 20	for 75
Carrots, chopped	1 tsp	1½ tbsp	¾ cup	2⅛ cups
Celery, chopped	1 tsp	2 tbsp	1⅓ cups	4⅓ cups
Onions, chopped	1	2	4½ cups	13½ cups
Garlic cloves, finely chopped	1	3	10	37
Veal shank pieces, 9 oz each	2	6	20	75
Flour	1½ tbsp	¼ cup	1¼ cups	3½ cups
Butter	1½ tbsp	7 tbsp	2 cups	6 cups
White wine	⅓ cup	1 cup	4½ cups	13½ cups
Dried bay leaves	2	4	½ oz	1½ oz
Tomato sauce (see page 42)	2 tsp	2 tbsp	scant 1½ cups	4½ cups
Beef stock (see page 58)	2¼ cups	6¼ cups	2 gallons	6¼ gallons
For the gremolata:				
Fresh parsley, finely chopped	2 tsp	2 tbsp	½ bunch	1 bunch
Garlic cloves, finely chopped	1	3	8½	24
Lemons	1	3	2	5
Oranges	1	3	2	5

Start →

Cut the carrots into sticks about ¼ inch thick, then cut into ¼-inch cubes.

Repeat with the celery.

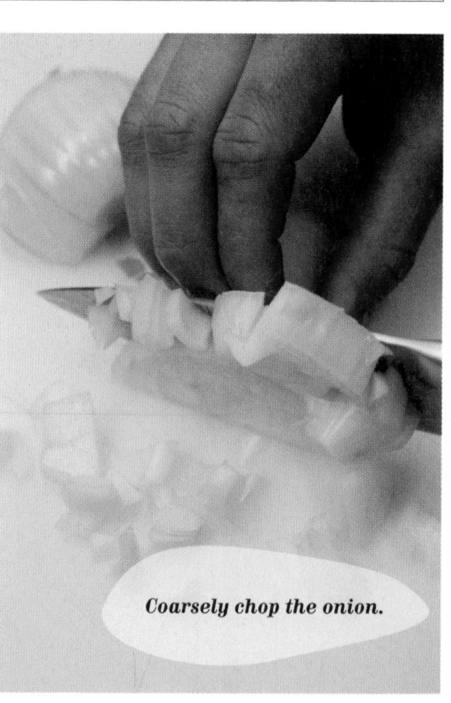

Coarsely chop the onion.

Continue →

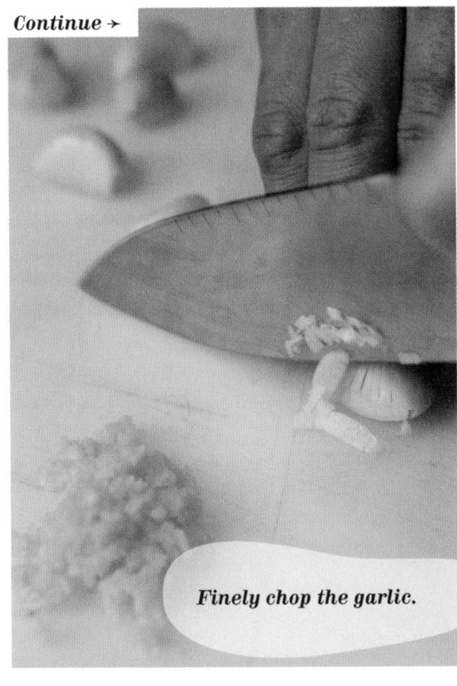

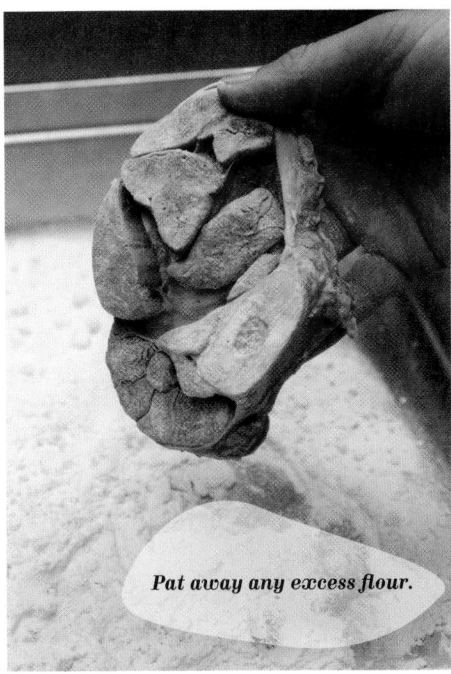

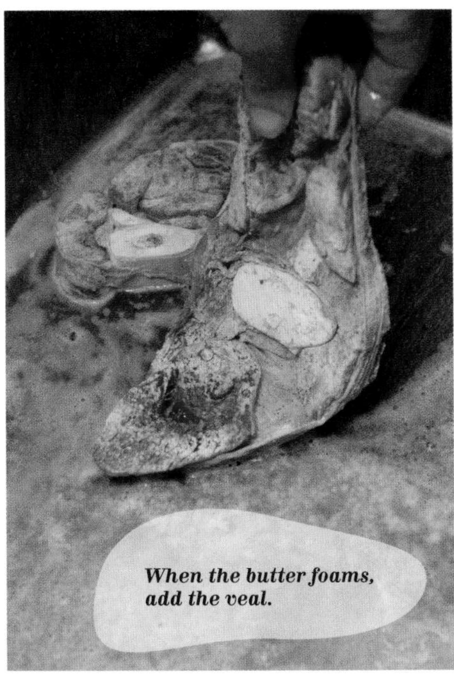

Continue →

Continue →

Add the onion, celery, and garlic, then cook gently for 10 minutes, stirring often, until the vegetables have softened.

Pour in the white wine and loosen any sediment from the bottom of the pan with a wooden spoon.
Preheat the oven to 400°F.

When the wine has almost evaporated, add the bay leaves and tomato sauce. Cook over medium heat for another 10 minutes, until thickened.

Put the browned veal into a roasting pan. Spoon over the vegetables, then pour in the beef stock or water.

Cover the pan with foil and cook in the oven for 2 hours, until the meat is very tender.

Meanwhile, prepare the gremolata. Finely chop the parsley and garlic, then mix in small bowl. Finely grate in the zest of the lemon and orange, then mix well.

Sprinkle the gremolata over the osso buco just before serving.

Piña colada

We like to serve this topped with more chopped pineapple, crushed meringues, freeze-dried fruit, or nuts.

•

To choose a ripe pineapple, look for one in which the central leaves can be pulled out easily.

	for 2	for 6	for 20	for 75
Pineapples	½	1	5 (7¾ lb)	18 (28½ lb)
Coconut milk	3 tbsp	½ cup	1½ cups	6⅛ cups
White rum	1½ tbsp	¼ cup	1 cup	6¾ cups

Start →

–

Meal 10

–

Miso soup with clams

–

Mackerel with vinaigrette

–

Almond cookies

Miso soup with clams

Mackerel with vinaigrette

INGREDIENTS

BUY FRESH
* small round clams
* silken tofu
* fresh mackerel
* ripe tomatoes
* fresh basil
* fresh thyme
* black olive paste

IN THE PANTRY
* dashi powder
* red miso paste
* small dried chiles
* extra-virgin olive oil
* pickled capers
* salt
* black pepper
* sugar
* ground almonds
* whole toasted Marcona almonds

IN THE FRIDGE
* eggs

IN THE FREEZER
* ice cream

Almond cookies

ORGANIZING THE MENU	Hours before the meal
	4
	3½
	3
	2½
	2
	1½
1 hour before Soak the clams in salted water Make and bake the almond cookies Prepare all the ingredients for the fish	1
	½
15 minutes before Make the miso soup base and cut the tofu into cubes	
5 minutes before Add the clams to the soup. Blend the soup and remaining tofu	
	Start of the meal
Just before main course Fry the fish Take the ice cream out of the freezer so that it is soft enough to scoop	
	Main course

Miso soup with clams

Before cooking, pick over the clams, discarding any that are damaged. Put the clams into a large bowl, cover with salted cold water, and let stand for 1 hour. This will help the clams to purge themselves of any sand.

•

You could also use other types of clam or mussels, increasing the cooking time if they are larger.

	for 2	for 6	for 20	for 75
Water	¾ cup	5½ cups	1¼ gallons	3⅔ gallons
Dashi powder	½ tsp	2 tsp	¼ cup	1 cup
Red miso paste	2 tsp	½ cup	1½ cups	4 cups
Silken tofu	5 oz	1 lb	2¼ lb	15½ lb
Small round clams	4 oz	14 oz	3¼ lb	13¼ lb

Start →

Pour the water into a large pan and add the dashi powder and red miso paste.

Process with a hand-held blender until well mixed.

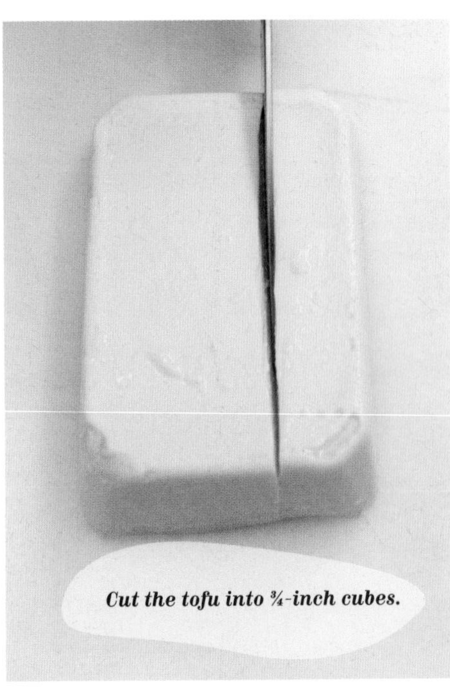

Cut the tofu into ¾-inch cubes.

Place tofu into serving bowls, allowing 5 per person.

Continue →

Rinse the clams
under cold water.

Bring the soup to a boil,
then add the clams.

Cook for 3 minutes
or until the clams open.
Remove from the heat.

Lift the clams out of the
soup with a slotted spoon.

Place the clams on top of
the tofu in the serving bowls,
discarding any that have
not opened.

Add the remaining tofu
to the soup and blend
until creamy and smooth.

Ladle the soup over the
clams and tofu and serve.

Mackerel with vinaigrette

Ask your fish supplier to clean, gut, and prepare the fish if you prefer.

•

Other types of small whole fish, such as sardines, can be used instead.

	for 2	for 6	for 20	for 75
Mackerel, 7 oz each	2	6	20	75
Ripe tomatoes	1	3	1¾ lb	4½ lb
Small dried chiles	1	3	15	40
Extra-virgin olive oil	½ cup, plus 2 tsp	1 cup, plus 1½ tbsp	4¼ cups, plus ½ cup	13½ cups, plus 1 cup
Pickled capers	2 tsp	2 tbsp	¾ cup	2½ cups
Sprigs fresh thyme	2	6	20	80
Black olive paste	1 tsp	2 tsp	¼ cup	¾ cup
Fresh basil	1 sprigs	3 sprigs	1 bunch	2 bunches

Start →

Cut the fins from the fish with kitchen scissors. Cut out the gills.

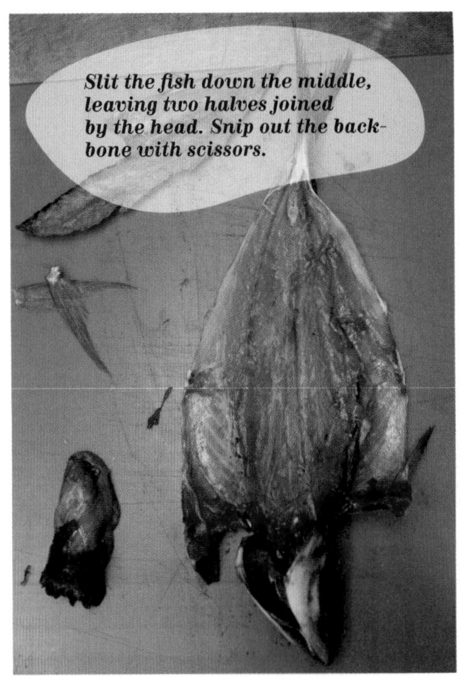

Slit the fish down the middle, leaving two halves joined by the head. Snip out the backbone with scissors.

Cut a small cross into the bottom of each tomato, then blanch them in a pot of boiling water for 30 seconds.

Plunge into a bowl of iced water.

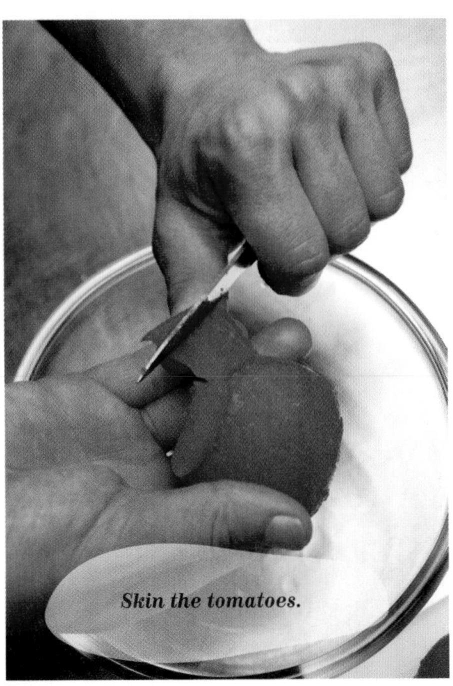

Skin the tomatoes.

Cut in half, scoop out the seeds, and cut into ¼-inch cubes.

Continue →

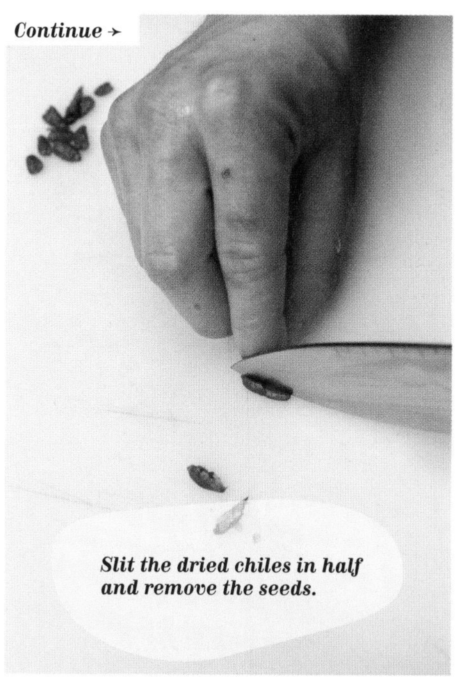

Slit the dried chiles in half and remove the seeds.

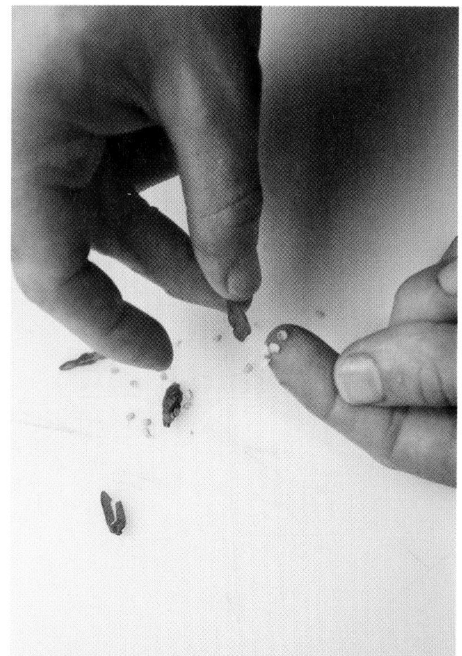

Finely shred the chiles.

Put the diced tomato into a bowl, add the first quantity of olive oil, the shredded chiles, capers, and thyme sprigs.

Season with salt and pepper.

Loosen the black olive paste with most of the remaining olive oil.

Place a large frying pan over medium heat, add a little oil, and put the fish in the pan skin-side down. Fry the fish for 3 minutes, or until golden underneath.

Cook on the second side for 3 minutes, then transfer the fish to a serving plate, flesh facing upward. It should be golden and juicy.

Pick the smallest leaves from the basil sprigs. Spoon the tomato vinaigrette over the fish, scatter with the basil leaves, then add a few spots of black olive paste.

Almond cookies

We do not recommend making any less than the quantity given for 12 cookies. Any leftover cookies will keep in an airtight container for several days.

•

The cookies can be served with any flavor of ice cream, but we like to serve them with nougat ice cream.

•

Marcona almonds are a sweet variety from Spain. Any good-quality almonds can be substituted.

	for 2	for 6 (makes 12 almond cookies)	for 20	for 75
Egg whites	-	1	3	8½
Sugar	-	⅔ cup	1½ cups	4½ cups
Ground almonds	-	1⅛ cup	2¾ cups	8⅓ cups
Whole toasted Marcona almonds	-	12	1 cup	3½ cups
Ice cream	-	2½ cups	15 cups (about 1 gal.)	38 cups (about 24 gal.)

Start →

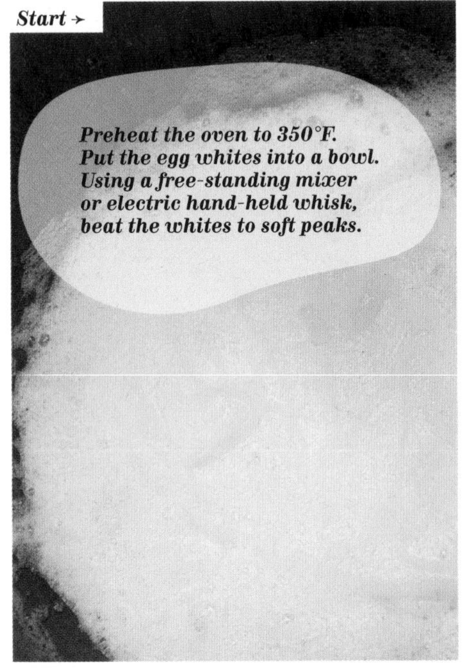

Preheat the oven to 350°F. Put the egg whites into a bowl. Using a free-standing mixer or electric hand-held whisk, beat the whites to soft peaks.

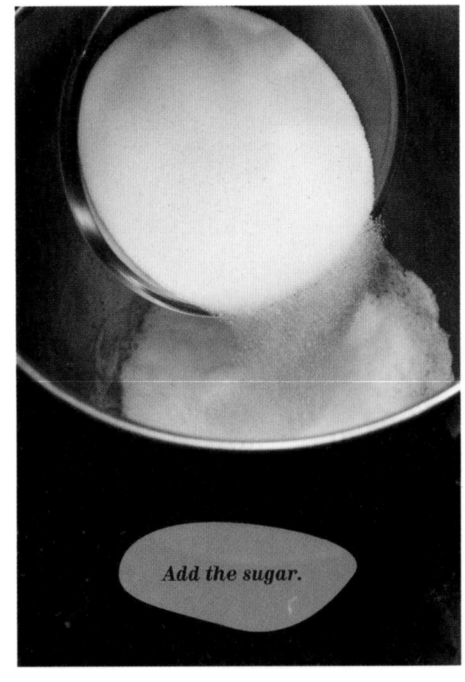

Add the sugar.

Whisk the whites again until stiff and glossy.

Add the ground almonds, then use a rubber spatula to fold them carefully into the meringue until evenly combined.

Try to preserve as much of the air in the meringue as possible.

Continue →

Line a baking sheet with parchment paper. Scoop tablespoons of the mixture onto the sheet, spacing them well apart.

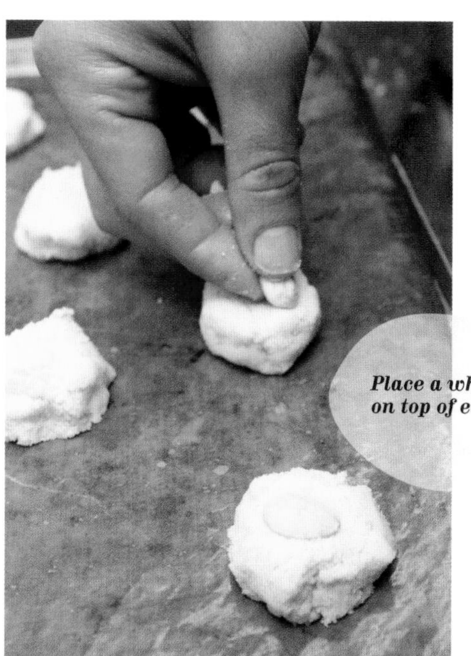

Place a whole almond on top of each mound.

Bake in the oven for 14 minutes, or until pale golden and slightly cracked.

Cool on the baking sheet, then transfer to a rack to cool completely.

Serve alone or with ice cream.

–

Meal 11

–

Fried eggs with asparagus

–

Chicken wings with mushrooms

–

Sangria with fruit

Fried eggs with asparagus

Chicken wings with mushrooms

INGREDIENTS

BUY FRESH

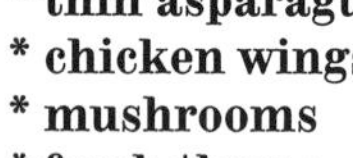

* thin asparagus spears
* chicken wings
* mushrooms
* fresh thyme
* pink grapefruit
* oranges
* lemons
* apples
* pears
* peaches
* fresh mint

IN THE PANTRY
* olive oil
* salt
* black peppercorns
* garlic
* dried bay leaves
* white wine
* red wine
* sugar
* Cointreau
* ground cinnamon

IN THE FRIDGE
* eggs

Sangria with fruit

ORGANIZING THE MENU	Hours before the meal
	4
	3½
	3
	2½
	2
	1½
1¼ hours before **Make the sangria and chill in the fridge**	1
40 minutes before **Brown the chicken wings** **Trim the asparagus** **Prepare the fruit for the sangria and chill in the fridge**	½
10 minutes before **Heat the oil for the eggs and cook the asparagus** **Finish cooking the chicken wings**	
Just before eating **Fry the eggs and serve with the asparagus**	
	Start of the meal
Just before dessert **Put the fruit into serving bowls, pour in the sangria, and finish with mint leaves**	
	Dessert

Fried eggs with asparagus

You can replace the asparagus with shavings of cured ham, sautéed mushrooms or Padrón peppers, if you like.

•

The oil used for frying the eggs can be strained and used to fry other things, such as bell peppers.

•

When preparing for large numbers, we like to break the eggs into individual cups before we start cooking.

	for 2	for 6	for 20	for 75
Thin asparagus spears	14	42	140	525
Olive oil	1 cup	2¼ cups	8½ cups	1¼ gallons
Eggs	4	12	40	150

Start →

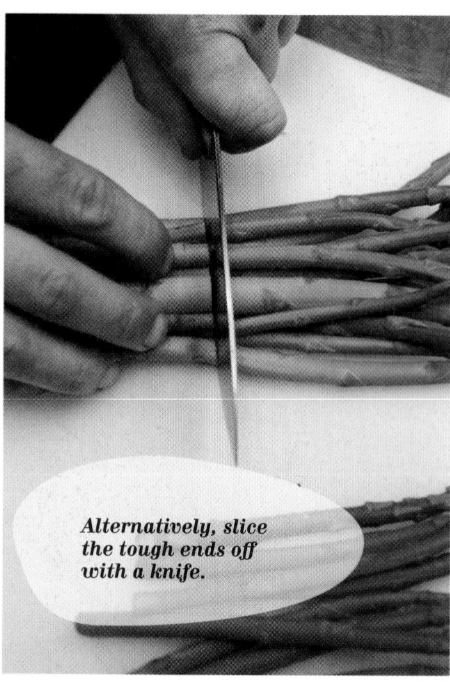

Continue →

Break the eggs into cups, then carefully slide them one at a time into the hot oil.

Fry the eggs for 1½ minutes, until the whites are crisp at the edges but the yolks are still soft.

Remove the eggs from the oil using a slotted spoon. Drain well, then place on top of the asparagus. Season with salt before serving.

The eggs can also be served with sautéed mushrooms (left) or Padrón peppers (right) instead of asparagus.

Chicken wings with mushrooms

Farmed mushrooms, such as white mushrooms, king trumpet, and shimeji (pictured) are ideal for this recipe, and available all year round. Wild mushrooms such as chanterelles, are reasonably priced when in season, and would make the dish even better.

	for 2	for 6	for 20	for 75
Chicken wings	6	18	60	225
Olive oil	¼ cup	scant ½ cup	4 cups	9 cups
Mushrooms	4 oz	12½ oz	2¼ lb	10 lb
Garlic cloves	10	30	14¼ oz	3 lb 2 oz
Dried bay leaves	1	3	14	38
Fresh thyme sprigs	1	3	10	30
White wine	¼ cup	¾ cup	4 cups	9½ cups
Water	3½ tbsp	⅔ cup	1¼ cup	4¼ cups

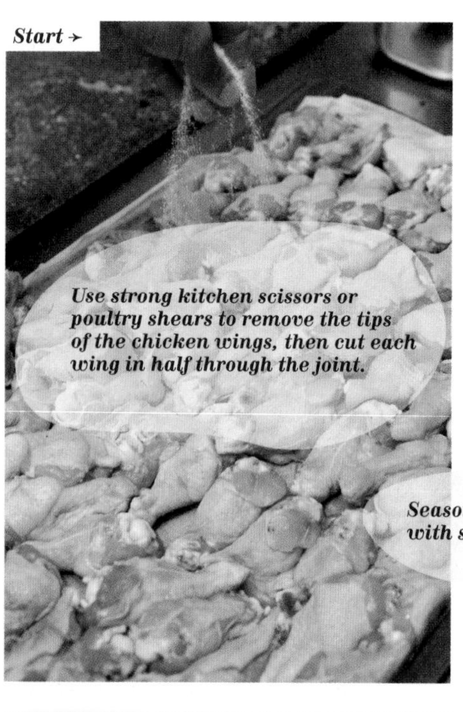

Continue →

Slice any that
are large.

Coarsely slice the garlic.

Add the garlic to the
chicken and cook for
5 more minutes.

Add the bay leaves
and thyme.

Pour in the white wine.

Turn up the heat and cook
until the wine has reduced
a little.

Add the mushrooms and cook
for 2 minutes, stirring.

Pour in the water, then let
simmer for 5 minutes, until
the mushrooms are just tender.

Serve the chicken
wings and mushrooms
together.

Sangria with fruit

We like to use Granny Smith apples and Blanquilla pears, but you could use other varieties.

	for 2	for 6	for 20	for 75
Orange juice, freshly squeezed	2 tbsp	6 tbsp	3¾ cups	10 cups
Red wine	¼ cup	1 cup	3½ cups	8½ cups
Sugar	2 tsp	2 tbsp	1 cup	3½ cups
Cointreau	2 tsp	1½ tbsp	½ cup	1½ cups
Ground cinnamon	1 pinch	2 pinches	scant 1 tsp	1 tbsp
Lemons	½	1	2	5
Pink grapefruit	½	1	5	15
Oranges	½	1	5	15
Apples	½	1	5	15
Pears	½	1	5	15
Peaches	½	1	5	15
Fresh mint	4 leaves	12 leaves	½ bunch	1 bunch

Start →

Squeeze the oranges.

Strain the juice through a fine-mesh strainer.

Add the red wine.

Add the sugar.

Now add the Cointreau.

Continue →

Stir in the cinnamon.

Finely grate in the lemon zest. Let steep while you prepare the fruit.

Cut the top and bottom from the grapefruit and oranges, then remove the pith and skin.

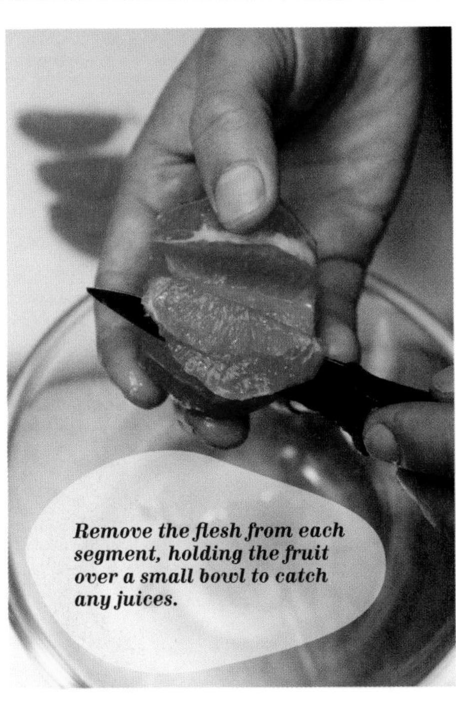
Remove the flesh from each segment, holding the fruit over a small bowl to catch any juices.

Peel and core the apples and cut into ½-inch wedges.

Peel and core the pears and cut into ½-inch wedges.

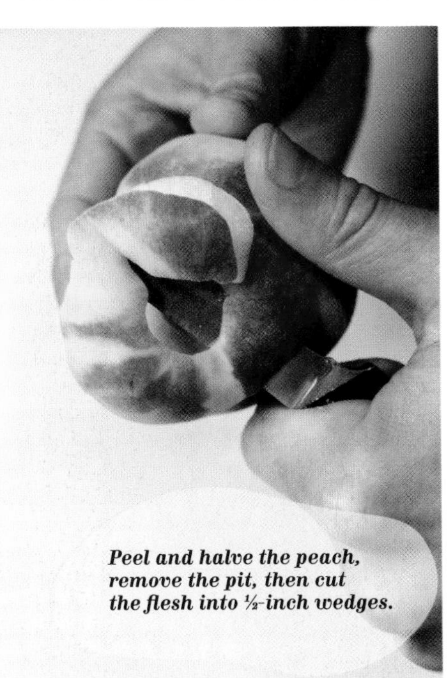
Peel and halve the peach, remove the pit, then cut the flesh into ½-inch wedges.

Add the fruit to the sangria and let marinate for 1 hour.

Scoop out the fruit and place in a bowl with a few mint leaves. Pour the sangria on top.

–

Meal 12

–

Potato salad

–

Thai beef curry

–

Strawberries in vinegar

–

Potato salad

–

INGREDIENTS

BUY FRESH
* large new potatoes
* fresh chives
* small green onions or scallions
* frankfurters
* blade steaks
* fresh ginger
* cilantro
* medium strawberries

IN THE PANTRY
* salt
* pickled gherkins
* pickled capers
* Dijon mustard
* black peppercorns
* olive oil
* yellow Thai curry paste
* coconut milk
* sugar
* red wine vinegar

IN THE FRIDGE
* mayonnaise
* whipping cream, 35% fat

Thai beef curry

Strawberries in vinegar

ORGANIZING THE MENU	Hours before the meal
	4
3½ hours before Make the curry (if using the oven method)	3½
	3
	2½
2 hours before Make the caramel and let cool in the fridge	2
1½ hours before Boil the potatoes for the salad, then wrap in foil and cool	1½
1 hour before Make the curry (if using a pressure cooker) Mix the strawberries and vinegar caramel and marinate in the fridge	1
30 minutes before Peel and chop the potatoes and prepare the salad ingredients	½
Just before eating Mix the dressing into the potatoes, sprinkle with the chives, and serve Finish the Thai beef curry with the coconut milk and cilantro	—
	Start of the meal
Just before dessert Spoon the strawberries in vinegar into small bowls or glasses	—
	Dessert

Potato salad

This German-style potato salad makes a good accompaniment to a main meal or a good addition to a picnic.

•

Wrapping the potatoes in foil after cooking keeps them warm and makes them easier to peel.

	for 2	for 6	for 20	for 75
Large new potatoes	2	2½ lb	8¾ lb	33 lb
Finely chopped fresh chives	1 tsp	1½ tbsp	⅞ cup	3 cups
Small green onions (or use the white parts from a bunch of scallions)	½	2	9 oz	2 lb 6 oz
Medium pickled gherkins, drained	2	6	11 oz	2¼ lb
Frankfurters	1	4	13	44
Mayonnaise	2 tbsp	1½ cups	4¼ cups	3½ quarts
Whipping cream, 35% fat	1½ tbsp	⅔ cup	1¼ cups	4 cups
Dijon mustard	1½ tbsp	½ cup	1½ cups	5½ cups
Pickled capers, drained	2 tsp	1½ tbsp	1¼ cups	4¼ cups

Start →

Bring a large pan of water to a boil, season with salt and add the potatoes. Cook for 20 minutes until tender.

Drain the potatoes and wrap individually in aluminum foil.

Meanwhile, finely chop the chives.

Trim the stems off the scallions.

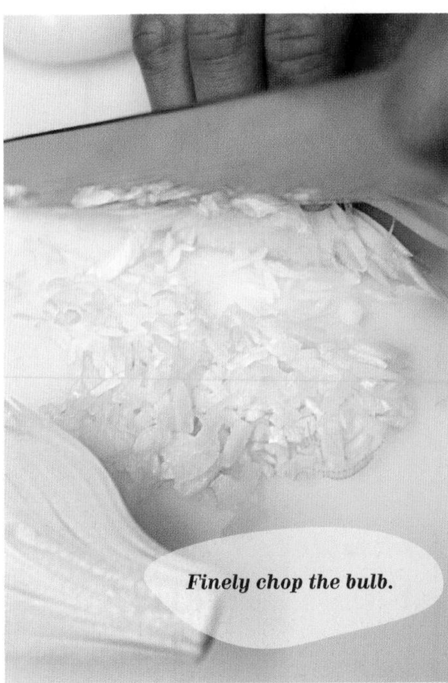

Finely chop the bulb.

Cut the gherkins into ½-inch slices.

Continue →

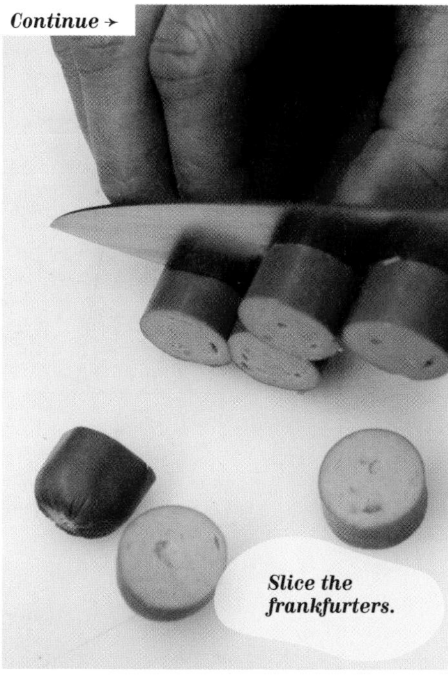
Slice the
frankfurters.

Using a balloon whisk,
mix together the mayonnaise,
cream, and mustard. Season
with salt and pepper.

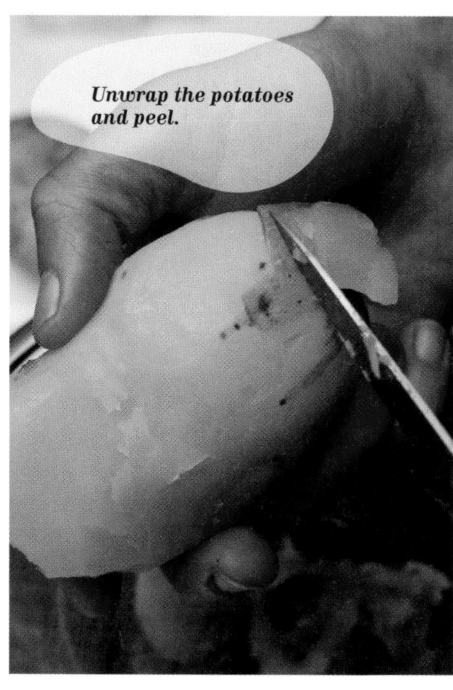
Unwrap the potatoes
and peel.

Cut the potatoes into 1-inch
cubes and put into a large bowl.

Add the onion, gherkins, capers,
and sausages to the potatoes.

Spoon the sauce on top, then
mix together, being careful
not to break up the potatoes.

Season the salad
with salt and pepper.

Sprinkle with the chopped
chives and serve.

Thai beef curry

A pressure cooker is ideal for cooking tough cuts of meat. If you do not own a pressure cooker, make the curry in the oven, preheated to 325°F. Make the curry in a flameproof casserole, then cover and cook in the oven for 3 hours, until the beef is very tender. Remove the beef, then simmer the sauce until thickened and tasty.

•

If you cannot find blade steak, try using shank or cheek instead.

	for 2	for 6	for 20	for 75
Blade steak	¾ lb	2 lb	6½ lb	26½ lb
Fresh ginger	½ slice	2 slices	2½ oz	9½ oz
Olive oil	2 tbsp	5 tbsp	scant ½ cup	2¼ cups
Yellow Thai curry paste	½ tsp	1 tsp	⅓ cup	3 cups
Cilantro, leaves picked	10 leaves	1 bunch	12 oz	2 lb 4 oz
Water	2¼ cups	6¼ cups	3½ quarts	3½ gallons
Coconut milk	scant ½ cup	1¼ cups	5½ cups	1⅓ gallons

Start →

Cut the beef into slices about ¼ inch thick, to give 3 slices per person.

Season with salt and pepper.

Finely slice and then chop the ginger, without peeling it.

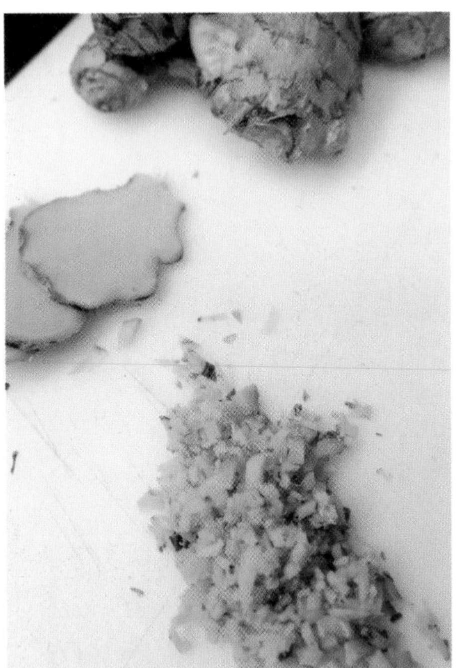

Place the bottom of the pressure cooker over medium heat.

Add the oil, followed by the ginger. Fry gently for 2 minutes, until fragrant.

Add the curry paste and stir through.

Continue →

Add half of the cilantro.

Add the water.

Next, add three-quarters of the coconut milk.

Add the beef.

Put the lid on the pressure cooker, then cook over medium heat for 50 minutes. Remove the lid, then simmer until the sauce is thickened and tasty.

Add the rest of the coconut milk.

Add the remaining cilantro leaves, then season to taste with salt if needed.

Serve the curry.

Strawberries in vinegar

We suggest Cabernet Sauvignon vinegar, but you could use balsamic vinegar instead if you like.

	for 2	for 6	for 20	for 75
Sugar	3 tbsp	¾ cup	3 cups	11 cups
Boiling water	1 tbsp	¼ cup	¾ cup	3⅓ cups
Red wine vinegar	2 tbsp	⅓ cup	1 cup	3¾ cups
Medium strawberries	10	1 lb 5 oz	4½ lb	16½ lb

Start →

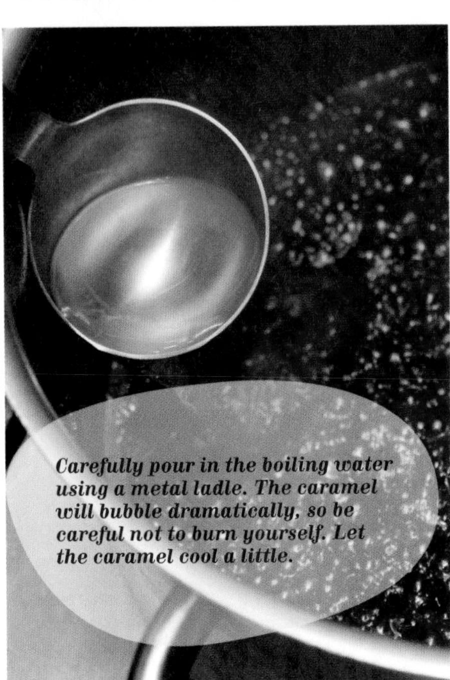

Continue →

Cool the caramel in the fridge. It will become thick.

Hull (remove the stems and leaves from) the strawberries, then cut in half lengthwise.

Put the strawberries into a bowl, then pour over the vinegar caramel.

Marinate in the fridge for 1 hour before serving.

–

Meal 13

–

Farfalle with pesto

–

Japanese-style bream

–

Mandarins with Cointreau

Farfalle with pesto

Japanese-style bream

INGREDIENTS

BUY FRESH
* gilthead bream
* scallions
* fresh cilantro
* fresh ginger
* mandarin oranges

IN THE PANTRY
* salt
* farfalle
* extra-virgin olive oil
* sunflower oil
* soy sauce
* Cointreau
* demerara or turbinado sugar

IN THE FRIDGE
* Parmesan cheese

IN THE FREEZER
* pesto sauce (see page 46)
* vanilla ice cream

Mandarins with Cointreau

ORGANIZING THE MENU	Hours before the meal
	4
	3½
	3
	2½
	2
	1½
1 hour before Clean and gut the fish. Wrap in wax paper and keep in the fridge	1
30 minutes before Slice the onion, cilantro, and ginger for the fish	½
25 minutes before Juice and peel the mandarin oranges	
10 minutes before Cook the pasta Bring the water to a boil in the steamer	
Just before eating Loosen the pesto sauce with the pasta water	
Steam the fish while eating the pasta	Start of the meal
Just before main course Heat the oil and fry the ginger Spoon the flavorings over the fish	
	Main course
Just before dessert Pour the Cointreau and juice over the oranges	
	Dessert

Farfalle with pesto

Pesto sauce (see page 46) can be made ahead and frozen. Do not forget to defrost it in advance.

•

Before serving, add 2 tbsp of the reserved cooking water to every ⅔ cup of pesto. This helps to loosen and warm up the pesto.

•

You can use any kind of pasta shape you like.

	for 2	for 6	for 20	for 75
Water	6¼ cups	12½ cups	1½ gallons	5¾ gallons
Salt	1 pinch	2 pinches	5 tbsp	1 cup
Farfalle	7 oz	1 lb 5 oz	4½ lb	16½ lb
Finely grated Parmesan cheese	⅔ cup	2⅛ cups	7 cups	3 lb
Extra-virgin olive oil	3 tbsp	½ cup	1¾ cups	6¼ cups
Pesto sauce (see page 46)	⅔ cup	2 cups	6½ cups	1½ gallons

Start →

Bring the water to a boil in a large pan. Season with the salt, then add the farfalle.

Stir once, then boil the pasta for 8–10 minutes, until tender but still firm to the bite (check the directions on the package).

Grate the Parmesan cheese while you cook the pasta.

Reserve some of the cooking water. For 2 servings, reserve 2 tablespoons of water; for 6 servings, reserve 6 tablespoons; for 20, reserve 1¼ cups; and for 75 reserve 4¼ cups. Drain the pasta.

Continue →

Put the pasta back into its pan, then stir in the oil to prevent it from sticking together.

Spoon over the pesto sauce.

Japanese-style bream

Ask your fish supplier to clean and gut the fish for you if you prefer.

•

You can broil the fish if you prefer.

•

You can use other kinds of fish, such as sea bass, hake, or megrim.

	for 2	for 6	for 20	for 75
Gilt-head bream, 12 oz each	2	6	20	75
Scallions (or use the white parts of a bunch of small green onions), thinly sliced	1	2	11 oz	2¼ lb
Cilantro	6 sprigs	30 sprigs	3 oz	11 oz
Fresh ginger	¾ oz	2⅛ oz	7 oz	1 lb 10 oz
Sunflower oil	3 tbsp	⅔ cup	1¾ cups	6¼ cups
Soy sauce	1½ tbsp	¼ cup	1 cup	3 cups

Start →

To scale the fish, run the back of a knife firmly along the length of the fish from the tail to the head.

Using kitchen scissors, cut the fins away from the body.

Cut along the belly from the small opening near the tail to just under the head.

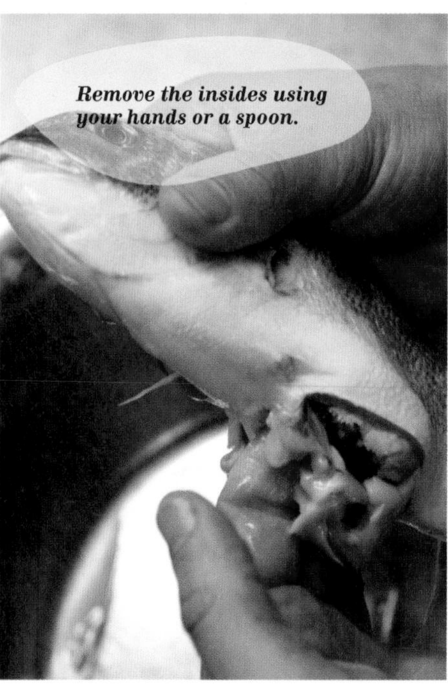

Remove the insides using your hands or a spoon.

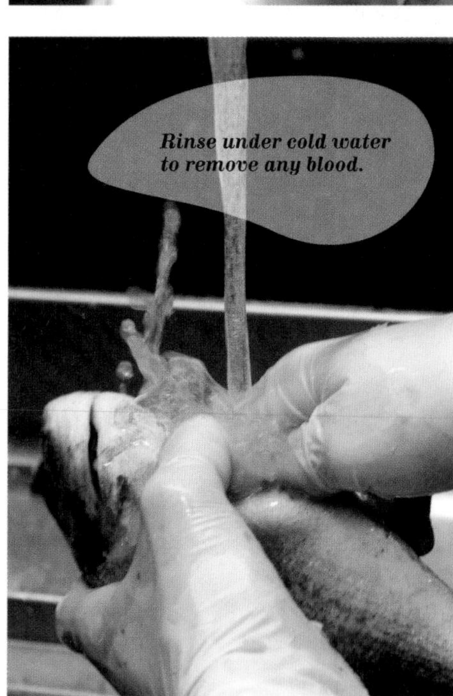

Rinse under cold water to remove any blood.

Continue →

Continue →

Continue →

Wrap each fish loosely
in a large square
of parchment paper.
Fill the bottom
of a steamer with
water and bring
it to a boil.

Season the fish with salt
and steam for 12 minutes,
until the flesh is opaque
and flakes easily from
the back bone.

While the fish is cooking,
pour the oil into a saucepan
with the ginger and cook
over medium heat until
the ginger begins to fry.

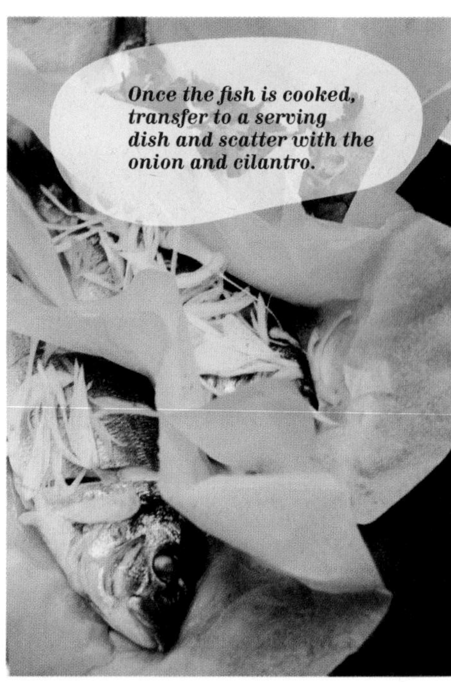
Once the fish is cooked,
transfer to a serving
dish and scatter with the
onion and cilantro.

Carefully spoon
over the hot ginger
oil so that the
onion and cilantro
start to sizzle.

Finish with a tablespoon
of soy sauce over each fish.

Mandarins with Cointreau

To make scooping the ice cream easier, take the tub out of the freezer 10 minutes before serving so that it softens a little.

•

If you cannot find mandarins, try using satsumas or clementines, and Grand Marnier can be substituted for Cointreau.

	for 2	for 6	for 20	for 75
Mandarins	3	9	30	112
Cointreau	1½ tbsp	¼ cup	⅓ cup	1¼ cups
Demerara or turbinado sugar	1 tbsp	2 tbsp	¼ cup	1 cup
Vanilla ice cream	2 scoops	6 scoops	1 lb 2 oz	4½ lb

Start →

–

Meal 14

–

Tomato & basil salad

–

Crab & rice stew

–

Coconut flan

Tomato & basil salad

INGREDIENTS

BUY FRESH
* very large ripe tomatoes
* fresh basil
* small whole crabs
* coconut milk
* dried or fresh coconut

IN THE PANTRY
* salt
* extra-virgin olive oil
* sherry vinegar
* olive oil
* paella rice
* white wine
* black peppercorns
* sugar

IN THE FRIDGE
* eggs

IN THE FREEZER
* fish stock (see page 56)
* sofrito (see page 43)
* picada (see page 41)

Crab & rice stew

Coconut flan

ORGANIZING THE MENU	Hours before the meal
Up to 4 hours before **Make the coconut crème caramel and chill in the fridge**	4
	3½
	3
	2½
	2
	1½
	1
30 minutes before **Brown the crabs and set aside. Start cooking the rice** **While the rice is cooking, prepare the tomatoes for the salad and pick the basil**	½
Just before eating **Finish the tomato salad with the oil and vinegar**	
	Start of the meal
Just before main course **Return the crabs to the rice and add the picada**	
	Main course
Just before dessert **Remove the flan from the molds**	
	Dessert

Tomato & basil salad

This recipe is ideal when tomatoes are ripe in summer, although there are some varieties that are still excellent in winter.

•

Use sea salt flakes to season the tomatoes if you prefer their flaky texture and slight crunch.

	for 2	for 6	for 20	for 75
Very large ripe tomatoes	3	9	5½ lb	17½ lb
Fresh basil	30 leaves	1⅓ cups	2 bunches	5 bunches
Extra-virgin olive oil	¼ cup	¾ cup	2½ cups	½ gallon
Sherry vinegar	2 tsp	1½ tbsp	5 tbsp	⅔ cup

Start →

Using the tip of a small knife, remove the stem and any fibrous green parts from the tops of the tomatoes.

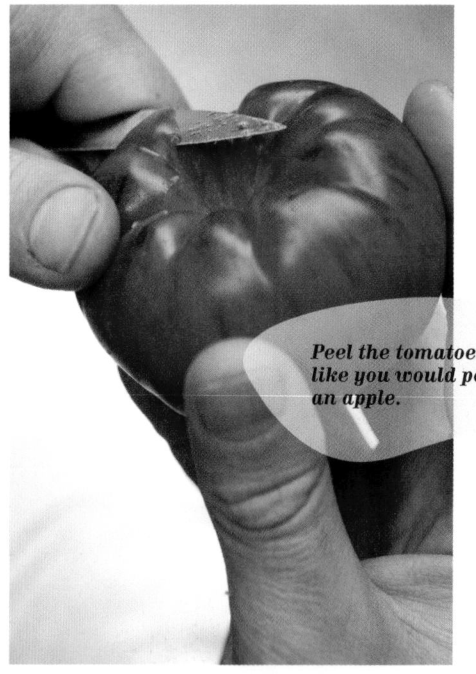

Peel the tomatoes like you would peel an apple.

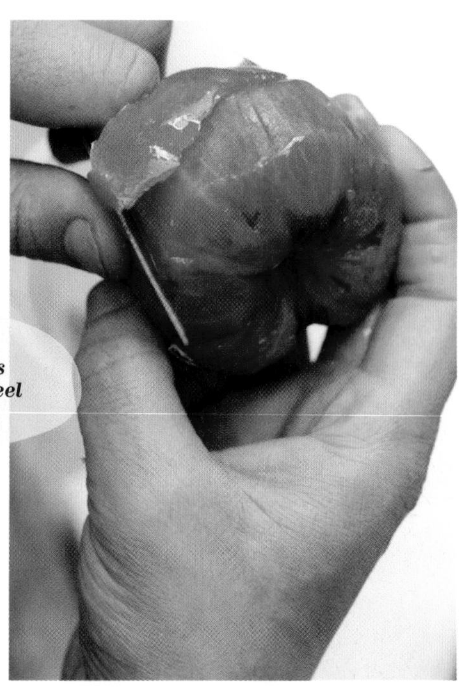

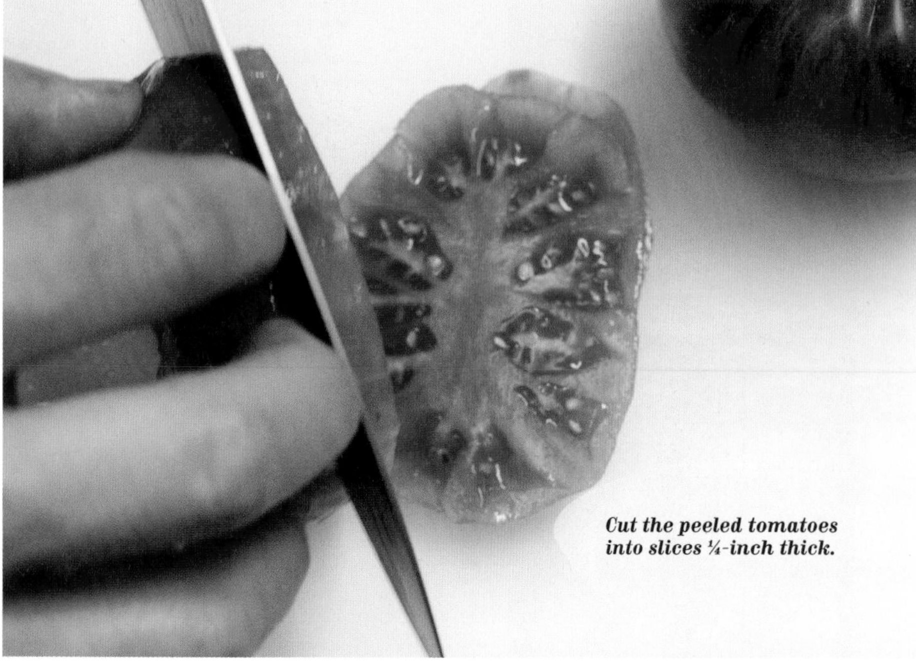

Cut the peeled tomatoes into slices ¼-inch thick.

Continue →

Arrange on a plate.

Season with salt.

Pick the leaves from the basil, tearing any larger ones into small pieces.

Dress with the oil and scatter the basil.

Sprinkle with the sherry vinegar.

–

Crab & rice stew

–

Small crabs are very delicate. Avoid stirring the rice once they have been added back to the pan, because the legs can easily break.

•

If the crabs are very small, remove the legs and only add the bodies, otherwise it could make eating this dish difficult.

•

You can use aioli (see page 53) instead of picada.

	for 2	for 6	for 20	for 75
Fish stock (see page 56)	5 cups	15¼ cups	2⅓ gallons	8 gallons
Olive oil	1½ tbsp	scant ½ cup	2¼ cups	4¼ cups
Small whole crabs	15	1 lb 8½ oz	5½ lb	18¾ lb
Sofrito (see page 43)	1½ tbsp	¾ cup	2¾ cups	7¼ cups
Paella rice	1 cup	3 cups	9½ cups	14½ lb
White wine	1½ tbsp	¼ cup	⅔ cup	2¼ cups
Picada (see page 41)	2 tsp	2 tbsp	½ cup	1¾ cups

Start →

Continue →

Fry for 2 minutes, stirring to coat the rice in the sofrito.

Pour in the white wine, then scrape up any sediment from the bottom of the pan.

When most of the wine has boiled away, add a ladle of stock.

Once the stock has been absorbed, add another ladle and repeat the process for 3 minutes.
Add all the remaining stock to the rice, then simmer for 12 more minutes, stirring often.

Return the crabs to the pan. Season with salt and pepper.

Add the picada.

Serve the stew in shallow bowls.

Coconut flan

We do not recommend making less than the quantity given to serve 5. If you are serving fewer people, any leftover flan will keep in the fridge for up to 3 days.

•

You can use fresh or unsweetened dried coconut.

•

You can also make the flans in small individual molds or timbales, in which case reduce the cooking time to 15–20 minutes.

	for 2	for 5	for 20	for 75
For the caramel:				
Water	-	2 tsp	2 tbsp	scant ½ cup
Sugar	-	2½ tbsp	½ cup	5 cups
For the coconut flan:				
Eggs	-	2	8	32
Coconut milk	-	1 cup	4½ cups	1 gallon
Grated coconut	-	2⅔ tbsp	⅔ cup	5¼ cups
Sugar	-	2 tbsp	½ cup	2 cups

Start →

Continue →

Cover the tops of the molds
with foil, then transfer
to a roasting pan.

Pour enough cold water into the
roasting pan to come halfway
up the sides of the molds. Bake
for 30 minutes, making sure
the water does not boil.
Once the crème caramel is cooked
(it will be just firm to the touch),
let cool in the water. Remove from
the water and chill in the fridge.

When ready to serve,
loosen the flan with
a round-bladed knife.

Carefully turn the crème
caramel out of the molds.

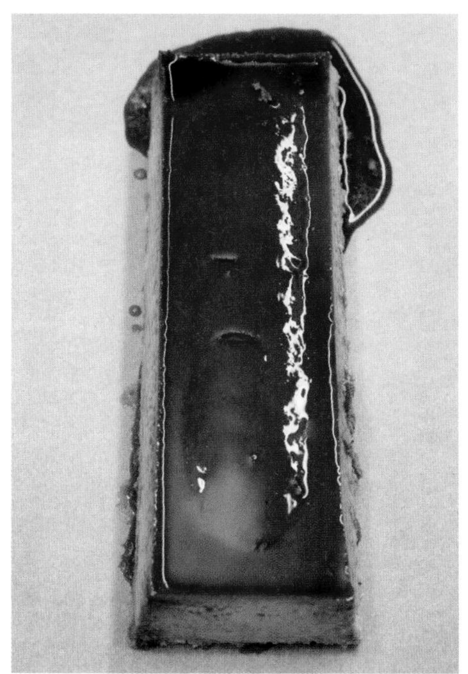

Slice into ¾-inch slices.

Serve the slices surrounded with
a few spoons of coconut milk.

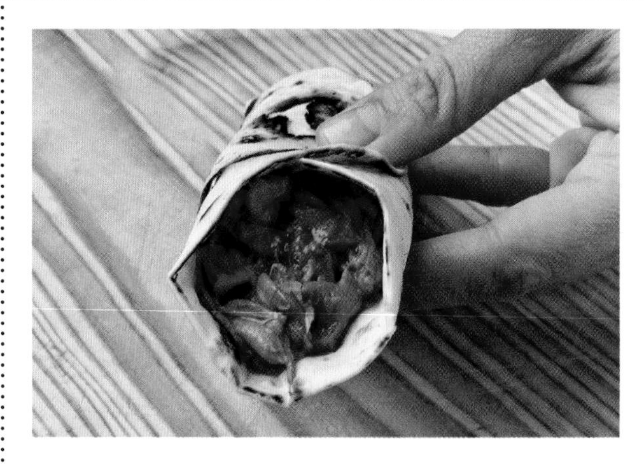

–

Meal 15

–

Bread & garlic soup

–

Mexican-style slow-cooked pork

–

Figs with cream & kirsch

Bread & garlic soup

Mexican-style slow-cooked pork

INGREDIENTS

BUY FRESH
* white country-style loaf
* boned and tied pork shoulder roast
* red onions
* small habanero chiles
* figs
* oranges
* limes

IN THE PANTRY
* olive oil
* garlic
* salt
* black peppercorns
* mild paprika
* dried oregano
* ground cumin
* white wine vinegar
* *achiote* paste
* onions
* flour tortillas
* kirsch
* sugar

IN THE FRIDGE
* eggs
* whipping cream, 35% fat

IN THE FREEZER
* chicken stock (see page 57)

Figs with cream & kirsch

ORGANIZING THE MENU	Hours before the meal
Up to 12 hours before Make the marinade for the pork and leave to marinate	
4 hours before Put the pork in the oven	4
	3½
	3
	2½
	2
	1½
	1
30 minutes before Make the bread and garlic soup Chop the red onions and chiles for the pork Prepare the figs and put into bowls. Splash with a little kirsch Whip the cream and kirsch, and keep in the fridge	½
5 minutes before Cook the eggs to your liking, then serve with the soup Shred the pork shoulder and place on a serving dish Toast the tortillas in a frying pan	
	Start of the meal
Just before dessert Spoon the kirsch cream onto the figs to serve	
	Dessert

–

Bread & garlic soup

–

This dish is good topped with either a boiled or poached egg, or we sometimes cook the egg in its shell in a low-temperature water bath called a Roner. This gives a very soft and silky result. To boil or poach an egg, see page 21.

•

Spanish *choricero* pepper paste can be used instead of paprika. It is available from specialty Spanish food stores and delicatessens.

	for 2	for 6	for 20	for 75
Olive oil	⅓ cup	1 cup	3⅓ cups	12¾ cups
1-lb white country-style loaf, cut into 2-oz slices	4 slices	12 slices	2 loaves	6 loaves
Garlic cloves	2	6	20	75
Mild paprika	2 tsp	4 tsp	3 tbsp	⅔ cup
Chicken stock (see page 57)	1¾ cups	6¼ cups	1¼ gallons	4¼ gallons
Eggs	2	6	20	75

Start →

Continue →

Add the fried bread
and chicken stock.

Season with salt and pepper.

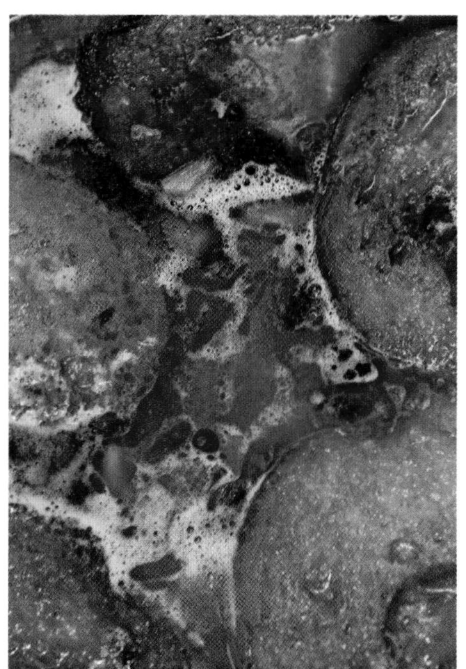

Simmer for 20 minutes,
then process with
a hand-held blender.
Meanwhile, cook the
eggs to your liking
(see note).

The soup will be
smooth and tasty.

Serve the soup with
the cooked egg.

Mexican-style slow-cooked pork

The original name of this dish is *cochinita pibil*, and it comes from Mexico's Yucatan Peninsula. Cider vinegar is used in Mexico instead of white wine vinegar.

•

If you have time, marinate the pork shoulder for 12 hours in the fridge. If you are short of time, you can marinate it for 30 minutes.

•

Achiote (or annatto) is a shrub native to Mexico and Peru. Its fruit is used as coloring and flavoring in many dishes. The paste is available from specialty food stores and delicatessens. If you cannot find it, you could try making a mixture of orange and lemon juice, pepper, and saffron, although the results will be different.

•

You can use flour or corn tortillas.

	for 2	for 6	for 20	for 75
Orange juice	¼ cup	⅔ cup	2¼ cups	6¼ cups
Dried oregano	1 pinch	2 pinches	½ tsp	2 tsp
Ground cumin	1 pinch	2 pinches	¼ tsp	1 tsp
White wine vinegar	2 tsp	2 tbsp	⅓ cup	1¼ cups
Achiote paste	2¼ oz	6¼ oz	1 lb 5 oz	4½ lb
Olive oil	1½ tbsp	¼ cup	⅔ cup	2¼ cups
Boned and tied pork shoulder roast	12 oz	2¼ lb	7¾ lb	26½ lb
Salt	1 pinch	2 pinches	⅔ cup	2⅛ cups
White onions	¼	1 small	1	3
Red onions	½	2	5	5½ lb
Small habanero chiles	¼	½	1	2
Lime juice, freshly squeezed	1 tbsp	3 tbsp	¼ cup	scant 1 cup
Flour tortillas	2	6	20	75

For 2 people you will need 1 orange and ½ lime. For 6 people you will need 2 oranges and 1 lime.

Start →

In a small bowl, whisk together the the orange juice, oregano, cumin, white wine vinegar, achiote paste, and oil.

Process with a hand-held blender until smooth.

Prick the meat several times with a fine-pointed knife to help the marinade penetrate deep into the meat. Season with salt and pepper.

Continue →

Line a roasting pan with a large sheet of aluminum foil. Put the meat in the middle of the foil and bring up the sides a little.

Pour over the marinade.

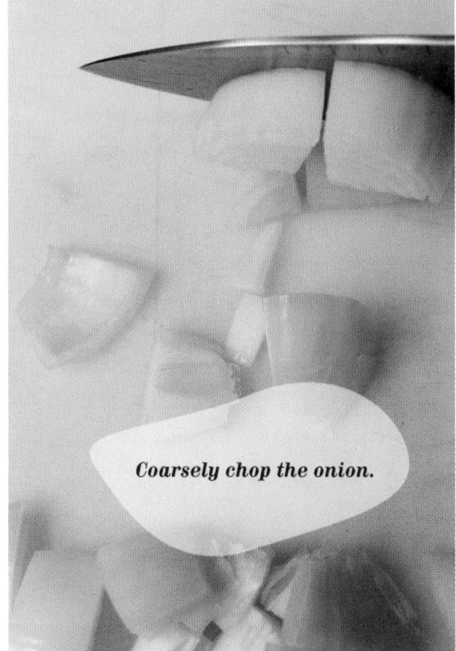

Coarsely chop the onion.

Scatter the white onions over the meat.

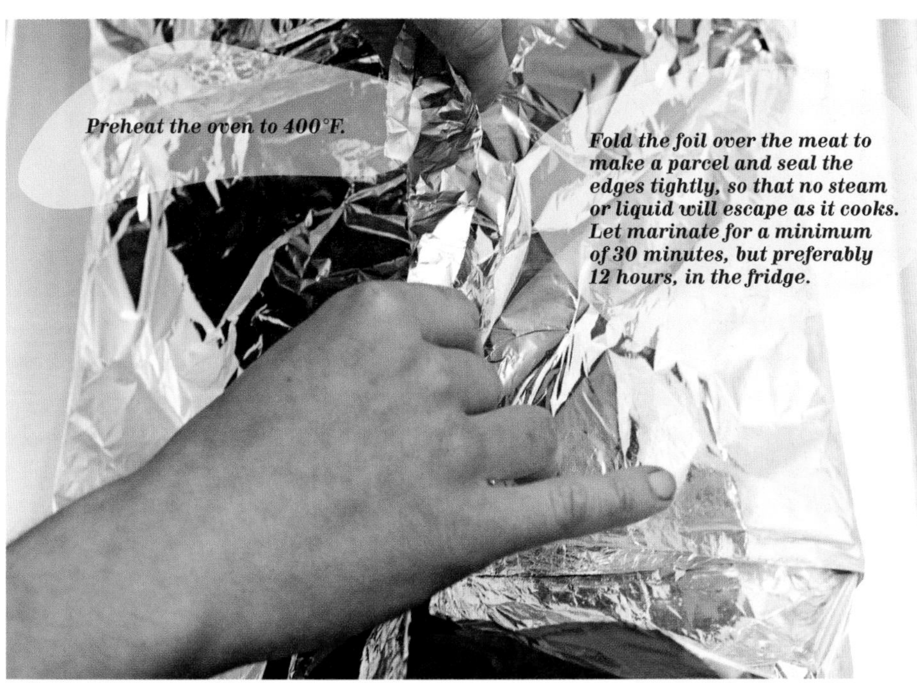

Preheat the oven to 400°F.

Fold the foil over the meat to make a parcel and seal the edges tightly, so that no steam or liquid will escape as it cooks. Let marinate for a minimum of 30 minutes, but preferably 12 hours, in the fridge.

Roast the pork shoulder for 4 hours. While it cooks, finely chop the red onion.

Continue →

Continue ➛

Remove the seeds from the habanero chile and chop the flesh finely.

Mix the chile with the onions. Add the lime juice, then season with salt.

Once cooked, take the meat out of the oven and let it rest for 20 minutes.
While you wait, toast the tortillas in a dry frying pan and wrap in foil to keep warm.

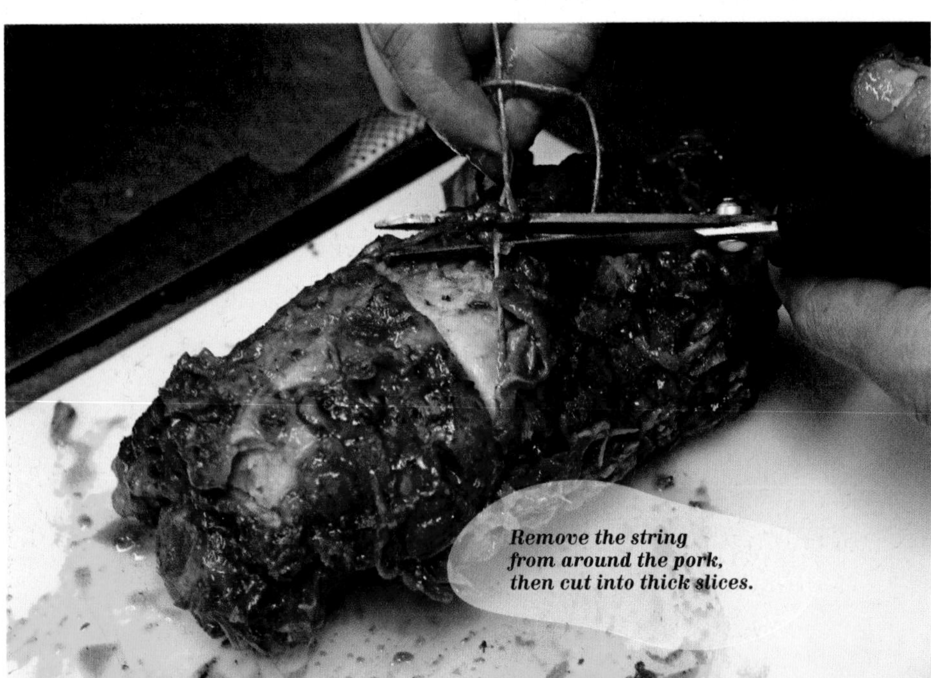
Remove the string from around the pork, then cut into thick slices.

Spread the pork over a serving platter and pull the meat to shreds with your fingers.

Spoon over the sauce from the pan.

Serve the pork with the warm tortillas and red onion salsa.

Figs with cream & kirsch

Kirsch is a cherry brandy with a high alcohol content. It is typical of Germany, Switzerland, Austria, and regions in France, such as Alsace and Franche-Comté.

•

If no kirsch is available, use another white distilled spirit, such as maraschino liqueur or white rum.

	for 2	for 6	for 20	for 75
Ripe figs	3	9	35	120
Kirsch, for the figs	2 tsp	2 tbsp	¼ cup	1 cup
Whipping cream, 35% fat	¼ cup	¾ cup	2½ cups	8½ cups
Sugar	1 tsp	1½ tbsp	scant ½ cup	1½ cups
Kirsch, for the cream	1 tsp	2 tsp	1 tbsp	¼ cup

Start →

–

Meal 16

–

Noodles with shiitake & ginger

–

Duck with chimichurri sauce

–

Pistachio custard

Noodles with shiitake & ginger

INGREDIENTS

BUY FRESH
* bacon
* scallions
* fresh ginger
* bean sprouts
* duck breasts

IN THE PANTRY
* dried shiitake mushrooms
* oyster sauce
* soy sauce
* Chinese Shaoxing wine
* sesame oil
* medium egg noodles
* olive oil
* *shichimi togarashi* spice mix
* salt
* black peppercorns
* sugar
* shelled pistachios

IN THE FRIDGE
* chimichurri sauce (see page 51)
* eggs
* whole milk
* whipping cream, 35% fat

Duck with chimichurri sauce

Pistachio custard

ORGANIZING THE MENU

	Hours before the meal
The day before Soak the shiitake mushrooms in water for 12 hours	
	4
	3½
	3
	2½
2 hours before Make the custard and chill in the fridge	2
	1½
	1
30 minutes before Boil the noodles, then chill in iced water Prepare the rest of the noodle ingredients	½
20 minutes before Brown the duck and wrap in foil Fry the bacon for the noodles, then cook the ginger, mushrooms, and onions	
5 minutes before Add the drained noodles and bean sprouts to the vegetables, fry for 5 minutes, then add the sauce	
	Start of the meal
Just before main course Slice the duck and arrange in a serving dish with the chimichurri	
	Main course

Noodles with shiitake & ginger

At elBulli, we often use ginger oil instead of fresh ginger.

•

Shichimi togarashi is a mix of seven spices used in Japanese cooking and characterized by its hot flavor. If you cannot find it in the stores, use freshly ground black pepper and a little chili powder instead.

•

Shaoxing rice wine, shiitake mushrooms, *shichimi togarashi*, oyster sauce, and the noodles can all be purchased from stores specializing in Asian food, and from some larger supermarkets.

	for 2	for 6	for 20	for 75
Dried shiitake mushrooms	6	3 oz	5½ oz	1 lb 5 oz
Oyster sauce	3 tsp	½ cup	1¾ cup	6 cups
Soy sauce	3 tsp	½ cup	1½ cup	6 cups
Chinese Shaoxing rice wine	3 tsp	½ cup	1½ cup	6 cups
Sesame oil	1 tbsp	¼ cup	¾ cup	2¾ cups
Medium egg noodles	4 oz	12½ oz	2½ lb	8¾ lb
Bacon	3 oz	8½ oz	1¾ lb	6½ lb
Small scallions, roughly chopped (or use the white parts from a bunch of scallions)	1	2	2½ lb	8¾ lb
Bean sprouts	¼ cups	1 cup	3¼ cups	11 cups
Finely chopped fresh ginger	1 tsp	4½ tsp	2¼ tbsp	scant ½ cup
Olive oil	2 tsp	2 tbsp	1¼ cups	4¼ cups
Shichimi togarashi	1 pinch	2 pinches	2½ tsp	2¾ tbsp

Start →

Put the shiitake mushrooms into a large bowl, cover with plenty of cold water, and let soak for 12 hours.

Continue →

Continue →

Continue →

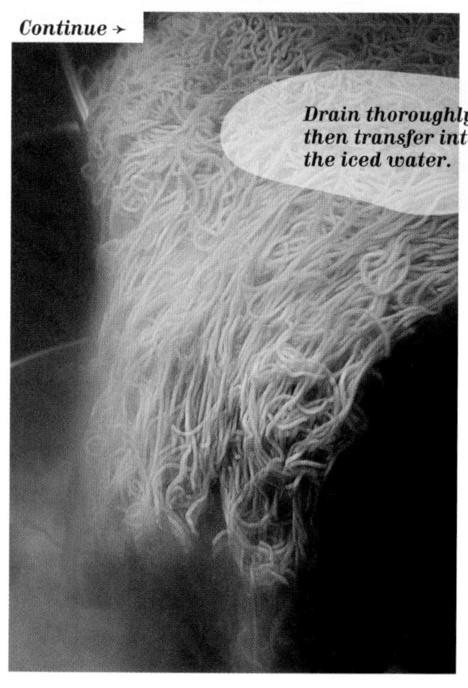
Drain thoroughly,
then transfer into
the iced water.

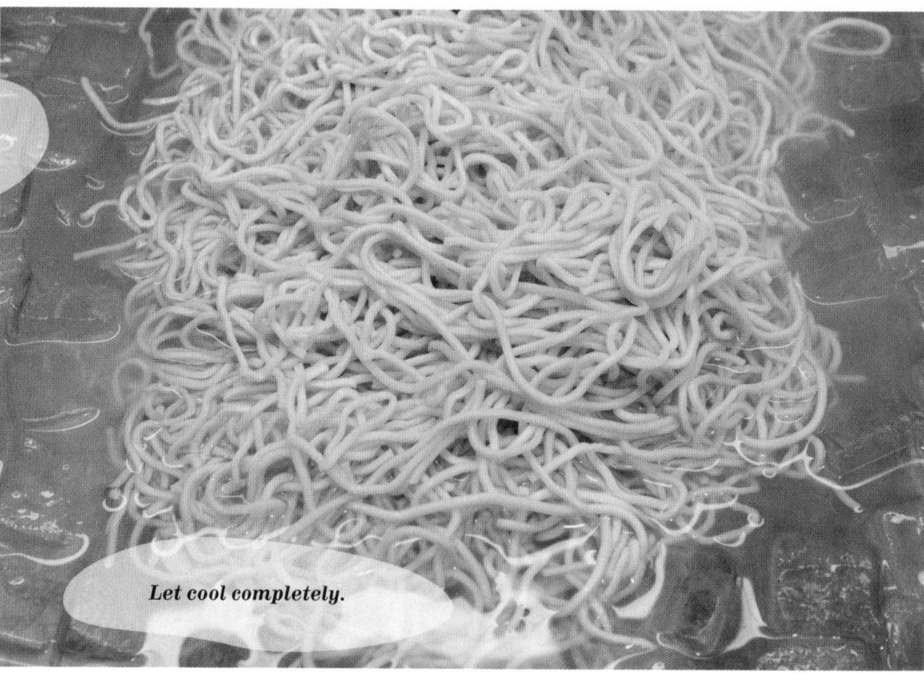
Let cool completely.

Slice the excess fat
off the bacon.

Cut the bacon thin strips.

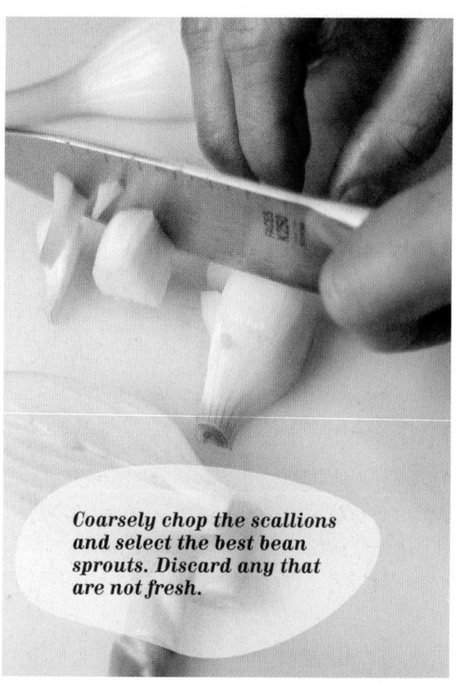
Coarsely chop the scallions
and select the best bean
sprouts. Discard any that
are not fresh.

Peel the ginger
using a teaspoon.

Slice and finely
chop the ginger.

Heat the oil in a large pan
or wok, then add the bacon
and fry until golden brown.

Continue →
Add the chopped ginger
and shiitake mushrooms
and fry for 1–2 minutes.
Add the chopped
scallions and fry
until browned,
stirring frequently.
Drain the noodles.
Add the bean sprouts
and noodles to the pan.
Stir-fry for 5 minutes,
then add the soy sauce
mixture, mixing well
to coat the noodles.
Serve the noodles on a plate,
then sprinkle with a little
shichimi togarashi.

Duck with chimichurri sauce

Chimichurri is a sauce made from parsley, garlic, spices, olive oil, and vinegar (see page 51). It comes from South America, where it is often served with steak, but it is also good with duck.

	for 2	for 6	for 20	for 75
Duck breasts	1	3	8	25
Chimichurri sauce (see page 51)	½ cup	1⅓ cups	4½ cups	1 gallon

Pistachio custard

If you have a kitchen thermometer, use it to check when the custard is ready—it will thicken at 170°F. If you do not have a thermometer, check the back of the spoon; the custard is ready when it is thick enough to coat it.

	for 2	for 6	for 20	for 75
Whole milk	scant 1 cup	2⅓ cups	8 cups	8½ quarts
Whipping cream, 35% fat	¼ cup	⅔ cup	2¼ cups	8 cups
Egg yolks	2	6	28	112
Sugar	½ cup	⅔ cup	2 cups	9 cups
Shelled pistachios	¼ cup	¾ cup	2⅔ cups	10½ cups

Start →

–

Meal 17

–

Baked potatoes with romesco sauce

–

Whiting in salsa verde

–

Rice pudding

Baked potatoes with romesco sauce

Whiting in salsa verde

INGREDIENTS

BUY FRESH
* small new potatoes
* fresh whole whiting
* fresh parsley
* lemons

IN THE PANTRY
* small onions
* garlic
* salt
* extra-virgin olive oil
* flour
* short-grain rice
* sugar
* ground cinnamon

IN THE FRIDGE
* whole milk
* butter
* whipping cream, 35% fat

IN THE FREEZER
* romesco sauce (see page 45)
* fish stock (see page 56)

Rice pudding

ORGANIZING THE MENU	Hours before the meal
	4
	3½
	3
	2½
	2
At least 1 hour before **Cook the rice pudding and chill in the fridge**	1½
1 hour before **Bake the potatoes and onions**	1
Cut the fish into pieces and chop the garlic and parsley	½
25 minutes before **Cook the whiting in salsa verde**	
Just before eating **Cut the baked potatoes and onions in half**	
	Start of the meal
Just before main course **Arrange the fish on a plate and cover with the salsa verde**	
	Main course
Just before dessert **Sprinkle cinnamon over the rice pudding**	
	Dessert

Baked potatoes with romesco sauce

Romesco is a traditional sauce from Tarragona in Catalonia. It is made from hazelnuts, red peppers, sherry vinegar and olive oil, and it is usually served with seafood, vegetables or chicken.

	for 2	for 6	for 20	for 75
Small new potatoes	4	12	6½ lb	22 lb
Small onions, left in their skins	2	6	4½ lb	16½ lb
Romesco sauce (see page 45)	½ cup	1¾ cups	5¾ cups	1¼ gallons

Start →

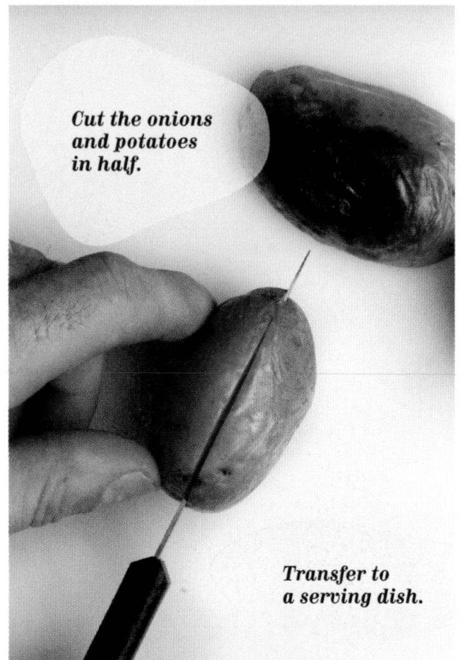

—

Whiting in salsa verde

—

Ask your fish supplier to clean and gut the fish for you if you prefer.

•

You can use other kinds of white fish in this recipe, such as sea bream or even shellfish. Cook in the sauce for 3–5 minutes.

	for 2	for 6	for 20	for 75
Fresh whole whiting, cleaned and gutted, 9 oz each	2	6	20	75
Salt	1 pinch	2 pinches	3⅓ tsp	scant ½ cup
Garlic cloves, finely chopped	1	3	1½ oz	4¾ oz
Fresh parsley, finely chopped	1½ tbsp	4 tbsp	1 bunch	3 bunches
Extra-virgin olive oil	1½ tbsp	5 tbsp	scant 1½ cups	4¼ cups
Flour	1 tsp	1½ tbsp	¾ cup	1¾ cups
Water	¾ cup	2¼ cups	6¼ cups	1 gallon

Start →

Cut the heads from the whiting, then cut the each body into two equal pieces. Season with a little of the salt.

To make the salsa verde, first finely chop the garlic.

Place a large pan over low heat, then pour in the oil. Add the garlic and fry it gently for 1–2 minutes, until softened but not browned.

Finely chop the parsley.

Continue →

Continue ➛

Stir the flour into the oil and garlic, and fry for 30 seconds. Add half of the chopped parsley.

Pour in the water.

Simmer the sauce for 10 minutes, stirring occasionally, until it thickens slightly.

Place the fish in the sauce and simmer for 10 minutes, until the flesh flakes easily.

Season the sauce with salt, then scatter with the rest of the parsley.

Transfer the fish onto serving plates, then spoon over the salsa verde.

Rice pudding

Rice pudding is a common dessert in many European, Latin American, and Asian countries. The cooking method is universal—what sets the recipes apart is the flavorings used, which can include vanilla, cinnamon, lemon zest, *dulce de leche* (milk caramel), saffron, cardamom, or port.

•

You could use any short-grain rice for this recipe.

	for 2	for 6	for 20	for 75
Whole milk	1⅓ cups	4½ cups	14¾ cups	scant 3½ gallons
Whipping cream, 35% fat	¼ cup	¾ cup	3⅓ cups	12 cups
Lemon zest in 2-inch strips	1 strip	2 strips	½ lemon	1 lemon
Cinnamon sticks	¼	½	1	2
Short-grain rice	⅓ cup	1 cup	3¾ cups	14 cups
Sugar	¼ cup	⅔ cup	3 cups	9 cups
Butter	4¼ tsp	4½ tbsp	7 tbsp	3 cups
Ground cinnamon	1 pinch	2 pinches	3 tbsp	⅔ cup

Start →

–

Meal 18

–

Guacamole with tortilla chips

–

Mexican-style chicken with rice

–

Watermelon with menthol candies

INGREDIENTS

BUY FRESH
* ripe tomatoes
* avocados
* cilantro
* lemons
* chicken leg quarters
* watermelon

IN THE PANTRY
* salt
* tortilla chips
* sesame seeds
* onions
* olive oil
* paella rice
* red mole paste
* canned corn
* sugar
* hard menthol candies
* N_2O cartridges for the siphon

IN THE FRIDGE
* butter

–

Guacamole with tortilla chips

–

–

Mexican-style chicken with rice

–

Watermelon with menthol candies

ORGANIZING THE MENU	Hours before the meal
	4
	3½
	3
	2½
	2
1½ hours before Simmer the chicken leg quarters	1½
Make the mole sauce	1
Prepare the tomatoes and onion for the guacamole. Puree the onion and cilantro for the rice	
30 minutes before Cut up the watermelon, marinate in the syrup, and chill in the fridge	½
Crush the candies	
Cover the chicken with the sauce and cook in the oven	
20 minutes before Cook the Mexican rice	—
While the rice and chicken are cooking, finish the guacamole	
Just before eating Finish the rice with the corn, butter, and cilantro	
	Start of the meal
Just before dessert Drain the watermelon and place on a serving dish	
	Dessert

Guacamole with tortilla chips

When making guacamole in small quantities, you can also use a mortar and pestle, which is the traditional method.

•

If the tomatoes are very ripe, you may not need to scald them before peeling.

	for 2	for 6	for 20	for 75
Ripe tomatoes, diced	1 tbsp	2 tbsp	14 oz	2½ lb
Cilantro, finely chopped	1½ tbsp	4 tbsp	½ cup	2 cups
Avocados	1	3	4½ lb	15½ lb
Medium onion, finely chopped	1 tbsp	3 tbsp	½ cup	1¾ cups
Lemon juice	1½ tbsp	¼ cup	⅔ cup	2¼ cups
Salt	1 pinch	1 generous pinch	¼ tsp	2 tsp
Tortilla chips	3½ oz	9 oz	1½ lb	5½ lb

To make it for 2 people you will need to buy 1 tomato and 1 onion; for 6, you will need 2 tomatoes and 1 onion.

Start →

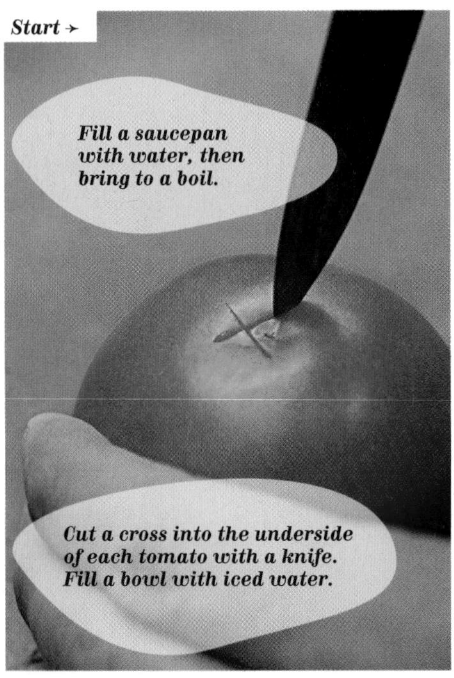

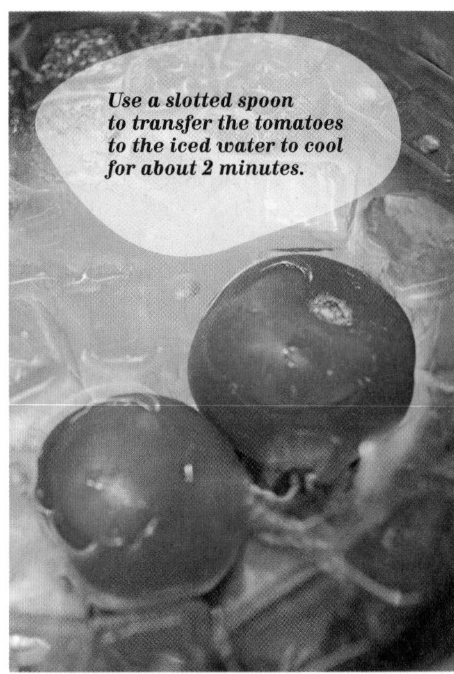

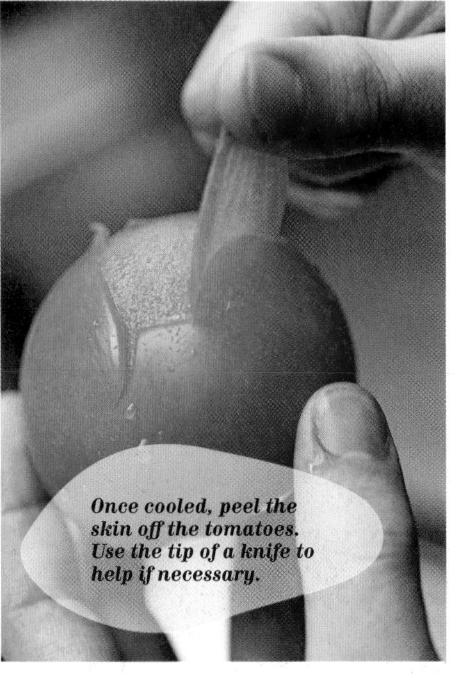

Continue →

Pick the leaves off the cilantro stems and chop them finely.

Cut the avocados in half and remove the pits. Scoop out the flesh with a spoon.

Mash the avocado using a whisk, fork, or hand-held blender.

Chop the onion finely.

Add the chopped tomato, onion, and cilantro to the avocados.

Pour in the lemon juice and stir. Season with salt.

Serve the guacamole with tortilla chips.

Mexican-style chicken with rice

Mole is a Mexican sauce containing chiles and spices, which usually accompanies meat.

•

There are many varieties of mole sauces, which differ according to the type of chile and other ingredients. Mole pastes are available from specialty stores and delicatessens.

•

When making it for 20 or 75, you could add ⅛ tsp Xanthan (see page 11) for every 4 cups of sauce to help thicken it.

	for 2	for 6	for 20	for 75
Chicken legs (thigh and drumstick connected)	2	6	20	75
Water	2½ cups	5 cups	1¼ gallons	4¾ gallons
Salt	1 pinch	2 pinches	1 tsp	3 tbsp
Sprigs cilantro	5	8	1¼ oz	3½ oz
Red mole paste	3½ oz	11 oz	2¼ lb	7¾ lb
Sesame seeds	2 tsp	2 tbsp	¼ cup	¾ cup plus 2 tbsp

Start →

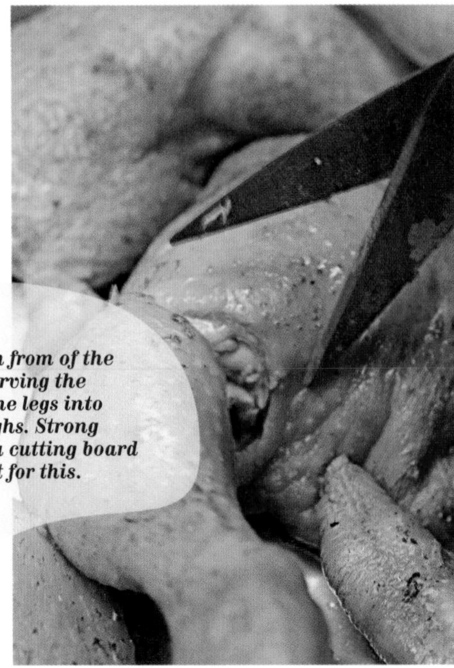

Continue →

Preheat the oven to 325°F.
Spoon the mole paste into a saucepan. Stir over low heat until it begins to melt.

Add one-third of the reserved chicken liquid.

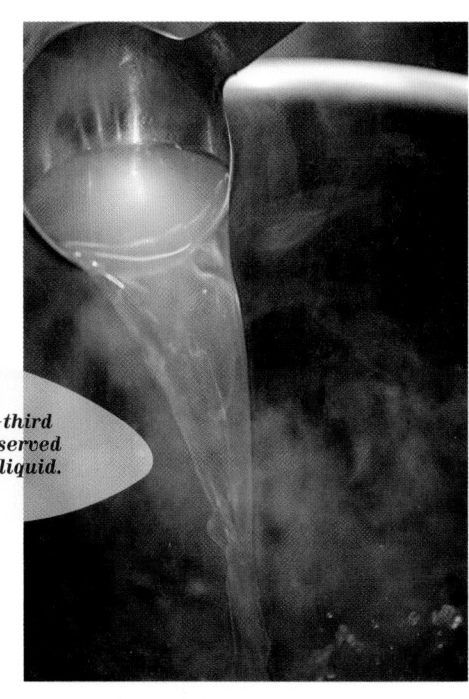

Boil for 15 minutes, until the sauce has a creamy consistency.

Cover the chicken with the sauce and roast for 30 minutes, until the sauce is thick and the chicken is very tender. To check, insert the tip of a sharp knife into the chicken flesh.

Meanwhile, toast the sesame seeds in a dry frying pan over low heat, stirring frequently. Remove from the pan as soon as they are ready.

Arrange the chicken on a serving dish. Cover with the sauce, then sprinkle with the toasted sesame seeds.

Serve with Mexican rice (page 244).

–

Mexican rice

–

Perfect as a side dish with Mexican-style chicken (see page 242), this dish also works as an appetizer with a few slices of avocado.

•

If you do not have a blender you can finely chop the onion and cilantro instead of pureeing them.

	for 2	for 6	for 20	for 75
Chicken stock (from the Mexican-style chicken recipe, page 242)	2½ cups	6¼ cups	1⅓ gallons	4¼ gallons
Small onions, roughly chopped	½	1½	5	12
Sprigs cilantro	2	1 handful	1½ bunches	5 bunches
Olive oil	2 tbsp	4 tbsp	⅔ cup	2¼ cups
Paella rice	¾ cup	2⅓ cups	7¾ cups	11 lb
Cannned corn, drained	⅓ cup	scant 1 cup	1⅓ cups	4⅔ cups
Butter	1 tbsp	¼ cup	¾ cup	2 cups

Start →

Pour the chicken stock into a saucepan and bring to a simmer. Meanwhile use a hand-held blender to puree the onion and half of the cilantro to make a smooth paste.

Pour the oil into a large saucepan over medium heat. Add the rice and cook for 1 minute, stirring.

Add the onion and cilantro mixture to the rice and continue to fry gently for 2 minutes.

Pour in the hot stock and simmer the rice for 20 minutes, stirring occasionally to prevent sticking.

Meanwhile, finely chop the remaining cilantro.

When the rice is nearly cooked (after about 17 minutes), add the drained corn.

When the time is up, turn off the heat. Add the butter and stir until the rice has a creamy texture.

Add the chopped cilantro, season with salt and pepper, and serve.

Watermelon with menthol candies

Our sense of taste perceives four basic flavors; sweet, salty, sour, and bitter, plus a series of nuances, collectively called "mouthfeel." Among these nuances is menthol, which gives the palate a feeling of freshness and works very well in this dish. Others include astringency, spiciness, tartness, and effervescence.

•

If you have a vacuum-packing machine, seal the watermelon and lemon syrup in a vacuum-pack bag. This will let the liquid penetrate more thoroughly into the fruit.

	for 2	for 6	for 20	for 75
Lemon juice	1½ tbsp	3 tbsp	1¼ cups	4¼ cups
Sugar	2 tbsp	6 tbsp	1½ cups	5 cups
Watermelon	1 wedge	½ melon	1½ melons	5 melons
Hard menthol candies	4	12	40 (7 oz)	150 (1½ lb)

Start →

Strain the lemon juice into a bowl and add the sugar. Stir to dissolve.

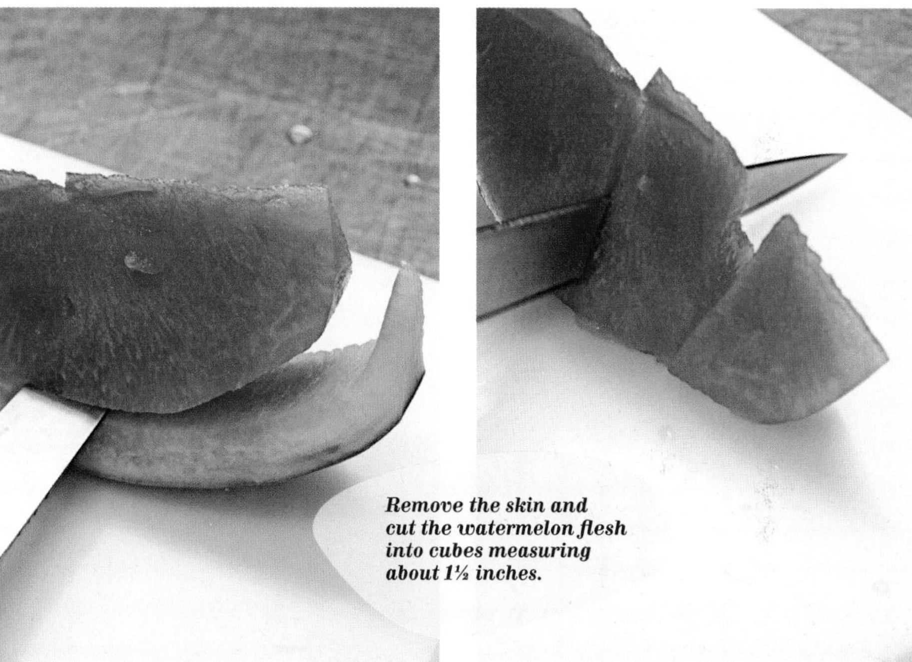

Remove the skin and cut the watermelon flesh into cubes measuring about 1½ inches.

Transfer the melon and lemon syrup into a resealable bag or nonreactive bowl, then marinate in the fridge for 30 minutes.

Put the candies between two sheets of parchment paper and crush with a rolling pin or other heavy utensil to make a fine powder.

Drain the watermelon pieces and arrange on a serving dish. You can serve it on crushed ice, if you like.

Serve the melon with the crushed candies in a separate bowl for guests to sprinkle.

–

Meal 19

–

Spaghetti with tomato & basil

–

Fried fish with garlic

–

Caramel foam

Spaghetti with tomato & basil

Fried fish with garlic

INGREDIENTS

BUY FRESH
- **fresh basil**
- **fresh whole fish, cleaned and gutted**

IN THE PANTRY
- **salt**
- **spaghetti**
- **extra-virgin olive oil**
- **olive oil**
- **garlic**
- **sherry vinegar**
- **sugar**
- **N_2O cartridges for the siphon**

IN THE FRIDGE
- **whipping cream, 35% fat**
- **Parmesan cheese**
- **whole milk**
- **eggs**

IN THE FREEZER
- **tomato sauce** **(see page 42)**

Caramel foam

ORGANIZING THE MENU	Hours before the meal
	4
	3½
	3
	2½
2 hours before **Make the caramel base for the foam**	2
Fill the siphon and chill in the fridge or in an ice bucket	1½
	1
30 minutes before **Trim the fins and remove the head from the fish** **Reheat the tomato sauce** **Fry the garlic and make the garlic dressing for the fish**	½
10 minutes before **Boil the spaghetti**	
5 minutes before **Cook the fish**	
Just before eating **Drain the pasta and toss with the oil** **Put the fish onto a serving plate, cover with the fried garlic, and spoon over the dressing**	
	Start of the meal
Just before dessert **Dispense the caramel foam into small bowls**	
	Dessert

Spaghetti with tomato & basil

The tomato sauce (see page 42) can be made ahead and frozen (or use a good-quality store-bought sauce instead). Do not forget to defrost it in advance.

•

As well as flavoring the pasta, the oil prevents the spaghetti strands from sticking together, which is especially useful for large quantities.

•

When cooking pasta, add 1 teaspoon salt per 4 cups of water.

	for 2	for 6	for 20	for 75
Tomato sauce (see page 42)	1 cup	2½ cups	8¾ cups	2 gallons
Fresh basil	20 leaves	60 leaves	1⅛ cups	3½ cups
Parmesan cheese	1¼ oz	3¾ oz	1 lb 5 oz	4½ lb
Water	2½ cups	8½ cups	4 gallons	15¾ gallons
Salt	1 tsp	1¼ tsp	⅔ cup	2½ cups
Spaghetti	7 oz	1 lb 5 oz	4½ oz	15½ lb
Extra-virgin olive oil	3 tbsp	½ cup	1¾ cups	6⅓ cups

Start →

In a saucepan over medium heat, bring the tomato sauce to a simmer.

Pick the basil leaves from their stems and set aside the smallest and best ones for finishing the dish.

Remove the tomato sauce from the heat and stir in the rest of the basil.

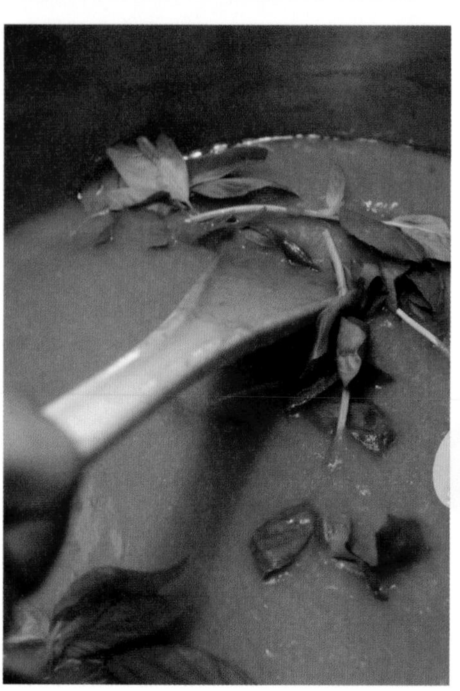

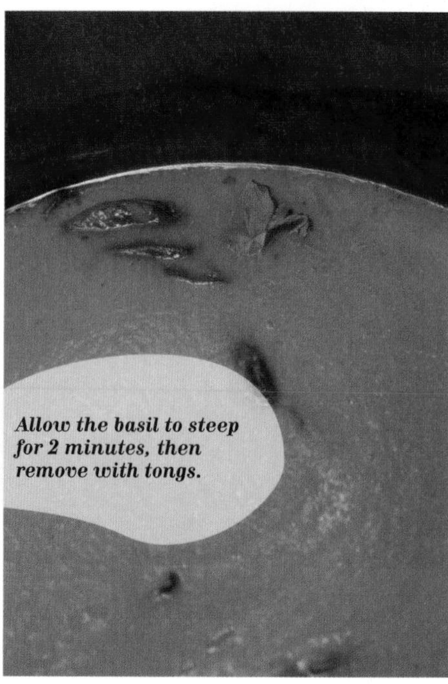

Allow the basil to steep for 2 minutes, then remove with tongs.

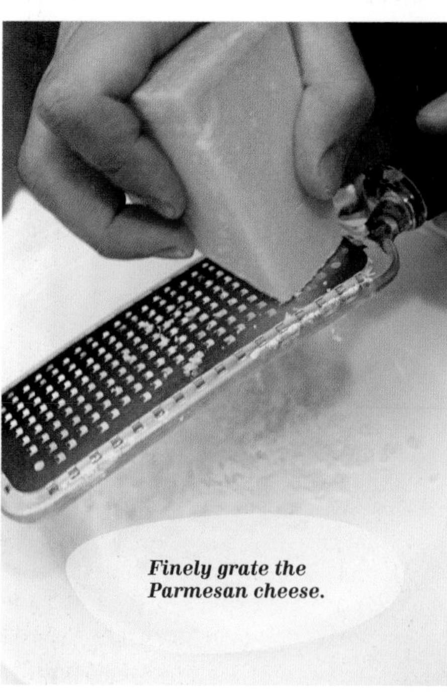

Finely grate the Parmesan cheese.

Continue →

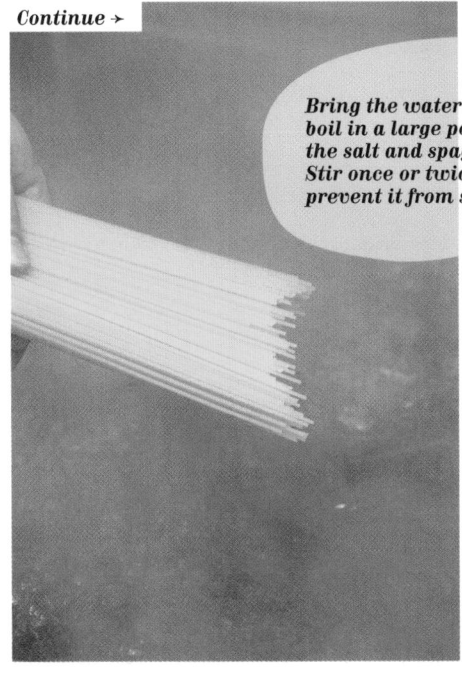

Bring the water to a boil in a large pot. Add the salt and spaghetti. Stir once or twice to prevent it from sticking.

Boil for 8–10 minutes, or until tender but still firm to the bite (check the directions on the package).

Transfer the pasta into a colander and drain well.

Transfer the pasta to a large serving dish and stir in the olive oil.

Using tongs or a wooden fork, divide the spaghetti among serving plates.

Spoon the tomato sauce over the top.

Scatter with the remaining basil leaves.

Finish with the grated Parmesan.

Fried fish with garlic

Ask your fish supplier to clean and gut the fish for you if you prefer.

•

At elBulli, we use a large flat griddle, but at home a large flat frying pan is fine.

•

Almost any small fish can be used for this dish. For thicker fish, the cooking time should be longer—it should be golden on both sides and tender and juicy in the middle.

	for 2	for 6	for 20	for 75
Fresh whole fish, cleaned and gutted, 6–9 oz each	2	6	20	75
Garlic cloves	3	9	30	112
Olive oil	¼ cup, plus extra to cook the fish	⅔ cup, plus extra to cook the fish	2¾ cups, plus extra to cook the fish	10½ cups, plus extra to cook the fish
Sherry vinegar	2 tsp	2 tbsp	⅔ cup	2¼ cups

Start →

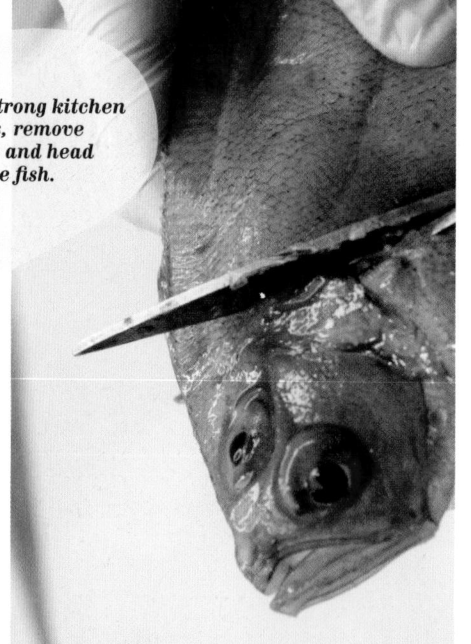

Using strong kitchen scissors, remove the fins and head from the fish.

Peel the garlic and slice very finely, using a mandoline or sharp knife.

Pour the oil into a small pan and add the garlic.

Put the pan over medium heat and gently fry the garlic until golden. Be careful not to let the garlic burn.

Drain the garlic through a fine-mesh metal strainer, reserving the oil.

Continue →
Transfer the garlic onto paper towels to absorb any excess oil.
Let the oil cool a little, then add the sherry vinegar and stir to make a dressing.
Season the fish with salt. Heat a large frying pan or flat griddle, add a little oil, and place the fish in it.
Fry the fish for 1 minute, or until golden underneath. Use a spatula to turn the fish.
Cook on the second side for 1 minute, then transfer to a serving dish.
Scatter the fried garlic over the fish. Give the oil-and-vinegar dressing a final stir.
Spoon a couple of tablespoons of dressing over each fish.

Caramel foam

A siphon is a restaurant tool that is definitely worth buying for home use. If you do not have a siphon, make caramel ice cream instead: follow this recipe and freeze the mixture in an ice-cream machine.

•

You can add your choice of topping to the foam, such as caramel sauce or crushed hard caramels.

•

If you are making this for more than 6–8 people, heat the milk and cream together before pouring into the caramel to avoid too much splashing.

	for 2	for 6–8	for 20	for 75
Sugar	-	⅓ cup	¾ cup	3 cups
Whipping cream, 35% fat	-	1⅓ cups	2⅔ cups	10 cups
Whole milk	-	6 tbsp	¾ cup	2½ cups
Egg yolks	-	4	10	30
N_2O cartridges for the siphon	-	2	4	14

The minimum quantity of foam you can make in a whipped-cream siphon is 6–8 portions. For 6–8, you will need a pint-size siphon. For 20, you will need 2 x 1-quart siphons, and for 75, you will need 7 x 1-quart siphons.

Continue →

Gradually pour the caramel mixture onto the yolks, whisking continuously. Transfer the mixture to a clean saucepan.

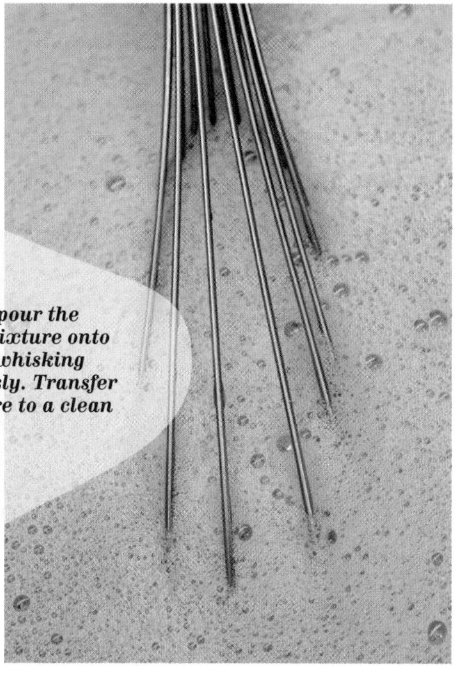

Cook very gently over low heat, stirring continuously with a whisk, until slightly thickened.
Do not let it boil.

Pass the mixture through a fine-mesh strainer.

Insert the cartridge into the siphon, then fill with the caramel mixture.

Chill in the fridge or a bucket of ice for 2 hours.

To serve the foam, first shake the siphon vigorously. Dispense the foam into bowls or glasses.

Add your choice of topping, such as caramel sauce or crushed caramels.

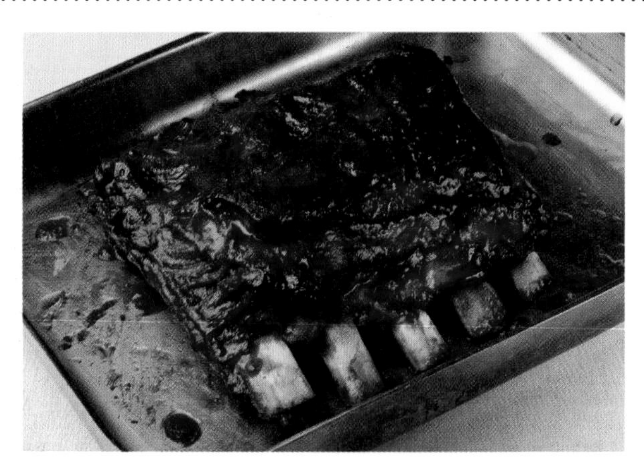

–

Meal 20

–

Cauliflower with béchamel

–

Pork ribs with barbecue sauce

–

Banana with lime

Cauliflower with béchamel

INGREDIENTS

BUY FRESH
* cauliflower
* pork rib racks
* oranges
* bananas
* limes

IN THE PANTRY
* flour
* onions
* cloves
* dried bay leaves
* white peppercorns
* ground nutmeg
* extra-virgin olive oil
* salt
* barbecue sauce
* sugar

IN THE FRIDGE
* Parmesan cheese
* whole milk
* butter

Pork ribs with barbecue sauce

Banana with lime

ORGANIZING THE MENU

	Hours before the meal
	4
	3½
	3
	2½
2 hours before Make the syrup for the bananas and cool	2
1½ hours before Roast the ribs in the oven	1½
1 hour before Slice the bananas and marinate in the syrup in the fridge Make the béchamel	1
30 minutes before Cut the cauliflower, then boil until just tender. Drain	½
5 minutes before Cover the cauliflower with the béchamel, then cook under the broiler Cut the ribs and sprinkle with orange zest	
	Start of the meal
Just before dessert Spoon the bananas and some of their syrup into serving bowls	
	Dessert

Cauliflower with béchamel

If cooking this dish for 2 people, omit the onion and clove from the béchamel, and reduce the cooking time to 5–10 minutes.

	for 2	for 6	for 20	for 75
Whole milk	1¼ cups	3⅓ cups	11¾ cups	2½ gallons
Butter	2 tsp	2 tbsp	7 tbsp	1½ cups plus 2 tbsp
Flour	2 tsp	2 tbsp	¾ cup	3 cups
Cloves	-	1	2	6
Small onions	-	1	1	1
Dried bay leaves	¼	½	3	6
Ground nutmeg	1 pinch	2 pinches	scant ⅛ tsp	scant ½ tsp
Cauliflowers	½	1½	4	15
Freshly ground white pepper	1 pinch	2 pinches	⅛ tsp	½ tsp
Extra-virgin olive oil	2 tsp	1¾ tbsp	⅓ cup	1¼ cups
Finely grated Parmesan cheese	⅓ cup	1 cup	4 cups	3 lb 5 oz

Start →

Continue →

To prepare
the cauliflower,
cut off the stem
and leaves.

Cut the head into florets
about 1 inch large.

Bring a large pan of water
to a boil. Add the cauliflower
florets and cook for 8 minutes,
or until just tender.

Drain the cauliflower, being
careful not to damage the
delicate florets.

Season with salt, white pepper
and extra-virgin olive oil.

Spoon a layer of béchamel
into a large heatproof
baking dish and arrange
the cauliflower over it,
then cover with the rest
of the sauce.

Heat the broiler to high.
Sprinkle the cauliflower
with the grated Parmesan.

Cook under the broiler
for a couple of minutes
until the cheese is golden
and the sauce is bubbling
around the edges.

Pork ribs with barbecue sauce

If you prefer to make your own barbecue sauce, see the recipe on page 48.

	for 2	for 6	for 20	for 75
Pork rib racks, whole, weighing about 3¼ lb each	⅓ (6 ribs)	1	4	15
Salt	1 pinch	2 pinches	1 tsp	1 tbsp
Barbecue sauce, either store-bought or homemade (see page 48)	½ cup	1¼ cups	4 cups	1 gallon
Water	½ cup	1¼ cups	4 cups	1 gallon
Oranges	½	1	2	4

Start →

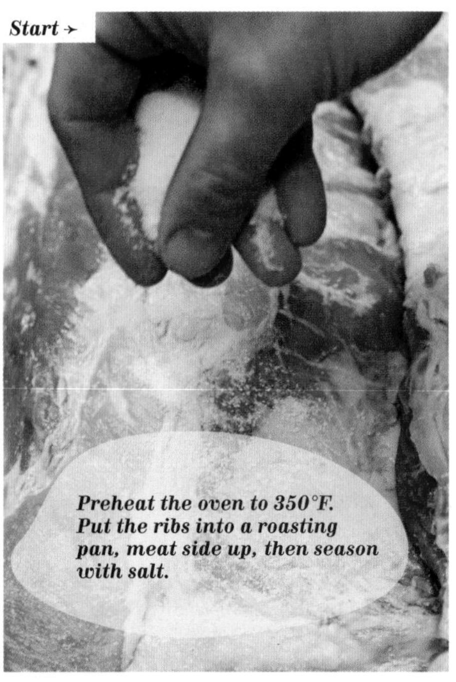

Preheat the oven to 350°F. Put the ribs into a roasting pan, meat side up, then season with salt.

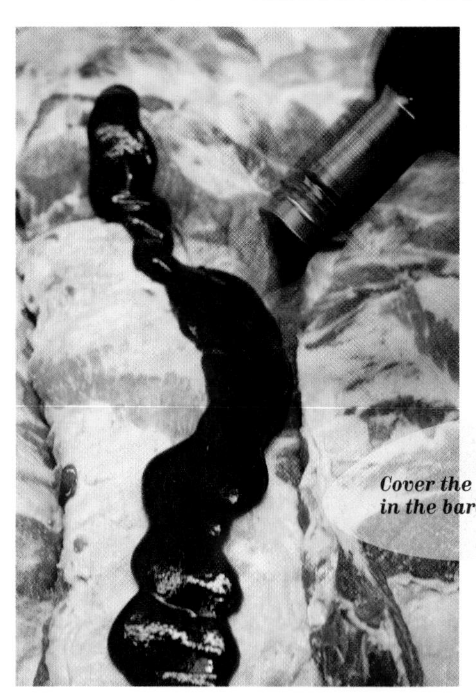

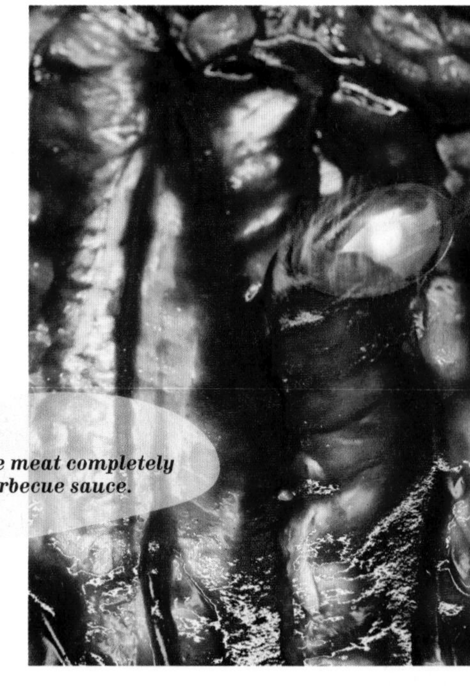

Cover the meat completely in the barbecue sauce.

Pour the water over the ribs to dilute the sauce a little.

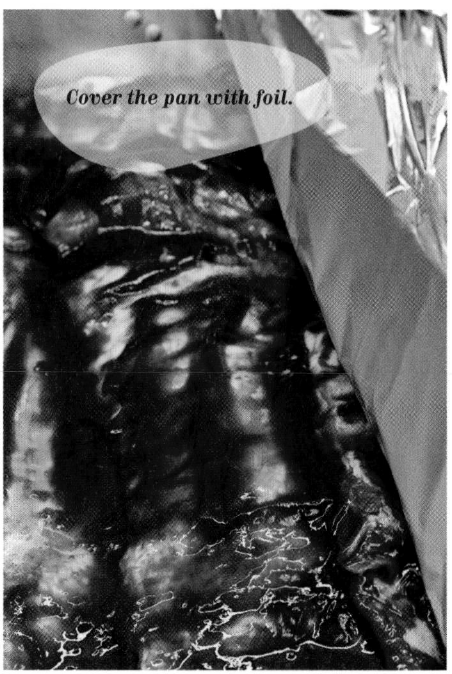

Cover the pan with foil.

Roast in the oven for 1½ hours.

Continue →

Baste with the barbecue sauce every 20 minutes to make sure the meat stays moist.

The racks are ready when they are dark, golden, and the meat is falling away from the bone.

Once cooked, separate the ribs and place them in a serving dish.

Finish with a fine grating of orange zest to serve.

Banana with lime

This simple recipe is a good dessert to serve when few fresh fruits are in season.

•

For a special occasion, you could add rum to the syrup: substitute 1 tsp, 2 tbsp, ½ cup, or 1¾ cups of the water for rum for 2, 6, 20 or 75 people respectively.

•

You could also steep a cinnamon stick or vanilla bean in the syrup while it cools.

	for 2	for 6	for 20	for 75
Sugar	2 tbsp	6 tbsp	2½ cups	7⅓ cups
Water	3 tbsp	⅔ cup	3 cups	8 cups
Bananas	2	6	20	75
Limes	½	2	8	16

Start →

Continue →

Squeeze the lime juice
into the syrup and stir.
Peel, then thinly slice the bananas.
Put the banana slices
into the syrup and marinate
in the fridge for 1 hour
before serving.
Serve in a small
bowl with a couple of
spoonfuls of syrup.

–

Meal 21

–

Gazpacho

–

Black rice with squid

–

Bread with chocolate & olive oil

INGREDIENTS

BUY FRESH
* small cucumbers
* red bell peppers
* ripe tomatoes
* white country-style loaf
* fresh squid, cleaned, with own ink (if possible)

IN THE PANTRY
* garlic
* onions
* extra-virgin olive oil
* olive oil
* sherry vinegar
* salt
* black pepper
* croutons
* paella rice
* dark chocolate, 60% cocoa
* sea salt flakes

IN THE FRIDGE
* mayonnaise

IN THE FREEZER
* fish stock (see page 56)
* sofrito (see page 43)
* squid ink (optional, see page 272)
* picada (see page 41)

–

Gazpacho

–

–

Black rice with squid

–

Bread with chocolate & olive oil

ORGANIZING THE MENU	Hours before the meal
	4
	3½
	3
	2½
	2
	1½
	1
45 minutes before Make the gazpacho and chill in the fridge	½
25 minutes before Cut up the squid and heat the stock	
20 minutes before Start cooking the black rice Grate the chocolate while the rice is cooking	
Just before eating Drizzle the gazpacho with oil and sprinkle with croutons	
	Start of the meal
Just before dessert Toast the bread and finish it with the chocolate, oil, and salt	
	Dessert

Gazpacho

Gazpacho can be made ahead and frozen. Defrost it in the fridge overnight.

•

Mayonnaise is an unusual ingredient, but we like the creaminess it adds to the soup.

•

For 2, you will need 4 tomatoes, 1 small cucumber, and 1 small red bell pepper. For 6, you will need 12 tomatoes, 1 cucumber and 1 red pepper.

	for 2	for 6	for 20	for 75
Garlic cloves	1	3	10	32
Onions	1	2	7	25
Cucumber	¾ oz	2¼ oz	7 oz	1¾ lb
Red bell pepper	1 oz	2⅞ oz	11 oz	2¼ lb
Ripe tomatoes	11½ oz	2¼ lb	7 lb	26½ lb
White country-style bread (without crusts)	¼ oz	1¼ oz	3 oz	11 oz
Water	¼ cup	½ cup	1¾ cups	6 cups
Olive oil, plus extra to serve	3 tbsp	⅓ cup	2½ cups	8 cups
Sherry vinegar	2 tsp	2 tbsp	⅓ cup	6 cups
Mayonnaise	2 tsp	1 tbsp	⅔ cup	2⅔ cups
Croutons (see page 52)	1½ oz	4 oz	14 oz	3¼ lb

Continue →

Halve the bell peppers, then remove the seeds and white membranes.

Chop the bell peppers, then set aside along with the cucumber and onion.

Cut the tomatoes into large wedges and put in a bowl with the onions, cucumbers, and bell peppers.

Add the bread, torn into pieces, then pour over the water.

Process everything together using a hand-held blender, or use a food processor.

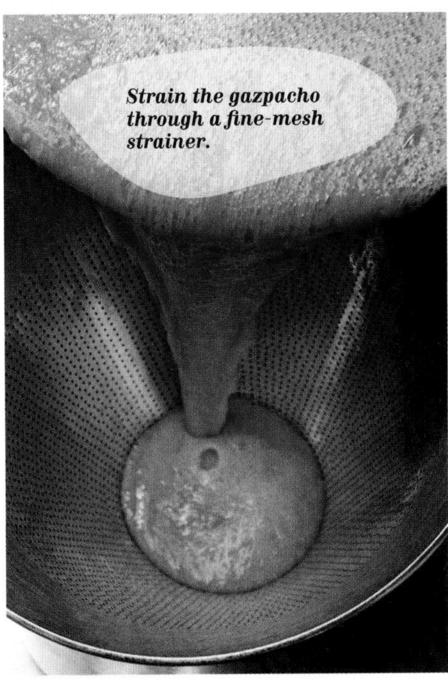
Strain the gazpacho through a fine-mesh strainer.

Add the oil, vinegar, and mayonnaise, then whisk or blend the soup until smooth and creamy.

Season with salt and pepper. Chill in the fridge before serving (at least 2 hours).

Serve the gazpacho in soup bowls with croutons, plus an extra drizzle of olive oil.

Black rice with squid

Ask your fish supplier to clean the squid for you, reserving the ink sacs and ink gland, which you use at the end of this recipe. Squid ink is also available in jars and individual packets.

•

A spoonful of aioli (see page 53) makes an ideal accompaniment for this dish.

	for 2	for 6	for 20	for 75
Fresh squid, cleaned	7 oz	1 lb 5 oz	4⅓ lb	15½ lb
Fish stock (see page 56)	2½ cups	8 cups	1½ gallons	5¾ gallons
Olive oil	1½ tbsp	⅓ cup	1 cup	3 cups
Sofrito (see page 43)	1½ tbsp	½ cup	2¼ cups	7¼ cups
Paella rice	1 cup	3 cups	10¾ cups	15½ lb
Squid ink (optional)	¼ oz	¾ oz	2¼ oz	7 oz
Picada (see page 41)	2 tsp	2 tbsp	½ cup	1¾ cups

Start →

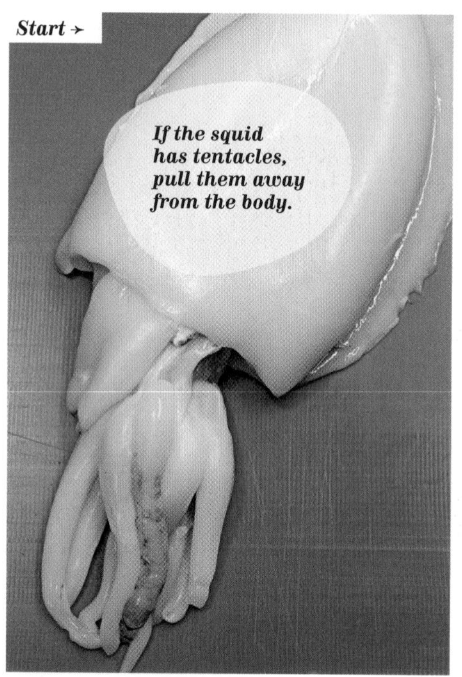

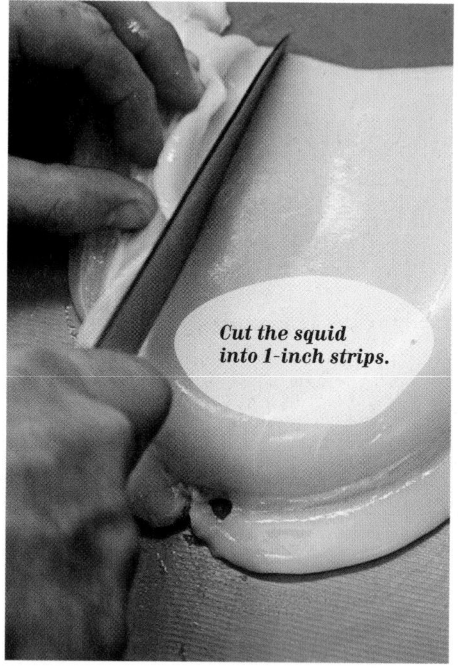

Continue →

Add the rice, stirring it into the squid. Fry for 10 minutes, stirring often.

Turn the heat to high and add a ladle of stock, stirring continuously. Once the stock has been absorbed, add another ladle and repeat until 5 minutes have passed.

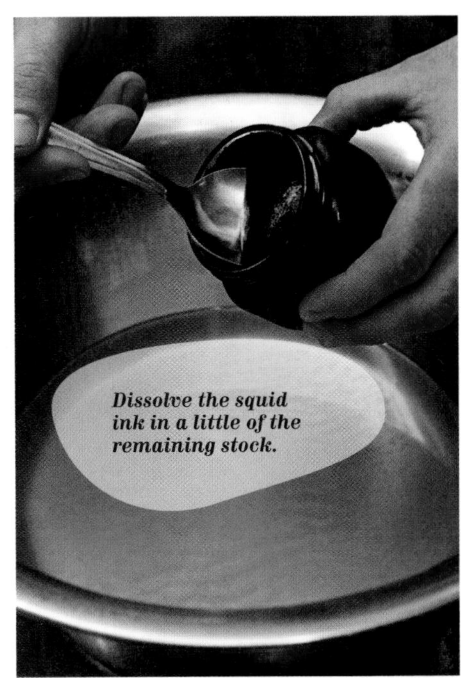
Dissolve the squid ink in a little of the remaining stock.

Add this to the rice, and then continue adding the rest of the stock.

Cook the rice for another 12 minutes, stirring frequently.

Add the picada and continue to cook for another 2 minutes, or until the rice has absorbed most of the liquid and is just tender to the bite.

Season with salt, then serve.

Bread with chocolate & olive oil

Bread with chocolate is a popular dessert in Catalonia. When we cook it at elBulli, we add extra-virgin olive oil and sea salt.

	for 2	for 6	for 20	for 75
Dark chocolate, 60% cocoa	2¼ oz	6 oz	1 lb 5 oz	4½ lb
1-lb white country-style loaf, cut into 8 slices	2 slices	6 slices	2 loaves	8 loaves
Extra-virgin olive oil	1½ tbsp	¼ cup	1 cup	3 cups
Sea salt flakes	1 pinch	½ tsp	2 tsp	2¼ tbsp

Start →

Preheat the oven or broiler to approximately 325°F.

Coarsely grate the chocolate onto a plate.

Place the bread on a baking sheet or heatproof plate.

Continue →

Toast under the broiler until golden on both sides.
Spoon the grated chocolate over the hot toast, covering it completely.
Pour the olive oil over the chocolate and sprinkle with the salt flakes.

–

Meal 22

–

Peas & ham

–

Roasted chicken with potato straws

–

Pineapple with molasses & lime

Peas & ham

Roasted chicken with potato straws

INGREDIENTS

BUY FRESH
* cured ham
* ham fat
* fresh mint
* whole chicken
* lemon
* pineapple
* lime

IN THE PANTRY
* olive oil
* cinnamon sticks
* onions
* dried bay leaves, rosemary, and thyme
* black peppercorns
* garlic
* white wine
* salt
* potato straws
* molasses

IN THE FREEZER
* frozen peas
* ham stock (see page 59)

Pineapple with molasses & lime

ORGANIZING THE MENU	Hours before the meal
	4
	3½
	3
	2½
	2
1½ hours before **Coat, stuff, and roast the chicken**	1½
1 hour before **Turn the chicken over**	1
30 minutes before **Start cooking the peas** **Cut up the pineapple and arrange in a serving dish**	½
10 minutes before **Make the gravy** **Carve the chicken**	
Just before eating **Finish off the peas and serve** **Place the chicken on a serving dish and cover with the gravy**	
	Start of the meal
Just before dessert **Finish the pineapple with the lime zest, juice, and molasses**	
	Dessert

Peas & ham

You can use Serrano, Iberico, Bayonne, Parma, or any other type of dry-cured ham for this recipe. If you cannot find ham fat, pancetta could be used instead.

•

The ham stock can be substituted with vegetable, chicken, or meat stock (see page 59).

•

When they are in season, you could also make this with fresh peas, although they may be more expensive. Follow the recipe, but deduct 4 minutes from the cooking time.

	for 2	for 6	for 20	for 75
Olive oil	2 tsp	2 tbsp	3 tbsp	⅔ cup
Small onions, finely sliced	1	3	11 oz	2¼ lb
Cured ham, thinly sliced	2	6	11 oz	2¼ lb
Ham fat	¼ oz	1 oz	4 oz	15 oz
Frozen peas	2 cups	6 cups	6½ lb	22 lb
Cinnamon sticks	1	2	4	25
Fresh mint	1 sprig	3 sprigs	⅓ bunch	1 bunch
Ham stock (see page 59)	⅓ cup	½ cup	1¾ cups	6¼ cups

Start →

Heat the oil in a large frying pan, then add the onion and cook gently for 10 minutes, until softened.

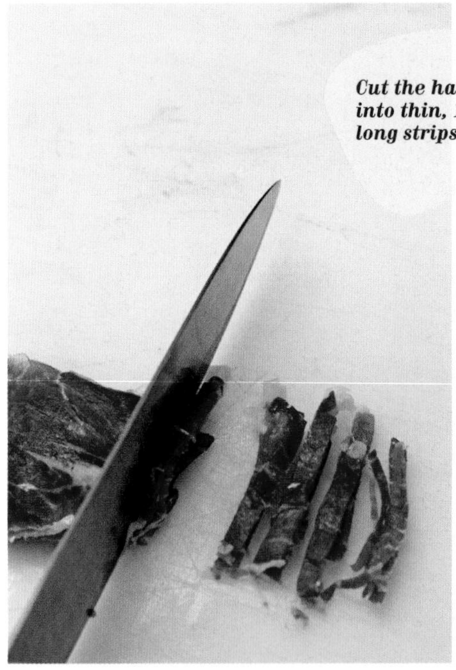

Cut the ham into thin, 1-inch long strips.

Chop the ham fat into very small pieces.

Add the chopped ham and fat to the onion.

Continue →

Fry gently for 2 minutes, or until the fat has melted and the ham and onion are golden.

Stir in the frozen peas and continue to cook for 4 minutes.

Add the cinnamon and mint, then cover the pan and cook over medium heat for 5 minutes.

Pour in the ham stock and simmer for another 5 minutes, covered, until the peas are very tender.

Turn off the heat and let stand, covered, for 5 minutes.
Remove one-tenth of the peas and process with a hand-held blender until creamy.

Add this back to the peas to make the sauce creamier.

Mix well.

Season to taste with salt and serve in soup plates.

Roasted chicken with potato straws

The Catalan name for this dish is *pollo a l'ast*. It is a traditional dish of spit-roasted chicken with lemon and herbs.

•

One chicken will serve four people. If you are cooking for two, the leftovers can be used in a salad the next day.

•

It is difficult to make the dried herb mixture in smaller quantities than those listed for 6–8, but the mixture will keep well in an airtight container.

	for 4	for 6–8	for 20	for 75
Chickens, whole, 4½ lb each	1	2	5	19
Olive oil	1 tbsp	2 tbsp	¾ cup	2¾ cups
Lemons	1	2	5	19
Dried bay leaves	-	20	70	175
Dried rosemary	-	3¾ tsp	2 cups	6½ cups
Dried thyme	-	⅓ cup	⅔ cup	2⅝ cups
Black peppercorns	-	⅔ tsp	2 tbsp	¼ cup
Garlic cloves	2	4	9	32
White wine	2 tbsp	4 tbsp	¼ cup	scant 1 cup
Water	3 tbsp	⅓ cup	½ cup	2 cups
Salt	¾ tsp	1½ tsp	2 tbsp	scant ½ cup
Potato straws	1 package (3½ oz)	7 oz	1 lb 2 oz	3¼ lb

Start →

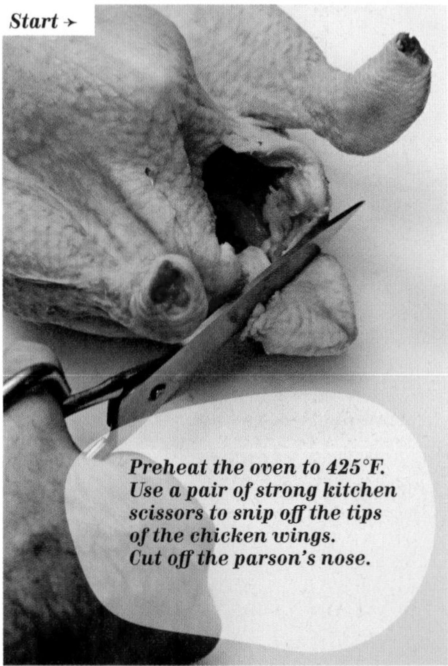

Preheat the oven to 425°F. Use a pair of strong kitchen scissors to snip off the tips of the chicken wings. Cut off the parson's nose.

Put the chicken in a roasting pan, season inside and out with salt, then rub with oil. Finely grate lemon zest over the breast and legs.

Cut the lemon into pieces and place inside the chicken.

Put the bay leaves, rosemary, thyme, and peppercorns into a small food processor or blender and process to a fine powder.

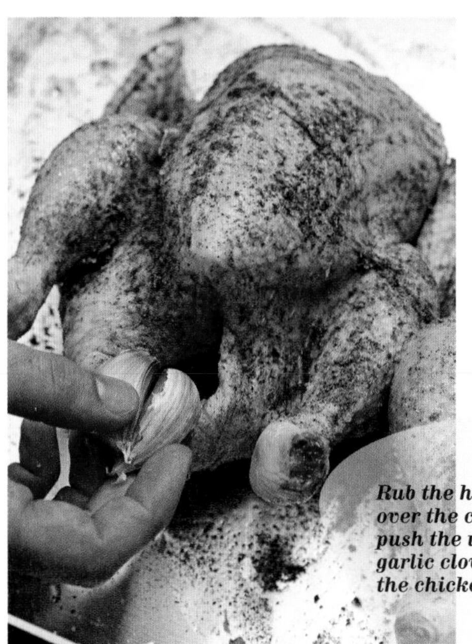

Rub the herb mixture over the chicken and push the unpeeled garlic cloves inside the chicken.

Continue →

Roast the chicken, breast facing down, for 25 minutes.

Turn the chicken over and roast for another 35 minutes, until golden and cooked through.

Remove the chicken and set aside to rest in a warm place. Place the roasting pan over medium-high heat on the stovetop.

Pour in the wine and water, and loosen any sediment with a wooden spoon. Boil the cooking juices, bubbling them down to make a tasty gravy.

Carve the chicken into pieces and place on a serving dish.

Alternatively, serve the chicken whole.
Pour the gravy over and serve with potato straws.

Pineapple with molasses & lime

Substitute the molasses with honey or dark cane syrup, if you like.

•

For an easier preparation, simply cut off the top and bottom of the pineapple, quarter, remove the inner core, and serve in its skin.

•

To choose a ripe pineapple, look for one in which the central leaves can be pulled out easily.

	for 2	for 6	for 20	for 75
Pineapples	½	1	3	6
Limes	½	1½	3	8
Molasses	1½ tbsp	¼ cup	scant 1 cup	3⅓ cups

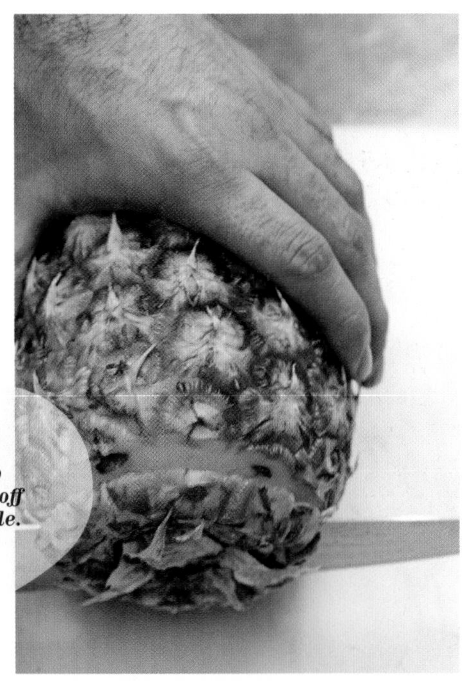

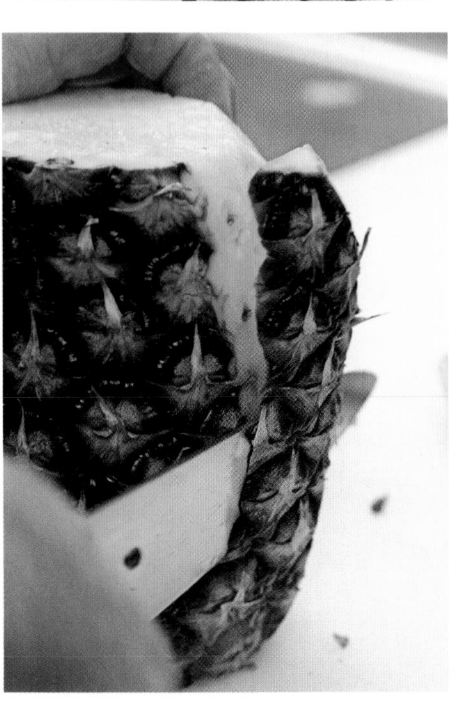

Continue →

Cut away the tough
inner core.

Slice each piece
into chunks about
½ inch thick.

Arrange evenly
on a serving dish.

Finely grate the lime zest
over the pineapple.

Squeeze over the
lime juice.

Finish with a drizzle
of the molasses to serve.

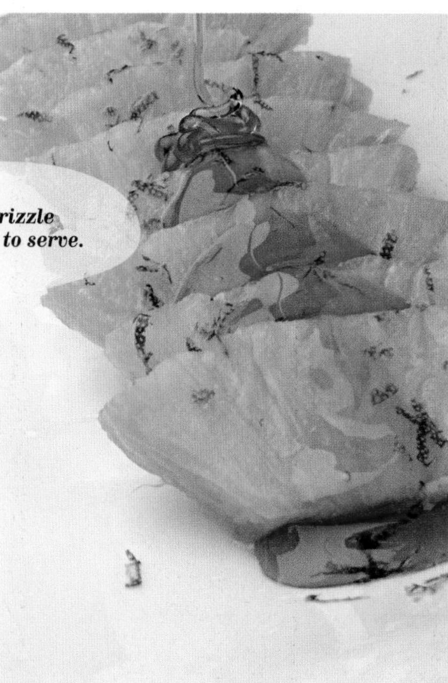

–

Meal 23

–

Tagliatelle carbonara

–

Cod & green pepper sandwich

–

Almond soup with ice cream

Tagliatelle carbonara

INGREDIENTS

BUY FRESH
* long, sweet green peppers
* fresh cod fillet
* white country-style loaf
* smoked bacon

IN THE PANTRY
* sunflower oil
* flour
* salt
* olive oil
* egg tagliatelle
* whole blanched almonds
* sugar
* whole caramelized almonds

IN THE FRIDGE
* eggs
* mayonnaise
* Parmesan cheese
* whipping cream, 35% fat

IN THE FREEZER
* ice cream

Cod & green pepper sandwich

Almond soup with ice cream

ORGANIZING THE MENU

	Hours before the meal
The day before	—
Chop, then soak the almonds in the fridge for 12 hours	4
	3½
	3
	2½
	2
	1½
	1
40 minutes before	—
Make the almond soup and chill in the fridge	
35 minutes before	—
Make the bacon cream for the carbonara	½
Cut the cod into pieces and get the flour, eggs, and oil ready	
20 minutes before	—
Fry the peppers	
Just before eating	—
Fry the cod, toast the bread, and assemble the sandwich	
	Start of the meal
Boil the pasta while you eat the sandwich	
Finish the pasta and serve with grated Parmesan	
Just before dessert	—
Scoop or quenelle the ice cream	
	Dessert

Tagliatelle carbonara

For small quantities, you can increase the amount of egg yolks for a richer flavor.

	for 2	for 6	for 20	for 75
Smoked bacon	4 oz	12½ oz	2½ lb	8¾ lb
Olive oil	1½ tbsp	⅓ cup	1¼ cups	4¼ cups
Whipping cream, 35% fat	1 cup	2½ cups	9¼ cups	2⅓ gallons
Water	2½ cups	7¾ cups	1½ gallons	5¾ gallons
Salt	1 tsp	1 tbsp	2½ tbsp	scant ½ cup
Egg tagliatelle	7 oz	1 lb 5 oz	4½ lb	16½ lb
Parmesan cheese, finely grated	½ cup	1⅔ cups	6 cups	4½ lb
Egg yolks	2	6	8	26

Start →

Continue →

Season with salt and pepper before removing from the heat.

Bring the water to a boil, then add the salt and pasta.

Cook for 7 minutes, or until the pasta is tender but still firm to the bite (check the directions on the package).

Grate the Parmesan cheese.

Whisk together the egg yolks and the reserved cream.

Drain the pasta, then return to the pan.

Add the bacon cream to the pasta.

Stirring continuously, add the egg yolk and cream mix. The eggs will thicken slightly as they come into contact with the hot pasta.

Serve with the grated Parmesan.

Cod & green pepper sandwich

In Spain, this dish is known as a *montadito*, which is a traditional dish consisting of various cooked ingredients on a slice of toasted country bread.

•

Ask your fish supplier to clean, gut, and fillet the fish for you if you prefer. Any white fish, such as hake or monkfish, can be used instead of cod.

•

When frying in large quantities, use a large saucepan, and never fill the pan more than halfway with oil.

	for 2	for 6	for 20	for 75
Sunflower oil	⅔ cup	2¼ cups	6¼ cups	1⅓ gallons
Long, sweet green peppers	2	6	20	75
Fresh cod fillet, skin on and scaled	11 oz	3¼ lb	11 lb	35¼ lb
Salt	1 pinch	½ tsp	1 tsp	2½ tbsp
Flour	1½ tbsp	¾ cup	2½ cups plus 2 tbsp	8 cups
Eggs	1	2	4	10
1-lb white country-style loaf, cut into 8 slices	2 slices	6 slices	2 loaves	6 loaves
Mayonnaise	2 tbsp	⅓ cup	1½ cups	4⅔ cups

Start →

Continue →

Pat the excess flour off the fish.

Beat the egg, then dip a piece of the floured cod into it. Let the excess drip away.

Repeat with all the pieces.

Carefully add the fish to the oil and fry for about 1 minute, turning half way through, until golden on both sides and juicy in the middle.

Lift the fried cod from the pan with a slotted spoon and drain on a paper towel. Preheat the broiler or oven to high.

Spread the bread over a baking sheet.

Toast the bread under the broiler or in the oven until golden on both sides.

To assemble the sandwich, top the toast with a green pepper followed by a piece of fried cod.

Serve with the mayonnaise.

Almond soup with ice cream

We do not recommend making any less than the quantity given for 6 people. Any leftover soup will keep well in the fridge.

•

Caramel or nut-flavored ice cream could be substituted for the nougat ice cream, and any other caramelized nut could be substituted for the almonds.

•

Marcona almonds are a Spanish, sweet-flavored variety. Any good-quality almond can be used.

	for 2	for 6	for 20	for 75
Whole blanched Marcona almonds	-	1⅔ cups	4 cups	6½ lb
Water	-	2½ cups	6¼ cups	2 gallons
Sugar	-	⅓ cup	heaping ¾ cup	3½ cups
Whole caramelized almonds	-	2 tbsp	1 cup	3½ cups
Nougat ice cream	-	1⅓ cup	4⅓ cups	4½ lb

Start →

Put the almonds into a food processor and coarsely chop.

Transfer them to a large bowl, then add the water.

Let soak for 12 hours or overnight in the fridge.

Use a hand-held blender or food processor to blend the almonds and water until smooth and creamy.

Continue →

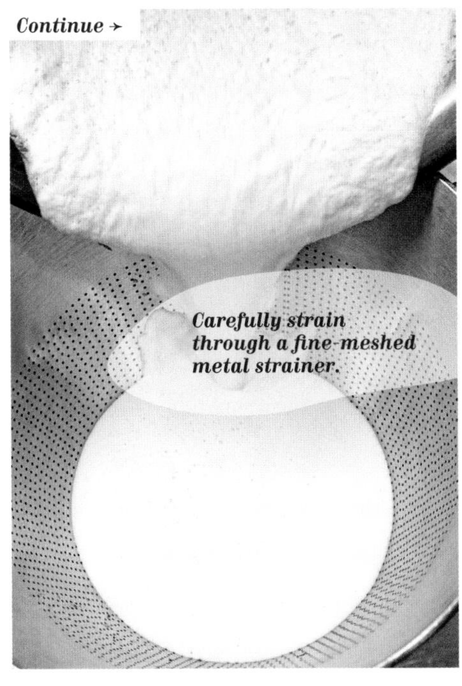

Carefully strain through a fine-meshed metal strainer.

Use the back of a ladle to help the soup pass through the strainer.

Add the sugar and whisk until it dissolves.

To serve, put a triangle of three caramelized almonds in the bottom of a bowl. Place a scoop of nougat ice cream in the center of the triangle.

Pour the almond soup around the ice cream.

–

Meal 24

–

Garbanzo beans with spinach & egg

–

Glazed teriyaki pork belly

–

Sweet potato with honey & cream

Garbanzo beans with spinach & egg

INGREDIENTS

BUY FRESH
* ripe tomatoes
* pork belly
* sweet potatoes

IN THE PANTRY
* olive oil
* garlic
* ground cumin
* cooked garbanzo beans
* salt
* black peppercorns
* cornstarch
* medium onions
* teriyaki sauce
* sugar
* honey

IN THE FRIDGE
* eggs
* whipping cream, 35% fat

IN THE FREEZER
* whole-leaf spinach
* chicken stock (see page 57)

Glazed teriyaki pork belly

Sweet potato with honey & cream

ORGANIZING THE MENU

Hours before the meal

4

3½

3

2½

2

2 hours before
Simmer the pork for 1½ hours

1½

Blend and drain the tomatoes and chop the garlic for the garbanzo beans

1

45 minutes before
Bake the sweet potatoes

½

30 minutes before
Cut the pork and cover with teriyaki sauce. Roast for 30 minutes, basting once

Chop, boil, and drain the spinach, then finish the garbanzo bean recipe

Just before eating
Boil or poach the eggs

Whip the cream to soft peaks and set aside in the fridge

Start of the meal

Just before dessert
Split the sweet potatoes and spread with the honey

Dessert

Garbanzo beans with spinach & egg

This dish is good topped with either a boiled or poached egg, or we sometimes cook the egg in its shell in a low-temperature water bath called a Roner. This gives a very soft and silky result. To boil or poach an egg, see page 19.

•

To substitute fresh, raw spinach for frozen spinach, allow for 3½ oz for 2 people, 9½ oz for 6, 1¾ lb for 20 and 7 lb for 75. The cooking time will be slightly longer.

	for 2	for 6	for 20	for 75
Frozen whole-leaf spinach, defrosted	2½ oz	7 oz	1 lb 5 oz	9½ lb
Ripe tomatoes	2	5	2½ lb	8¾ lb
Garlic cloves	2	6	1½ oz	4¼ oz
Olive oil	2 tbsp	⅓ cup	1¼ cups	4⅓ cups
Cooked garbanzo beans, drained	2 cups	6 cups	7 lb	26½ lb
Ground cumin	1 pinch	2 pinches	⅛ tsp	⅔ tsp
Chicken stock (see page 57)	1 cup	2½ cups	8 cups	1¾ gallons
Cornstarch	1 tsp	3 tsp	1 tbsp	½ cup
Eggs	2	6	20	75

Start →

Bring a medium pan of water to a boil. Cut the spinach into 1-inch pieces and boil for 1 minute.

Drain the spinach and set aside.

Process the tomatoes to a puree using a hand-held blender or food processor.

Set a fine-mesh strainer over a pan. Pour the tomatoes into the strainer and let drain for 15 minutes without pressing.

Continue →

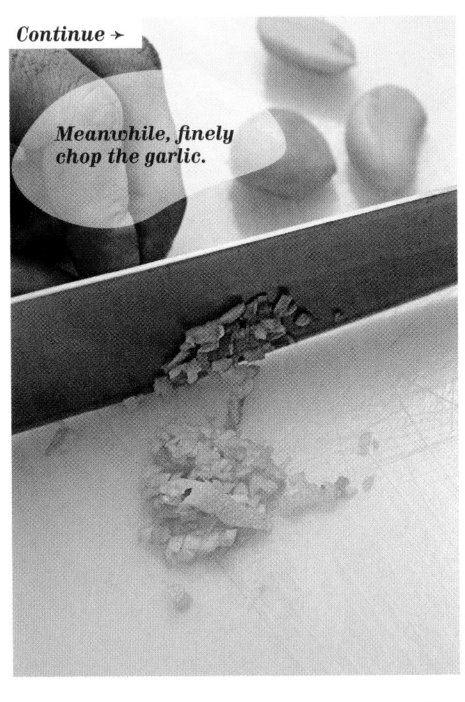
Meanwhile, finely chop the garlic.

Heat the oil over medium heat in a large pan, then add the garlic and the tomato pulp.

Add the garbanzo beans and cumin and cook for 30 seconds.

Add the stock and bring to a boil.
Meanwhile, cook the eggs to your liking (see note.)

Stir in the spinach and season with salt and pepper.

Mix the cornstarch with a little cold water until smooth, then add to the beans and spinach. Stir until slightly thickened.

Spoon the garbanzo beans into serving dishes, and top with the eggs.

Glazed teriyaki pork belly

Teriyaki is a sweet Japanese sauce used for marinating before roasting or broiling.

•

You can make the teriyaki sauce yourself (see page 50), or use a good-quality, store-bought sauce.

	for 2	for 6	for 20	for 75
Pork belly	14 oz	2½ lb	8¾ lb	33 lb
Water	4¼ cups	10½ cups	2½ gallons	10½ gallons
Salt	2 pinches	2 tsp	2½ tbsp	scant ½ cup
Black peppercorns	4	12	1 tsp	1 tbsp
Garlic cloves	1	3	6	18
Onions, roughly chopped	¼	1	4½ oz	1 lb
Teriyaki sauce (see page 50)	1 cup	2½ cups	8½ cups	2 gallons

Start →

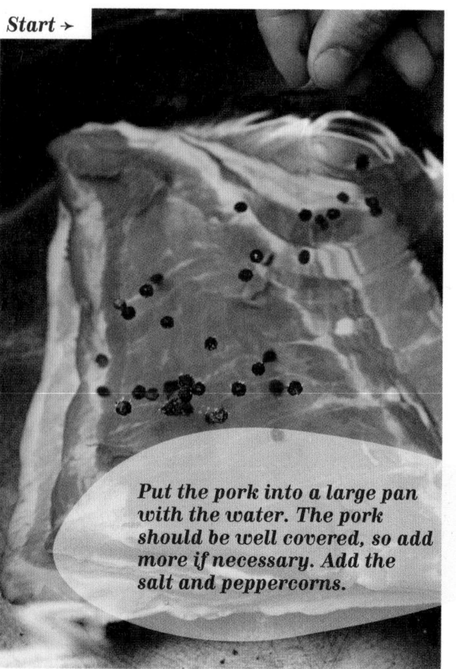

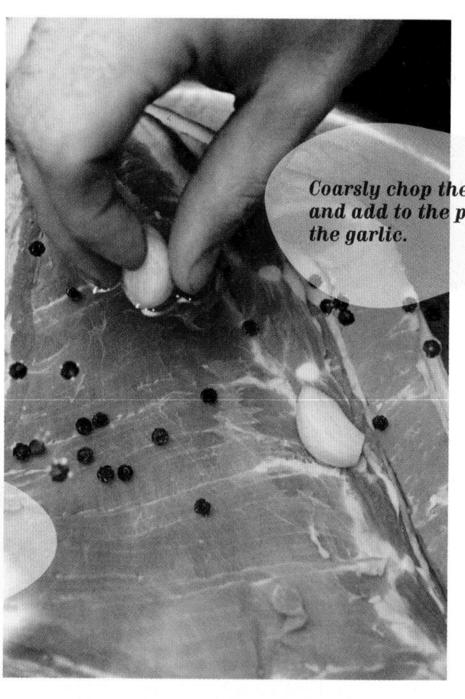

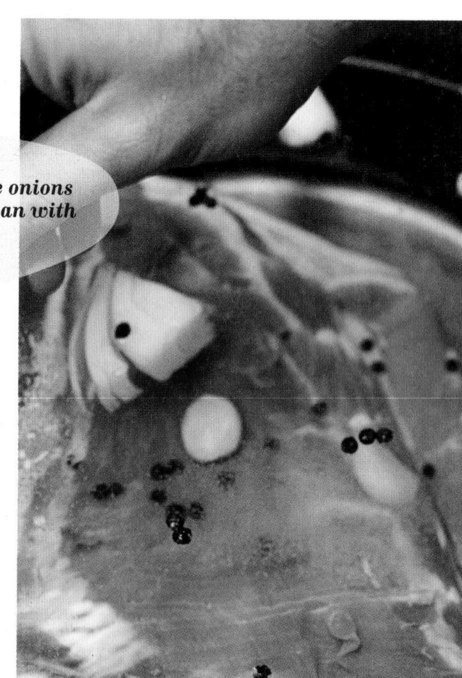

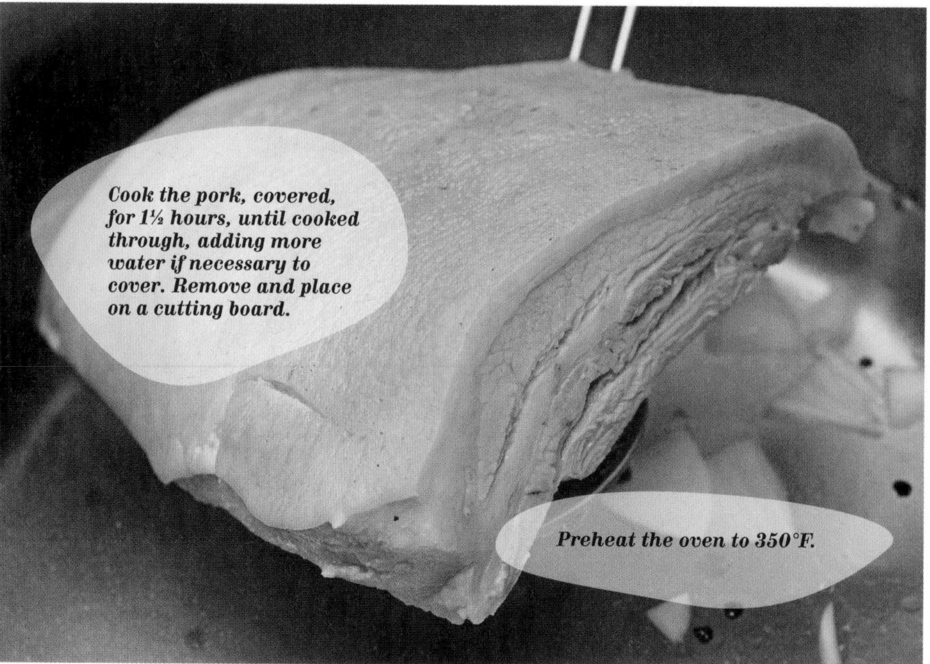

Continue →

Cut the pork into strips about ¾ inch thick.

Place the pork in a roasting pan in a single layer, then cover with the teriyaki sauce.

Roast the pork for 30 minutes, regularly basting with the teriyaki sauce to glaze.

Serve the pork with spoonfuls of the teriyaki sauce.

Sweet potato with honey & cream

The sweet potato is native to central and South America, where it is used in both sweet and savory dishes. This simple recipe shows how well it works as a dessert.

	for 2	for 6	for 20	for 75
Sweet potatoes, 3½ oz each	2	6	20	75
Whipping cream, 35% fat	¼ cup	¾ cup	2½ cups	8¼ cups
Sugar	1½ tsp	5 tsp	scant ½ cup	1½ cups
Honey	2 tbsp	⅓ cup	1¼ cups	4¼ cups

Start →

Continue →

Use a whisk or free-standing mixer to whip the cream to soft peaks.

Remove the sweet potatoes from the oven. They will be crisp on the outside and tender in the middle.

Cut them in half lengthwise.

Put the sweet potatoes cut side up on a serving plate, then pour over the honey.

Serve the hot sweet potatoes with the whipped cream.

–

Meal 25

–

Potatoes & green beans with Chantilly

–

Quails with couscous

–

Caramelized pears

Potatoes & green beans with Chantilly

Quails with couscous

INGREDIENTS

BUY FRESH
* flat green beans
* lemons
* quails
* spinach
* fresh mint
* Conference pears
* fruit sorbet or ice cream
* ras el hanout

IN THE PANTRY
* potatoes
* salt
* N_2O cartridges
* black peppercorns
* honey
* extra-virgin olive oil
* pine nuts
* raisins
* couscous
* sugar

IN THE FRIDGE
* mayonnaise
* butter
* whipping cream, 35% fat

IN THE FREEZER
* chicken stock (see page 57)

Caramelized pears

ORGANIZING THE MENU	Hours before the meal
	4
	3½
	3
	2½
	2
1½ hours before Prepare the quails and chill in the fridge Make the caramelized pears and let cool at room temperature	1½
	1
45 minutes before Cut up the potatoes and trim the beans	
30 minutes before Boil the potatoes Make the Chantilly foam, fill the siphon, and chill Start broiling the quails Heat the stock. Toast the pine nuts and add the raisins and couscous	½
10 minutes before Add the spinach, stock, and ras el hanout to the couscous. Cover and set aside Boil the beans, then drain	
	Start of the meal
Just before main course Finish with the lemon zest and juice	
	Main course

-

Potatoes & green beans with Chantilly

-

Perona beans are a variety of green beans commonly grown in Spain. Wax beans or other types of green beans would also work.

•

If you do not have a whipped-cream siphon, you can whip the cream into soft peaks and fold it through the mayonnaise instead, but of course the texture will not be quite the same.

	for 2	for 6	for 20	for 75
Medium potatoes	2	2½ lb	8¾ lb	35¼ lb
Green Perona beans	8½ oz	1½ lb	5⅓ lb	19¾ lb
For the Chantilly foam:				
Mayonnaise	⅔ cup	1¼ cups	2¼ cup	6¼ cups
Whipping cream, 35% fat	½ cup	½ cup	1¾ cups	5¼ cups
Lemon juice	1 tsp	1 tsp	⅔ cup	1½ cups
N_2O cartridges for the siphon	2	2	4	10

Start →

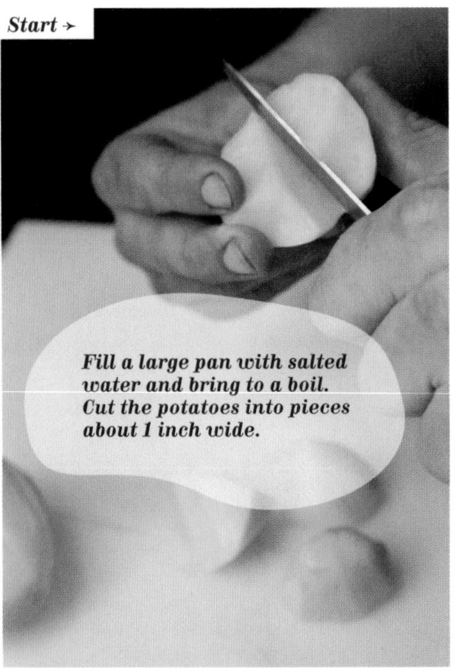

Fill a large pan with salted water and bring to a boil. Cut the potatoes into pieces about 1 inch wide.

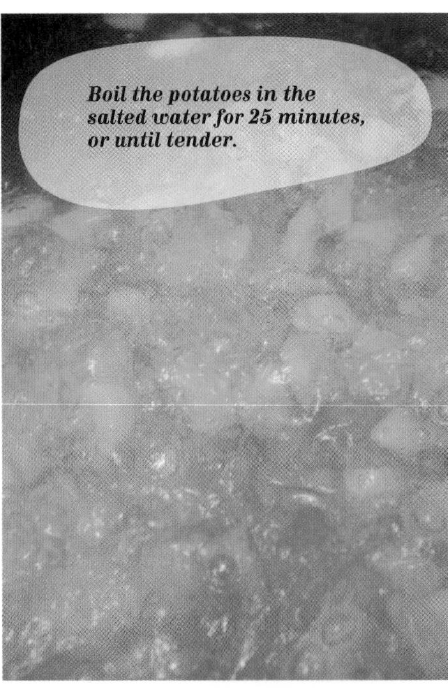

Boil the potatoes in the salted water for 25 minutes, or until tender.

While the potatoes are cooking, whisk together the mayonnaise and cream in a large bowl.

Squeeze the lemon juice, strain through a strainer, then add to the bowl. Whisk until evenly combined. Season with salt.

Continue →

Put the mixture
into the whipped-
cream siphon
and close the top.

Charge the siphon with
the cartridge, then chill
in the fridge until later.

Bring another pan
of salted water to
a boil.

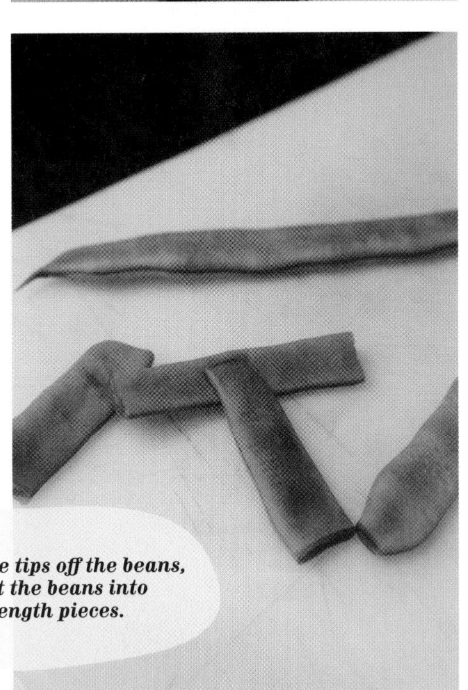
Trim the tips off the beans,
then cut the beans into
finger-length pieces.

Boil the green beans
for 4 minutes, or
until just tender.

Drain the potatoes
and beans.

Serve the potatoes in
a bowl, topped with the
beans. Dispense the
Chantilly foam on top
of the beans, or in a
separate dish on the side.

Quail with couscous

When cooking for 20 or 75, we recommend serving one quail per person. Chicken breasts can be substituted for the quail. For this dish, we split each quail down the middle, which helps the meat to cook quickly and evenly. If you prefer not to prepare the quail yourself, ask your butcher to do it.

•

Ras el hanout is a classic spice mixture used in Moroccan cuisine.

	for 2	for 6	for 20	for 75
Quails	4	12	20	75
Ras el hanout	1½ tsp	3½ tsp	¼ cup	¾ cup
Chicken stock	scant ½ cup	1¼ cups	5½ cups	1 gallon
Sprigs fresh mint	4	12	1 bunch	2 bunches
Honey	2 tsp	1½ tbsp	⅔ cup	1¾ cups
Extra-virgin olive oil	2 tsp	1½ tbsp	scant ½ cup	1¼ cups
Extra-virgin olive oil	1½ tbsp	¼ cup	½ cup	1½ cups
Pine nuts	2 tsp	2 tbsp	1⅔ cups	5 cups
Raisins	2 tsp	2 tbsp	1 cup	3½ cups
Couscous	⅓ cup	1 cup	6 cups	6 lb 11 oz
Spinach	¾ oz	2¼ oz	9 oz	1¾ lb
Lemons	½	1	2	6

Start →

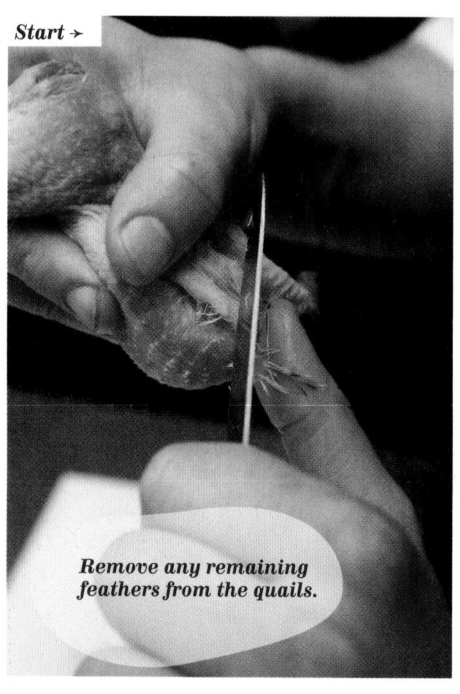

Remove any remaining feathers from the quails.

Use strong kitchen scissors or poultry shears to cut off the wing tips.

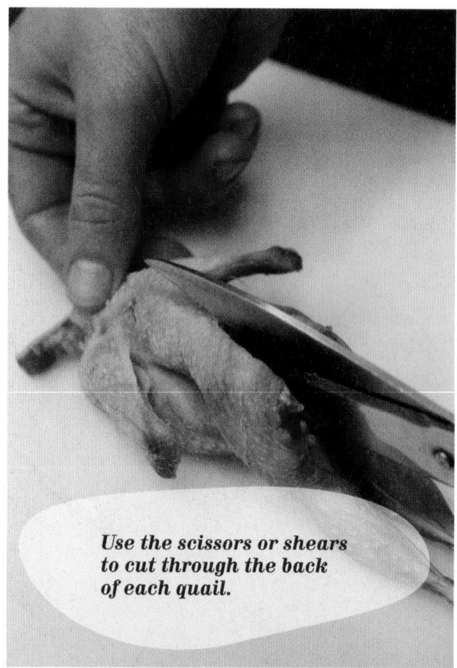

Use the scissors or shears to cut through the back of each quail.

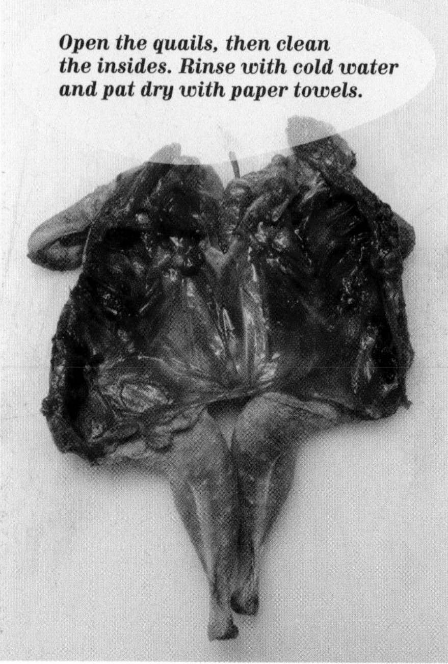

Open the quails, then clean the insides. Rinse with cold water and pat dry with paper towels.

Put the quails in a roasting pan, season with salt, pepper, and two-thirds of the ras el hanout. Chill for 1 hour.

Pour the chicken stock into a saucepan and bring to a boil. Heat the broiler to medium.

Pick the mint leaves from the stems and shred finely.

Continue →

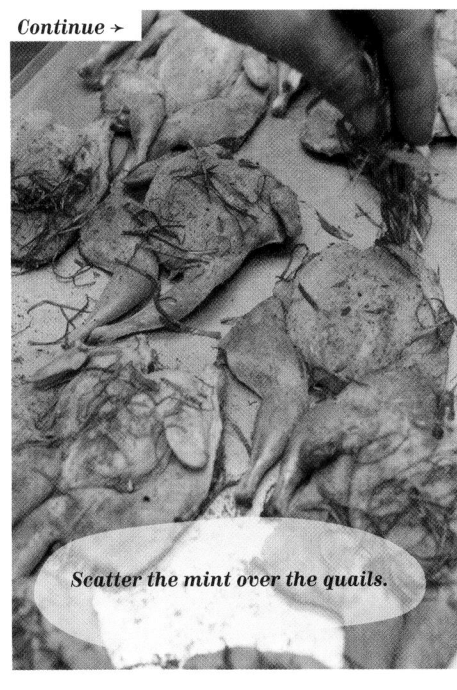
Scatter the mint over the quails.

Drizzle with the honey
and the first quantity of oil.

Broil the quails for 4 minutes,
turning from time to time, until
golden and juicy. Keep them
warm under aluminum foil.

Meanwhile, heat the second
quantity of oil in a wide pan,
then add the pine nuts. Cook
over low heat for 5 minutes,
stirring often, until golden.

Add the raisins to the pine nuts
and stir for 30 seconds. Add the
couscous and cook for 1 minute.

Add the spinach and remaining
ras el hanout and pour in the
chicken stock. Cover the pan,
remove from the heat and let
the couscous absorb the stock.

Stir the couscous
to separate the grains.

Spoon the couscous onto
a serving dish, then top with
the quails. Finish with the
finely grated zest and the juice
of the lemon.

Caramelized pears

These are delicious served with fruit sorbet, or vanilla or chocolate ice cream.

•

It is best to choose pears that have just ripened.

	for 2	for 6	for 20	for 75
Bosc or other cooking pears	1	3	10	38
Sugar	1½ tbsp	3½ tbsp	1¾ cups	5⅔ cups
Butter	2 tbsp	2 tbsp	scant 1 cup	2⅔ cups
Hot water	1 cup	2½ cups	2¼ cups	6¼ cups
Ice cream or sorbet	¾ cup	2½ cups	8 cups	7¾ lb
Sprigs fresh mint	1	3	10	38

Start →

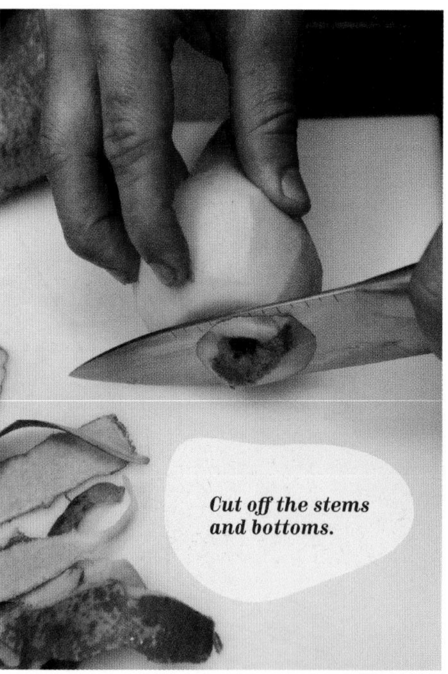

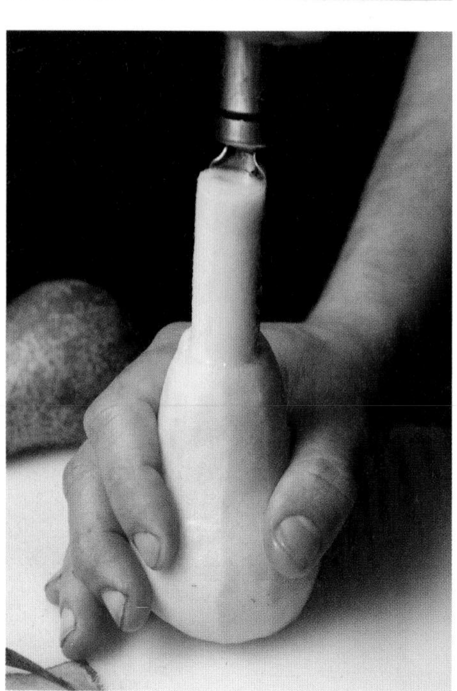

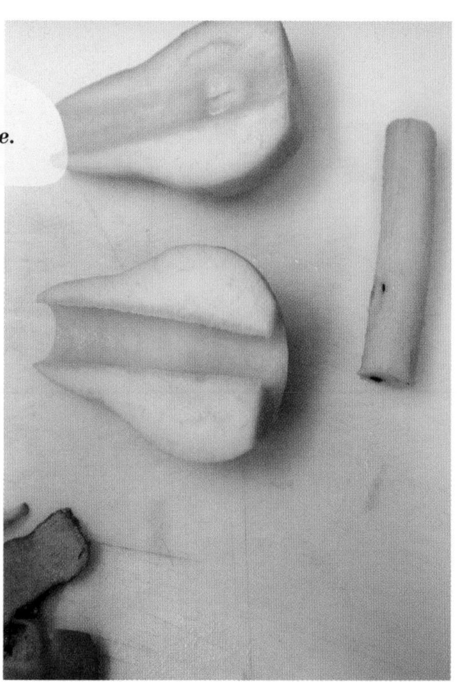

Continue →

Put the sugar into a wide pan,
then place the pan over low-
to-medium heat. You will
see darker patches of caramel
starting to appear.

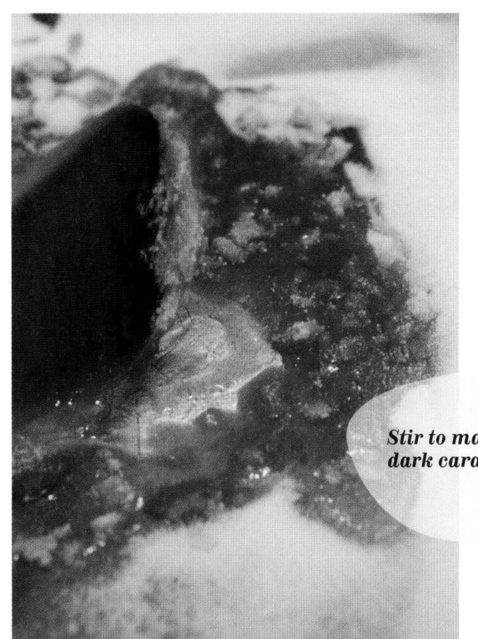

Stir to make an even,
dark caramel.

Add the butter to the caramel,
then stir until melted and even.

Carefully add the pears
to the pan, cut side down.

Pour in the hot water. The caramel
will bubble dramatically, so
be careful not to burn yourself.

Cook the pears for 5 minutes,
turning after 2½ minutes.

The pears will be soft and the
caramel sauce silky. Remove
from the heat and let cool
at room temperature.

Serve the pears and caramel
sauce with ice cream or sorbet.
Decorate with a few mint leaves.

–

Meal 26

–

Fish soup

–

Sausages with mushrooms

–

Oranges with honey, olive oil & salt

INGREDIENTS

BUY FRESH
* whole, fresh, cleaned fish from the market
* baguette (or use day-old bread)
* butifarra sausages or other good-quality coarse pork sausages
* fresh rosemary
* fresh thyme
* medium white mushrooms
* fresh parsley
* large oranges

IN THE PANTRY
* garlic
* extra-virgin olive oil
* olive oil
* mild paprika
* pastis, or any anise-base liqueur
* croutons
* *vino rancio* or dry sherry
* salt
* black peppercorns
* honey-flavor hard candies
* honey
* sea salt flakes

IN THE FREEZER
* sofrito (see page 43)
* picada (see page 41)

Fish soup

Sausages with mushrooms

Oranges with honey, olive oil & salt

ORGANIZING THE MENU	Hours before the meal
	4
	3½
	3
	2½
	2
	1½
1 hour (or up to 2 days) before Make the soup	1
30 minutes before Pinch the sausage meat into balls and fry for a few minutes Slice the mushrooms Peel and slice the oranges, then set aside in the fridge Crush the candies	½
20 minutes before Fry the mushrooms and finish cooking the sausages with the herbs and seasoning	
5 minutes before Reheat the soup Put the sausages and mushrooms in a dish and keep warm	
	Start of the meal
Just before dessert Dress the oranges with the honey, olive oil, crushed candies, and salt flakes	
	Dessert

Fish soup

Any anise-base liqueur can be used instead of pastis, or you could add a little chopped fennel to the pan just before serving.

•

Choose an economical mixture of fish, crabs, and crustaceans and use the whole fish to give a rich, deep flavor. Ask the fish supplier to clean and gut the fish for you if you prefer.

•

This soup is good served with croutons (see page 52).

	for 2	for 6	for 20	for 75
Garlic cloves	3	9	1 oz	3¼ oz
Olive oil	2 tbsp	⅓ cup	¾ cup	2¾ cups
Sofrito (see page 43)	1½ tbsp	4 tbsp	1¾ cups	5½ cups
Mix of fresh whole fish, already cleaned	11 oz	2 lb	6½ lb	22 lb
Sweet paprika	2 tsp	2 tbsp	¼ cup	¾ cup plus 1 tbsp
Water	3 cups	8½ cups	1⅓ gallons	4¼ gallons
Bread (day-old is good)	¾ slice	2¼ slices	4 slices	14 slices
Picada (see page 41)	2 tsp	2 tbsp	½ cup	1¾ cups
Pastis	1 dash	2 dashes	1 tsp	1½ tbsp

Continue →

Cook the soup
for 20 minutes
at a gentle simmer.

While the soup cooks, fry the
bread slices in a frying pan
with the remaining oil until
deep golden.

Strain the soup
into another
large saucepan.

Add the fried bread
and the picada to the
pan, then cook for
another 10 minutes.

Process the soup
with a hand-held
blender until smooth.
You could also use
a blender.

Season with salt.

Pour in the pastis
or other anise-
flavor liqueur.

Serve with croutons
if you like.

Sausages with mushrooms

Butifarra are traditional sausages from Catalonia. The original Catalan name for this dish is *butifarra esparracada*, which literally means "butifarra sausage broken into little pieces." Any good-quality pork sausage can be substituted.

•

You could use wild mushrooms instead of white mushrooms, and parsley oil could be substituted for the fresh parsley.

•

Vino rancio is a Catalan fortified oxidized wine. If you cannot find it, use dry sherry instead.

	for 2	for 6	for 20	for 75
Butifarra, or other good-quality coarse pork sausages	9 oz	1 lb 10 oz	5½ lb	21 lb
Olive oil	3 tbsp	⅓ cup	2½ cups	8 cups
Garlic cloves	4	12	40	150
Sprigs fresh rosemary	1	1	⅒ oz	¼ oz
Sprigs fresh thyme	1	1	⅒ oz	¼ oz
Medium white mushrooms	7 oz	1 lb 5 oz	4 lb	14 lb 5 oz
Vino rancio or dry sherry	3 tbsp	½ cup	¾ cup	3¼ cups
Fresh parsley, chopped	1 tsp	1 tbsp	4½ cups	1 lb 5¼ oz

Start →

Continue →

Meanwhile, clean, trim, and quarter the mushrooms.
Pour the vino rancio into the pan and scrape the bottom to loosen any sediment. Use a little water if needed. Remove the pan from the heat.
In another pan, fry the mushrooms in a little oil for 5 minutes, until golden.
Add the mushrooms to the sausages and cook over medium heat for 15 minutes, until they are cooked through.
Pick the leaves from the parsley stems and finely chop.
Stir in the chopped parsley, season with salt and pepper, and serve.

Oranges with honey, olive oil & salt

You can use coarse salt instead of salt flakes (although the texture will be more crunchy.)

	for 2	for 6	for 20	for 75
Honey-flavor hard candies	3	9	2½ oz	9 oz
Large oranges	2	6	20	75
Honey	1½ tbsp	¼ cup	⅔ cup	2¼ cups
Extra-virgin olive oil	2 tbsp	⅓ cup	⅔ cup	2¼ cups
Sea salt flakes	1 pinch	1 generous pinch	1 tsp	1 tbsp

Start →

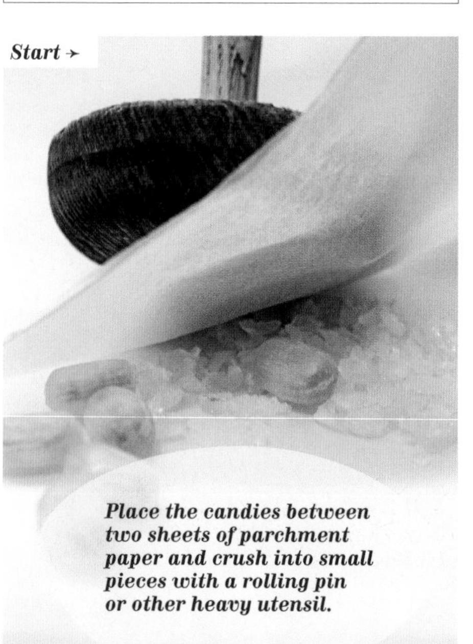

Place the candies between two sheets of parchment paper and crush into small pieces with a rolling pin or other heavy utensil.

Using a sharp knife, cut the ends off the oranges.

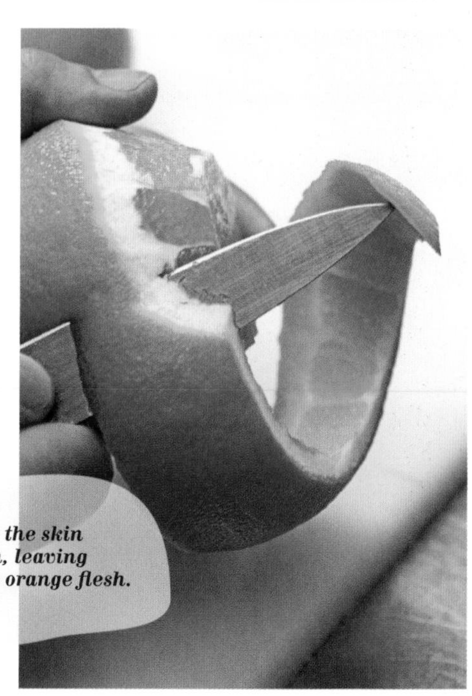

Remove the skin and pith, leaving only the orange flesh.

Continue →

Cut the oranges into slices about ¼ inch thick, then spread them out in a single layer in a serving dish.

Pour the honey over the oranges.

Drizzle with the olive oil.

Sprinkle with the sea salt flakes.

Scatter the crushed candies and serve.

Meal 27

Mussels with paprika

–

Baked sea bass

–

Caramel pudding

Mussels with paprika

INGREDIENTS

BUY FRESH
* medium mussels
* fresh parsley
* whole sea bass
* ripe tomatoes
* fresh thyme
* fresh rosemary
* potatoes

IN THE PANTRY
* onions
* garlic
* olive oil
* mild paprika
* flour
* salt
* black peppercorns
* sugar
* white rum

IN THE FRIDGE
* eggs
* whipping cream, 35% fat

Baked sea bass

Caramel pudding

ORGANIZING THE MENU	Hours before the meal
	4
	3½
	3
	2½
	2
	1½
1 hour before Prepare and steam the caramel puddings Prepare all the ingredients for the fish	1
45 minutes before Bake the potato, onion, and tomato for the fish Clean the mussels and prepare the sauce	½
15 minutes before Add the sea bass to the vegetables and put in the oven	
Just before eating Add the mussels to the sauce	
	Start of the meal
Drizzle the baked sea bass with olive oil	
	Main course
Just before dessert Whip the rum cream to soft peaks	
	Dessert

Mussels with paprika

It is essential to cook the mussels at the last minute so that they do not become tough.

•

Any mussels that do not open should be discarded.

	for 2	for 6	for 20	for 75
Mussels	1 lb 5 oz	3 lb	13¼ lb	40 lb
Garlic cloves	1	3	18	42
Olive oil	1½ tbsp	¼ cup	1¾ cups	5 cups
Mild paprika	½ tsp	1 tsp	2½ tsp	scant ½ cup
Flour	1 tsp	1 tbsp	⅔ cup	2½ cups
Water	1 cup	2 cups	5 cups	1 gallon
Fresh parsley, finely chopped	2½ sprigs	6 sprigs	1 bunch	3 bunches

Start →

Scrub and debeard the mussels under cold running water.

Finely chop the garlic.

Heat the oil in a saucepan, then add the garlic. Cook for 1 minute.

Add the paprika and cook for a couple of seconds.

Continue →

Stir in the flour.

Mix well.

Pour in the water, stirring to make a smooth sauce.
Boil for 10 minutes, or until the sauce is thickened and tasty.

Finely chop the parsley. Add half of the parsley to the sauce.

Add the cleaned mussels and cover the pan.

Cook for 5 minutes.

The mussels are ready when they have opened up completely. Discard any that have stayed shut.
Remove the pan from the heat.

Sprinkle with the rest of the parsley and serve. Season with salt.

Baked sea bass

Ask your fish supplier to clean and gut the fish for you if you prefer.

•

This dish can be made with other varieties of fish, such as bream.

	for 2	for 6	for 20	for 75
Sea bass, 11 oz each	2	6	20	75
Medium potatoes	2	6	6½ lb	31 lb
Ripe tomatoes	2	6	3¼ lb	11½ lb
Medium onions	1	3	2¼ lb	7½ lb
Garlic cloves	3	9	7¼ oz	1 lb 5½ oz
Olive oil	2 tbsp	⅓ cup	1¾ cups	5 cups
Sprigs fresh thyme	2	6	20	75
Sprigs fresh rosemary	2	6	20	75

Start →

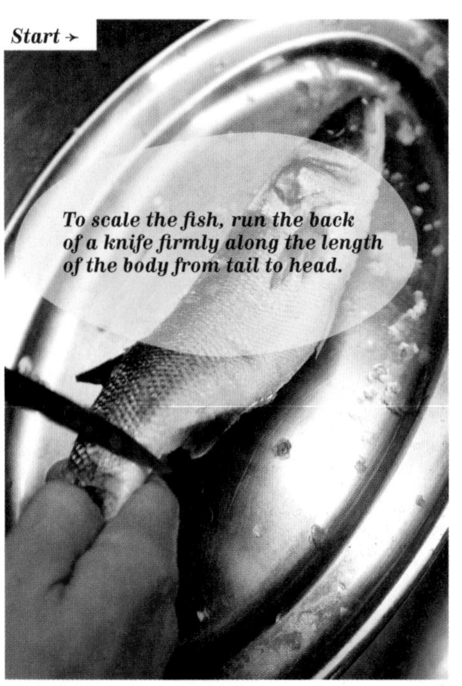

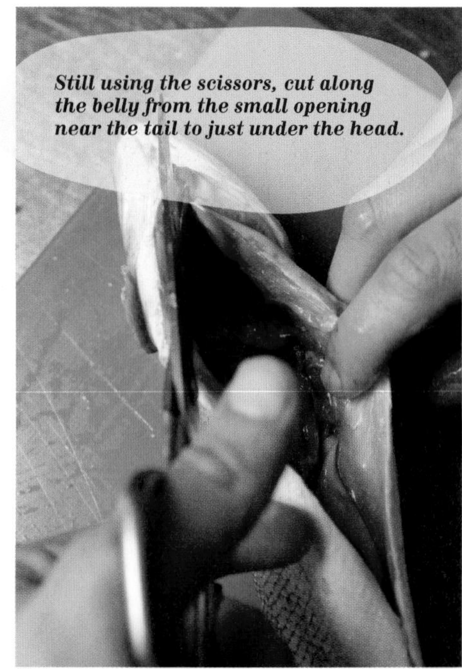

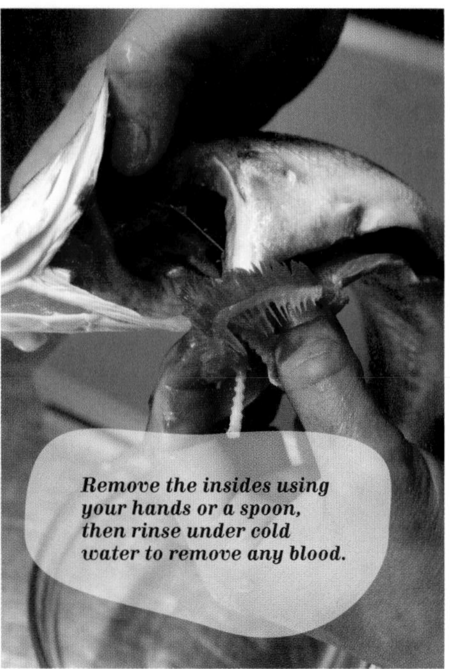

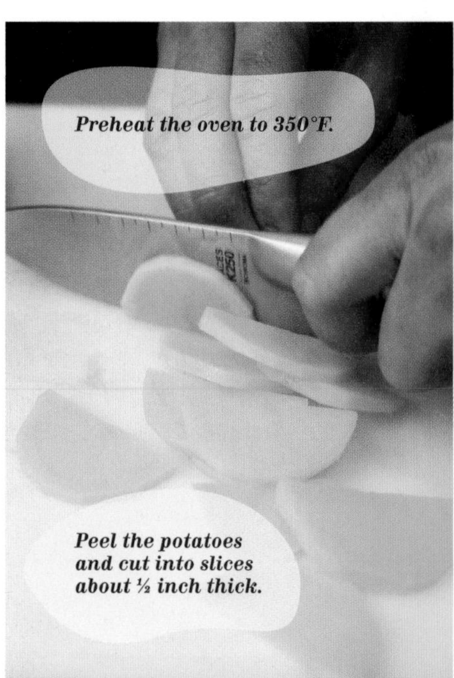

Continue →

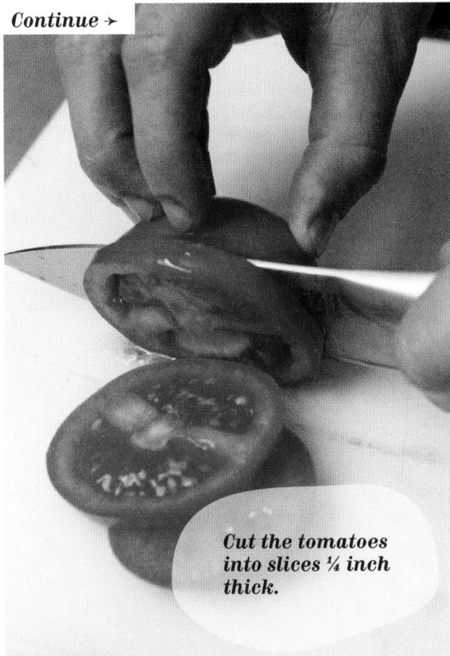
Cut the tomatoes into slices ¼ inch thick.

Thinly slice the onion.

Coarsely crush the whole garlic cloves, leaving the skins on.

Pour a little oil into a large roasting pan. Spread half of the potato in the pan, then half of the tomato and half of the onion.

Season with salt and pepper. Repeat the layers of potato, tomato and onion.
Scatter the garlic and herbs. Pour over most of the remaining oil. Cover the pan with foil, then bake in the oven for 30 minutes.

Season the sea bass inside and out. Remove the foil from the pan and put the fish on top of the vegetables. Turn the oven up to 375°F.

Return the pan to the oven, uncovered, for 12 minutes, or until the fish is opaque and flakes easily from the back bone.

Finish with a little more olive oil and a few sprigs of rosemary and thyme.

Caramel pudding

Depending on the size of your heatproof molds, you may need to let the puddings steam for longer.

•

The puddings are ready when they have a consistent texture, and when a knife inserted comes out clean.

	for 2	for 6	for 20	for 75
Sugar	scant ½ cup	1⅓ cup	4⅔ cups	14 cups
Water	¼ cup	⅔ cup	2¼ cups	6¼ cups
Egg yolks	4	12	40	120
Whipping cream, 35% fat	1 tsp	1½ tbsp	scant ½ cup	1¼ cups
For the rum cream:				
Whipping cream, 35% fat	1½ tbsp	scant ½ cup	2¼ cups	6¼ cups
White rum	½ tsp	2 tsp	scant ½ cup	1¼ cups

Start →

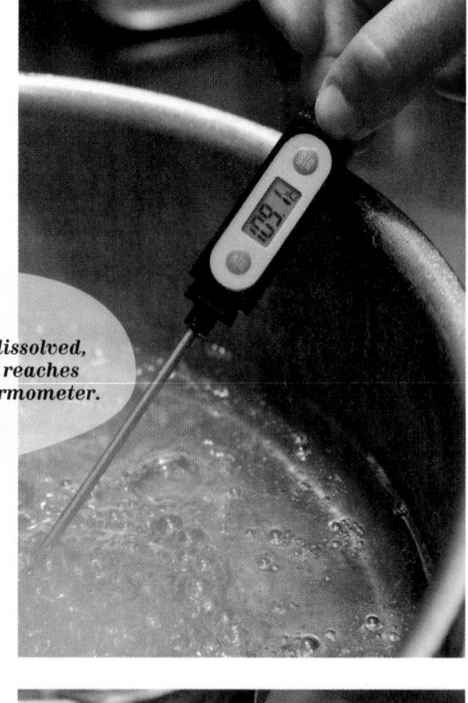

Continue →

Pour in the cream.

Stir in until evenly combined.

Pour into coffee cups, small glasses, or similar heatproof molds and cover with plastic wrap.

Place the cups or glasses in a steamer basket over a pan of boiling water. Cover and steam for 10 minutes.

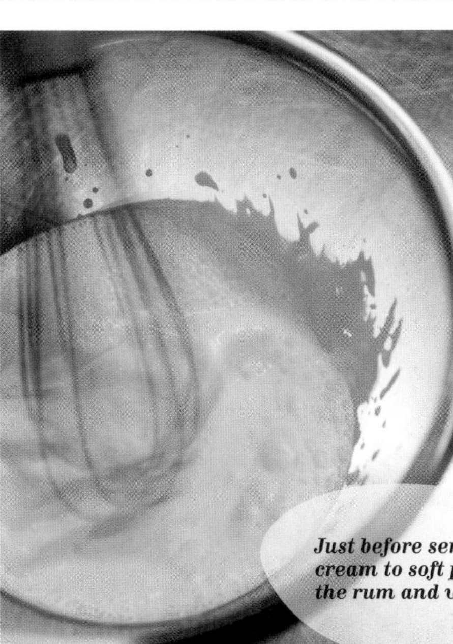

Just before serving, whip the cream to soft peaks, then add the rum and whip again.

Serve the puddings at room temperature.

–

Meal 28

–

Melon with cured ham

–

Rice with duck

–

Chocolate cake

Melon with cured ham

INGREDIENTS

BUY FRESH
* large ripe melon
* cured ham
* duck legs

IN THE PANTRY
* olive oil
* salt
* white wine
* paella rice
* black peppercorns
* dark chocolate, 60% cocoa
* sugar

IN THE FRIDGE
* butter
* eggs

IN THE FREEZER
* chicken stock (see page 57)
* sofrito (see page 43)
* picada (see page 41)

Rice with duck

Chocolate cake

ORGANIZING THE MENU

	Hours before the meal
	4
	3½
	3
	2½
	2
	1½
1 hour before Make the cake mixture and pipe into the molds	1
40 minutes before Boil the stock and cut up the duck, ready for the rice	
30 minutes before Start frying the duck Bake the chocolate cakes	½
20 minutes before Add the stock to the rice	
Just before eating Cut up the melon	
	Start of the meal
Just before dessert Remove the cakes from the molds and serve warm	
	Dessert

Melon with cured ham

The ham should be served at room temperature alongside the melon. Do not place slices of ham over the melon, or they will become soggy.

•

You can also serve this dish as a dessert.

•

The best melon varieties to choose are cantaloupe or *piel de sapo* (toad skin).

	for 2	for 6	for 20	for 75
Large ripe melon	¼	1	3	10
Cured ham, thinly sliced	6 slices	18 slices	1 lb 5 oz (60 slices)	5 lb (225 slices)

Start →

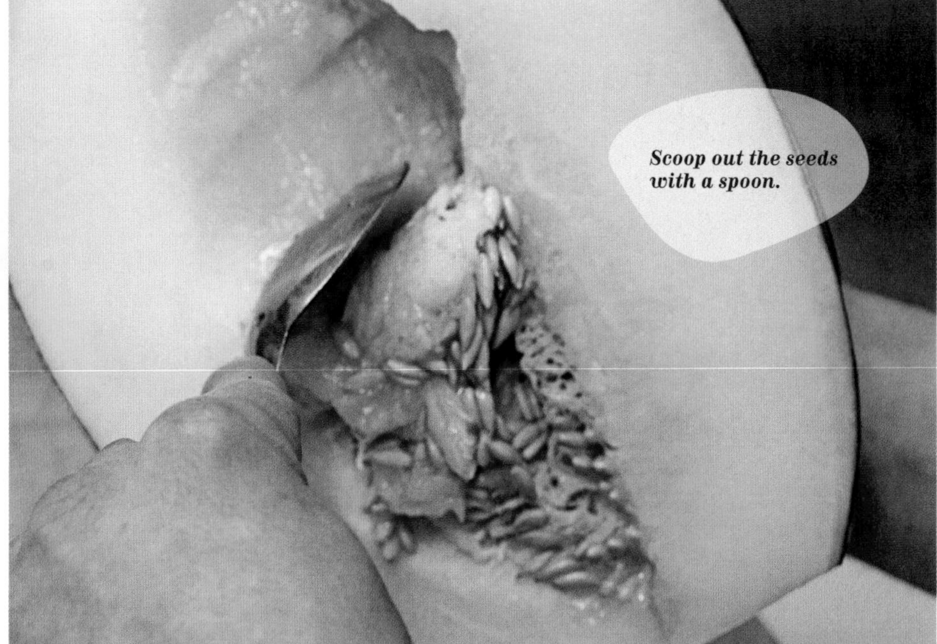

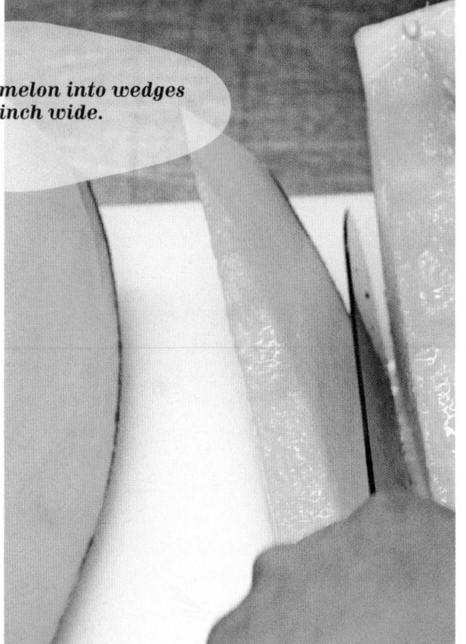

Continue →

You will need about
2 slices per person.

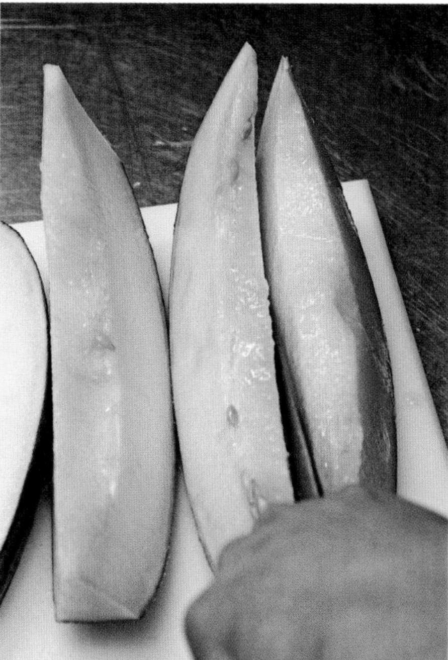

Place the melon wedges
on a serving dish.

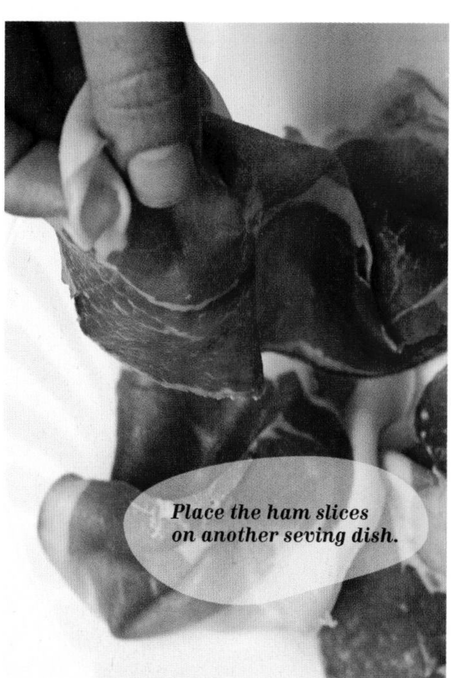
Place the ham slices
on another seving dish.

Serve the ham and
melon separately.

Rice with duck

We use sofrito and picada in many rice dishes. Make batches ahead of time and freeze in small quantities, ready for use.

•

With this rice dish, the texture should be creamy.

	for 2	for 6	for 20	for 75
Chicken stock (see page 57)	3⅛ cups	8 cups	1½ gallons	5¾ gallons
Duck legs	1	3	4½ lb	17½ lb
Olive oil	2 tbsp	¼ cup	½ cup plus 1 tsp	2 cups
White wine	1½ tbsp	¼ cup	½ cup plus 1 tsp	2 cups
Sofrito (see page 43)	1½ tbsp	1¼ cups	2⅓ cups	6¾ cups
Paella rice	1 cup	3 cups	9½ cups	14½ lb
Picada (see page 41)	2 tsp	2 tbsp	⅓ cup	1¾ cups

Start →

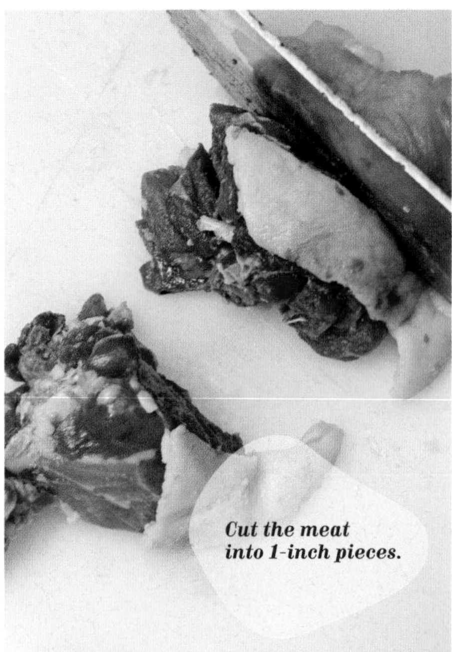

Continue →

When most of the wine has boiled away, add the sofrito.

Cook for 5 minutes, stirring.

Add the rice to the pan and cook for 3 minutes, stirring all the time.

Pour in the hot stock and cook the rice for 17 minutes, stirring frequently to prevent it from sticking.

Add the picada to the pan.

Season with salt and pepper.

Remove the pan from the heat and let the rice and duck stand for 3 minutes. The rice should be creamy but still with a little bite.

Serve in bowls.

Chocolate cake

There are many types of cake molds on the market. We recommend flexible silicone molds so you can be sure that your cake will not stick. If you only have metal molds, grease them well with butter before use. For this recipe, use circular molds about 4½ inches in diameter and 1½ inches deep.

•

This cake should be served lukewarm. We do not recommend making less than the quantity given for 6 people. Any leftover cakes will keep in an airtight container for up to 2 days.

	for 2	for 6	for 20	for 75
Dark chocolate, 60% cocoa	-	6⅓ oz	1 lb 5 oz	5 lb
Butter, at room temperature	-	6½ tbsp	1¼ cups plus 1 tbsp	5 cups
Egg whites	-	4¼ oz	14 oz	3 lb
Sugar	-	2 tbsp	½ cup	1½ cups
Egg yolks	-	½ oz	1¾ oz	6⅓ oz

Start →

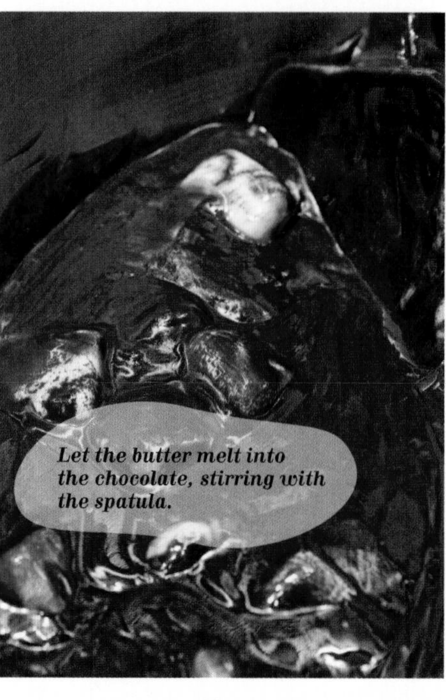

Continue →

In a separate bowl, whisk the egg yolks for a few seconds.

Pour the yolks over the meringue mixture, then fold together using a spatula or whisk.

Turn the meringue mixture into the buttery chocolate.

Fold everything together carefully with a spatula until even.

Spoon the cake mixture into a pastry bag and snip off the end. If you don't have a pastry bag, use two teaspoons instead.

Pipe or carefully spoon the mixture into circular silicone molds about 4½ inches across and 1½ inches deep.

Bake in the oven for 12 minutes, or until risen and shrinking away from the edges of the molds.

Let cool a little before removing from the molds.

Serve the cakes warm.

–

Meal 29

–

Roasted vegetables with olive oil

–

Salmon stewed with lentils

–

White chocolate cream

Roasted vegetables with olive oil

Salmon stewed with lentils

INGREDIENTS

BUY FRESH
* large eggplants
* large red bell peppers
* fresh salmon fillet
* fresh parsley
* cooked lentils
* shelled pistachios
* onions

IN THE PANTRY
* olive oil
* salt
* sherry vinegar
* black peppercorns
* white chocolate

IN THE FRIDGE
* eggs
* whipping cream, 35% fat

IN THE FREEZER
* sofrito (see page 43)
* fish stock (see page 56)
* picada (see page 41)

White chocolate cream

ORGANIZING THE MENU

	Hours before the meal
	4
	3½
	3
	2½
	2
1½ hours before Roast the vegetables, then let cool	1½
1 hour before Make the white chocolate cream and chill in the fridge	1
45 minutes before Prepare the salmon and parsley for the lentils	
	½
15 minutes before Start cooking the lentils	
10 minutes before Dress the vegetables with the vinaigrette	
Just before eating Add the salmon to the lentils	
	Start of the meal
Just before dessert Sprinkle the pistachios over the white chocolate cream	
	Dessert

Roasted vegetables with olive oil

In Spain, this dish is called *escalivada*. The name comes from the Catalan verb *escalivar*, which means to cook in hot ashes. It refers to a dish of vegetables roasted with olive oil.

•

If you do not have enough juices left from roasting the vegetables to make a vinaigrette, add more sherry vinegar and olive oil.

	for 2	for 6	for 20	for 75
Large eggplants	1	3	4½ lb	16½ lb
Large red bell peppers	1	3	4½ lb	16½ lb
Olive oil	2 tbsp	⅓ cup	1¼ cups	4 cups
Salt	1 pinch	2 pinches	1 tbsp	scant ½ cup
Medium onions	2	6	4½ lb	16½ lb
For the vinaigrette:				
Sherry vinegar	1 tsp	1 tbsp	2½ tbsp	scant ½ cup
Olive oil	2 tbsp	⅓ cup	1¼ cups	4 cups
Salt	1 pinch	2 pinches	3¾ tsp	¼ cup

Start →

Preheat the oven to 400°F.

Put the eggplants and bell peppers into a roasting pan, drizzle with the oil and sprinkle with the salt.

Wrap the onions in aluminum foil and add to the pan. Roast the vegetables all together for 45 minutes.

After 45 minutes, the bell pepper skins will be blackened and the eggplants very soft. Let cool enough to handle. Save any juices that have collected in the pan.

Peel the skin from the bell peppers and remove the seeds.

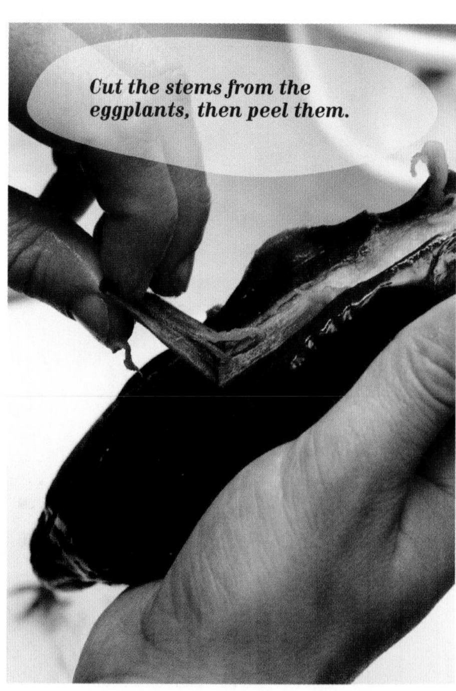

Cut the stems from the eggplants, then peel them.

Continue →

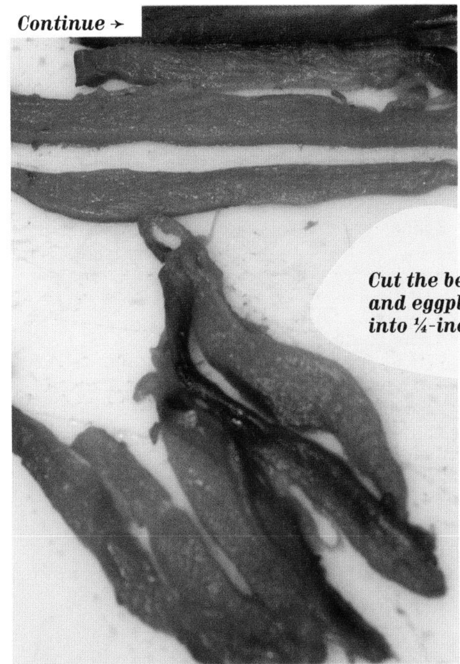
Cut the bell peppers
and eggplants
into ¼-inch strips.

Unwrap the onions, peel away
the skins, then cut the flesh
into quarters. Again, set aside
any juices released during cooking.

Arrange the vegetables
in separate piles
on a serving dish.

Make a vinaigrette by
mixing any juice from the
vegetables with the sherry
vinegar and oil.

Season
with salt.

Dress the vegetables
with the vinaigrette
and serve.

Salmon stewed with lentils

Ask your fish supplier to clean, gut, and skin the fish for you if you prefer.

•

This dish is also good with other types of oily fish, such as mackerel. To make it with shellfish, use small round clams, small razor clams, or mussels.

	for 2	for 6	for 20	for 75
Fresh salmon fillet	11 oz	2 lb	6½ lb	26½ lb
Fresh parsley	2½ sprigs	8 sprigs	1 bunch	3 bunches
Olive oil	2 tsp	2 tbsp	¼ cup	¾ cup
Sofrito (see page 43)	1 tbsp	3 tbsp	2¼ cups	7¼ cups
Fish stock (see page 56)	1¾ cups	5 cups	14¾ cups	2⅔ gallons
Canned lentils, drained	1¼ cups	4 cups	13 cups	2¾ gallons
Picada (see page 41)	2 tsp	2 tbsp	⅔ cup	1¾ cups
Salt	1 pinch	2 pinches	⅔ tsp	2 tsp

Start →

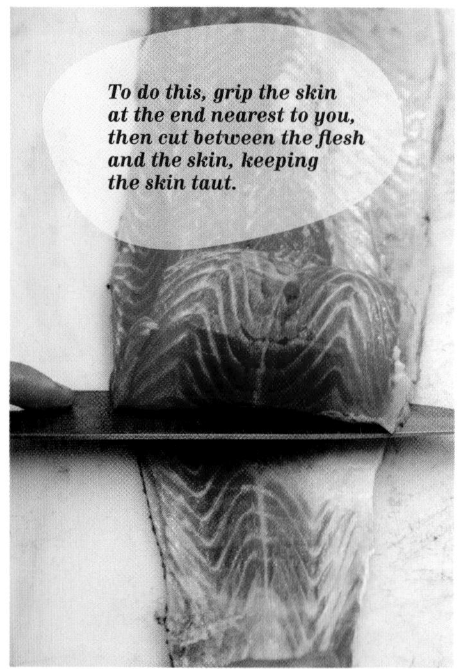

Continue →

Chop it finely.

Place a saucepan over medium heat, then pour in the oil and add the sofrito.

Cook for 1 minute.

Pour in the stock, bring to a boil, and add the lentils.

Add the picada and simmer for 10 minutes.

Season the salmon with salt and add to the pan.

After 1 minute, turn the salmon in the pan, being careful not to break it up, then season to taste with more salt if needed.

Sprinkle the chopped parsley into the pan and carefully stir in.

Serve the stew in shallow bowls.

White chocolate cream

We serve this topped with toasted pistachios, but they can be substituted with other toasted nuts, or fresh or freeze-dried raspberries or strawberries.

•

To toast the pistachios, put them in a frying pan over medium-high heat and cook for 2 minutes, stirring continuously until golden.

•

The white chocolate cream can be made the day before you want to eat it.

	for 2	for 6	for 20	for 75
White chocolate	2¾ oz	7¾ oz	1¾ lb	8 lb
Whipping cream, 35% fat	⅓ cup	1 cup	6 cups	1¼ gallons
Egg yolks	1	3	12	2 lb 3 oz
Shelled, toasted pistachios	3 tbsp	¾ tbsp	1 cup	5¼ cups

Start →

Continue →

If you have a kitchen thermometer, it will read 175°F when the mixture is ready.

Pour the hot mixture over the chocolate and let it melt for 2 minutes.

Whisk to make a smooth cream.

Ladle into bowls, then chill for 1 hour, until firm.

Sprinkle the pistachios over the top of the cream before serving.

–

Meal 30

–

Grilled lettuce hearts

–

Veal with red wine & mustard

–

Chocolate mousse

Grilled lettuce hearts

Veal with red wine & mustard

INGREDIENTS

BUY FRESH
* fresh mint
* lettuce hearts
* veal cheeks

IN THE PANTRY
* sherry vinegar
* wholegrain mustard
* olive oil
* salt
* black peppercorns
* brandy
* red wine
* sugar
* instant potato flakes
* dark chocolate, 60% cocoa
* N_2O cartridges
* caramelized hazelnuts

IN THE FRIDGE
* eggs
* whole milk
* butter
* whipping cream, 35% fat

Chocolate mousse

ORGANIZING THE MENU	Hours before the meal
	4
3½ hours before Brown and cook the veal cheeks (if using the oven method)	3½
	3
	2½
	2
	1½
1 hour before Brown and cook the veal cheeks (if using a pressure cooker)	1
Make the chocolate mousse mix and fill the siphon	½
20 minutes before Make the vinaigrette and cut the lettuce hearts	
10 minutes before Make the creamed potato	
Just before eating Cook the lettuce hearts and dress with the vinaigrette	Start of the meal
Just before main course Reduce the veal cheek sauce	Main course
Just before dessert Dispense the chocolate mousse and sprinkle with the hazelnuts	Dessert

Grilled lettuce hearts

When making the vinaigrette, it is important not to let it emulsify, so do not overwhisk it.

•

If lettuce hearts are not available, use Belgian endive instead.

	for 2	for 6	for 20	for 75
Fresh mint	8 sprigs	½ cup	⅓ bunch	1 bunch
Wholegrain mustard	1 tsp	1 tbsp	¾ cup	2¼ cups
Sherry vinegar	1 tbsp	3 tbsp	scant ½ cup	2½ cups
Egg yolks	1	3	8	25
Olive oil, plus extra for frying	⅓ cup	1 cup	3½ cups	11½ cups
Lettuce hearts, such as Boston	2	6	20	75

Start →

To make the dressing, put the mint leaves and mustard into a tall jar or pitcher.

Add the sherry vinegar.

Add the egg yolk.

Continue →

Add the oil while processing with a hand-held blender until the mint is finely chopped. Season with salt.

Cut the lettuce hearts in half lengthwise.

Heat a large frying pan over medium heat and add a little oil. Season the lettuce hearts with salt, then fry for about 5 minutes, until golden on both sides.

Cut the fried lettuce hearts in half again, then arrange 4 pieces on each serving plate.

Pour the mint vinaigrette over the lettuce just before serving.

Veal with red wine & mustard

A pressure cooker is ideal for cooking veal cheeks quickly. If you do not have one, this recipe can easily be made in the oven. Preheat the oven to 350°F. Brown the cheeks in a casserole, add the liquids, then cover and cook for 3 hours, until very tender, then finish with the mustard.

•

This dish can be made with pork cheeks or other cuts suitable for slow cooking, such as veal or beef shank.

	for 2	for 6	for 20	for 75
Veal cheeks	2	6	20	75
Olive oil	2 tsp	1½ tbsp	1 cup	2¼ cups
Brandy	3 tbsp	scant ½ cup	2¼ cups	6¼ cups
Sugar	2 tsp	1½ tbsp	scant ½ cup	1 cup
Red wine	2¼ cups	4¼ cups	12½ cups	9½ quarts
Water	4¼ cups	8½ cups	1 gallon	3 gallons
Wholegrain mustard	1 tsp	1½ tbsp	¼ cup	1 cup
Whole milk	1 cup	2¼ cups	10½ cups	2 gallons
Butter	2 tsp	5½ tsp	1 cup	3¼ cups
Instant potato granules	2½ tbsp	⅓ cup	1½ cups	4¼ cups

Start →

Continue →

Once the wine has reduced
and looks syrupy, add the water.

Add the mustard.

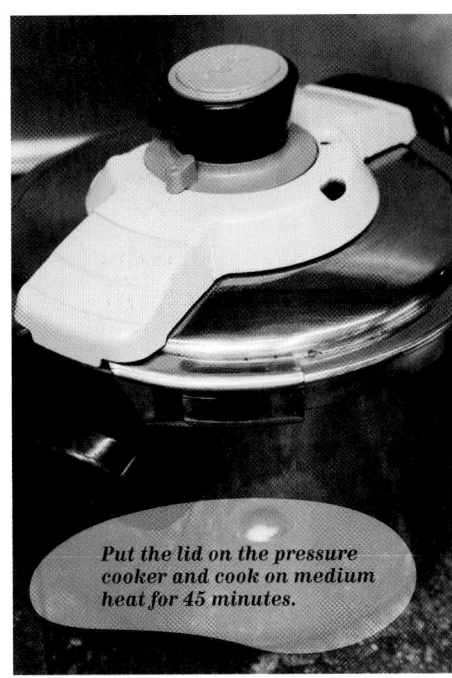
Put the lid on the pressure
cooker and cook on medium
heat for 45 minutes.

Meanwhile, make the
creamed potatoes.
Bring the milk to a boil
and add the butter.

Add the potato granules
and cook, stirring,until
thickened.

Blend to a smooth puree with
a hand-held blender or whisk.
Season with salt and pepper.

Remove the lid and simmer the
sauce until thickened and glossy.

Serve the veal cheeks whole,
covered with the wine and mustard
sauce, and with a dish of creamed
potatoes on the side.

Chocolate mousse

The minimum quantity of mousse you can make using a siphon is 6–8 portions. If you do not have a siphon, you could whisk the egg whites to stiff peaks and fold them through the chocolate mixture, although the texture will be very different.

•

Any kind of crunchy, nutty topping, such as crushed almond or peanut brittle, can be substituted for the caramelized hazelnuts.

	for 2	for 6-8	for 20	for 75
Dark chocolate, 60% cocoa	-	4½ oz	1 lb 6½ oz	5¼ lb
Whipping cream, 35% fat	-	½ cup	2½ cups	8 cups
Egg whites	-	4	2 cups	7½ cups
N_2O cartridges for the siphon	-	1	3	8
Caramelized hazelnuts	-	30	11 oz	2¼ lb

For 6–8 people, use a pint-size whipped-cream siphon. For the larger quantities use quart-sized siphons.

Start →

Finely chop the chocolate and put into a bowl.

Pour the cream into a saucepan, set over high heat, then bring to a boil.

Pour the boiling cream over the chocolate.

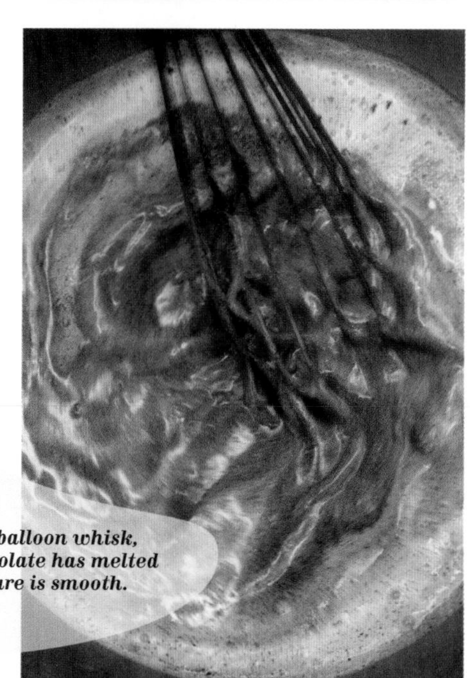

Beat, using a balloon whisk, until the chocolate has melted and the mixture is smooth.

Continue →

Set aside to cool a little.

Add the egg whites and stir
until thoroughly combined.

Pass the mixture through a
fine-meshed strainer, then pour
into the whipped-cream siphon.

Seal the top, then charge
the siphon with the cartridge.

Shake the siphon vigorously,
then set aside at room
temperature until needed.

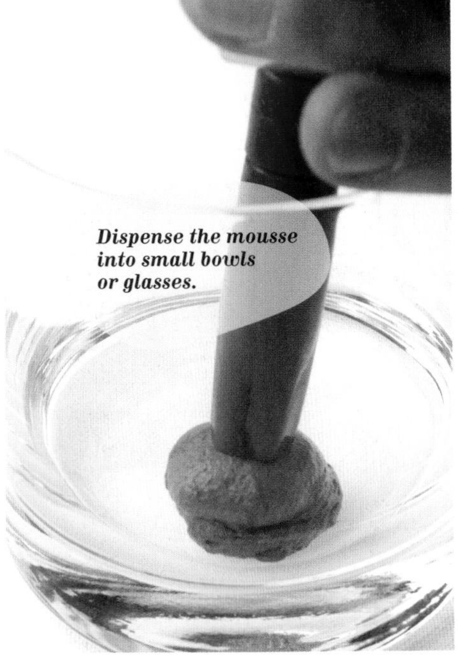
Dispense the mousse
into small bowls
or glasses.

Top with the
caramelized
hazelnuts or
your chosen
topping.

–

Meal 31

–

Waldorf salad

–

Noodle soup with mussels

–

Melon & mint soup with pink grapefruit

Waldorf salad

Noodle soup with mussels

INGREDIENTS

BUY FRESH
* celery
* lemons
* Golden Delicious apples
* small mussels
* large ripe melon, such as cantaloupe or *piel de sapo*
* pink grapefruit
* fresh mint

IN THE PANTRY
* walnut halves
* wholegrain mustard
* salt
* black peppercorns
* filini pasta
* olive oil
* white wine
* sugar

IN THE FRIDGE
* whipping cream, 35% fat
* mayonnaise

IN THE FREEZER
* fish stock (see page 56)
* sofrito (see page 43)
* picada (see page 41)

Melon & mint soup with pink grapefruit

ORGANIZING THE MENU	Hours before the meal
	4
	3½
	3
	2½
	2
	1½
1 hour before **Make the melon soup and segment and then chill the grapefruit** **Clean the mussels and return to the fridge**	1
30 minutes before **Bring the stock to a simmer** **Make the salad dressing** **Chop the celery, apple, and walnuts**	½
20 minutes before **Start cooking the pasta**	
10 minutes before **Add the sofrito, wine, stock, and picada to the pasta** **Finish preparing the salad**	
Just before eating **Add the mussels to the soup**	
	Start of the meal
Just before dessert **Put the grapefruit into bowls, then ladle over the melon soup**	
	Dessert

Waldorf salad

When making a large amount of salad, we toss the apple in ascorbic acid (vitamin C powder) to prevent the flesh from browning. You can use lemon juice to the same effect.

	for 2	for 6	for 20	for 75
Celery	2 stalks	8 stalks	2¼ lb	7¾ lb
Walnut halves	2 tbsp	⅓ cup	1 cup	7 cups
Mayonnaise	¼ cup	¾ cup	2¾ cups	9¼ cups
Wholegrain mustard	2 tsp	1½ tbsp	scant ½ cup	1⅛ cups
Whipping cream, 35% fat	1½ tbsp	¼ cup	⅔ cup	2¼ cups
Lemon juice, strained	1 tbsp	2 tbsp	⅓ cup	1 cup plus 3 tbsp
Golden Delicious apples	1	3	7	25

Start →

Trim the celery leaves, then remove the strings by peeling with a vegetable peeler.

Cut into ¼-inch slices.

Break the walnut halves in two.

For the dressing, put the mayonnaise into a bowl, then stir in the mustard.

Continue →

Stir in the cream and lemon juice, then season with salt.

Peel the apples.

Cut the apple flesh away from the core.

Cut into small cubes about ½ inch wide.

Mix the celery, apple, and walnuts in a salad bowl.

Spoon in the dressing and stir well until everything is well coated. Season the salad with salt and pepper.

Serve in small bowls.

Noodle soup with mussels

Sometimes we like to add paprika or saffron to this dish.

•

Baby clams can be used instead of mussels, and any short spaghetti-like noodles can be used instead of filini.

•

Keeping batches of fish stock, sofrito, and picada ready in the freezer makes this (and many other dishes) simple and quick to make.

	for 2	for 6	for 20	for 75
Small mussels	4 oz	12 oz	5 lb	18¾ lb
Fish stock (see page 56)	1¾ cups	5 cups	1 gallon	4¼ gallons
Olive oil	2 tsp	¼ cup	1 cup	2¾ cups
Filini pasta	6¼ oz	1 lb 3 oz	4 lb	15½ lb
Sofrito (see page 43)	¼ cup	⅔ cup	2¼ cups	7¼ cups
White wine	1½ tbsp	¼ cup	⅔ cup	2¼ cups
Picada (see page 41)	2 tsp	1½ tbsp	½ cup	1¾ cups

Start →

Continue →

Pour in the wine, loosening the sediment from the bottom of the pan.

Add the hot stock and then the picada. Boil for 10 minutes.

Drop the mussels into the soup, cover the pan, and simmer for 5 minutes.

The mussels are ready when they have opened up completely. Discard any that have stayed shut.

Remove the pan from the heat, season with salt and pepper, and serve.

Melon & mint soup with pink grapefruit

We do not recommend making a smaller quantity than that given for 6 people. Any leftover soup makes a delicious alternative to your fruit juice at breakfast the next day. Store it in the fridge overnight.

•

Cantaloupe or *piel de sapo* (toad skin) melons are good for this recipe. If the melon is ripe, the ends will yield slightly when pressed.

	for 2	for 6	for 20	for 75
Large ripe melon	-	1	3	10
Fresh mint	-	10 leaves	¼ bunch	⅔ bunch
Sugar	-	2 tbsp	¾ cup	2½ cups
Pink grapefruit	-	2	3¼ lb	11 lb

Start →

Cut the ends off the melon and slice in half.

Remove the seeds.

Slice each half into wedges, then remove the skin.

Cut each wedge into pieces.

Puree the melon with a hand-held blender or food processor to make a soup.

Continue →

Pick the mint leaves
off the stems, reserving
a few for the garnish.

Add the mint leaves,
blend until smooth, then
add the sugar and repeat.

Prepare half of the grape-
fruits by slicing off the top
and bottom and cutting off
the pith and skin.

Remove the flesh
from each segment
and set aside.

Squeeze the remaining
grapefruit.

Pour the juice
into the soup
and stir it in.

Strain the soup
through a fine
strainer.

To serve, put a few grapefruit
segments in the bottom of
each bowl, then add a few
sprigs of mint.

Pour the soup
over the grapefruit
and serve.

Glossary & Index

Glossary

ACHIOTE PASTE
A paste made from achiote (also known as annatto) seeds that come from the achiote shrub, which is common in South America.

BROWN
To pan-fry ingredients in very hot fat in order to color the surface.

BRAISE
To cook gently in a sealed pot with stock or thick sauce.

BLANCH
To cook briefly in boiling water. Usually followed by plunging straight into cold water to stop further cooking.

CARAMELIZE
To cook until golden. The point at which the natural sugars begin to turn to caramel. Often a blowtorch is used to caramelize the top of a custard.

CHANTILLY
A classic French preparation of cream whipped with sugar.

COAT
To cover a dish with a substance, such as a sauce.

CREAM
To beat eggs or butter and sugar together with a whisk or wooden spoon until they become thick and pale in color.

CRU
Denotes a procedure in which a solid substance is infused with a liquid, thus absorbing its flavor.

COUSCOUS
Tiny semolina pellets that have been rolled and coated with wheat flour.

DRAIN
To remove the liquid from a food, usually by tipping into a sieve or colander.

DRIZZLE
To pour a small amount of liquid over a surface.

EMULSIFY
To mix liquids of different densities to form a thicker liquid.

FOLD
To mix food gently from the bottom of the bowl to the top. A large metal spoon or spatula is best for this.

GREMOLATA
A chopped herb condiment made with lemon, garlic, and parsley, often served with *osso buco*.

GUT
To remove the entrails of a fish.

MARCONA ALMONDS
A sweet-flavored Spanish variety of almond.

MARINATE
To place raw meat or other foods in an aromatic liquid in order to tenderize prior to cooking, or to add extra flavor.

MISE EN PLACE
The culinary procedures and preparations that take place in a restaurant kitchen before service begins, such as preparing sauces and chopping vegetables.

N_2O CARTRIDGE
A steel cylinder that is filled with nitrous oxide. A cartridge charges the siphon.

PAELLA RICE
A short-grained, thick type of rice often used in Spain. Bomba is the best-known variety.

PLANCHADA BEANS
Long white beans typical of Spain. When cooked, they have a smooth creamy texture.

POACH
To cook gently in a liquid, such as water, stock, or milk.

PROCESS
To mix thoroughly with a blender or electric mixer.

PUREE
To reduce ingredients to a smooth paste in a food processor or blender. Also the name given to the paste itself.

QUENELLE
A small portion of food shaped with two spoons into an elongated sphere like a football.

RONER
A machine often used in professional kitchens to poach foods in liquid for long periods at a low and constant temperature.

RAS EL HANOUT
A classic spice mixture used in Moroccan cuisine. Typically includes cardamom, clove, cinnamon, peppercorn, peppers, cilantro and turmeric.

REDUCE
To boil or simmer a liquid to evaporate the water it contains, thereby concentrating the flavor and thickening it.

SALT COD
Cod that is packed in salt and dried in order to preserve it. It is said the whiter the cod, the better the quality.

SECOND STOCK
The liquid that results from reboiling the discarded meat from a stock. It can be used as the base for a new stock to intensify the flavor.

SHAOXING RICE WINE
China's best-known rice wine, made from fermented rice, millet and yeast. Available in Asian speciality shops.

SHICHIMI TOGARASHI
A mix of seven spices used in Japanese cooking and characterized by its hot flavor.

SIMMER
To cook slowly over a gentle heat, before the liquid comes to the boil.

SIPHON
Utensil designed to whip cream and which, in the mid-1990s, enabled the creation of foams at elBulli.

SKIM
To remove the frothy scum from the surface of a liquid using a ladle or large spoon.

SPRIG
A small shoot or twig from a plant or herb.

STAGE
A temporary work experience placement in a restaurant (those participating are known as "stagers").

STEAM
To cook in a perforated container set over boiling water with a tight-fitting lid.

STOCK
A flavored cooking liquid obtained by simmering beef, pork, poultry, or fish with vegetables and aromatics in water.

STRAINER
A kitchen utensil that separates food substances through a fine mesh or net, and is used for draining. Also referred to as "sieve."

THAI CURRY PASTE
A blend of herbs, chiles, and other aromatic ingredients used as a base for Thai curries, and available in three colors: red, green, and yellow.

THICKEN
To add ingredients, such as egg yolks or flour, to make a sauce or soup thicker.

TRIM
To remove all of the inedible or blemished parts from food.

VACUUM PACK
A method of packaging or storing food in an airless environment. Often used in professional kitchens.

VINO RANCIO
A Spanish fortified wine similar in flavor to sherry.

VIOLIN
The elBulli term for large oval platters upon which the family meals are served.

WHISK
To beat rapidly with a flexible tool to increase the volume and aerate the ingredients.

ZEST
The thin outer layer of a citrus fruit, on top of the white pith. Usually grated.

Index

Underlined page numbers refer to the recipe instructions.

H

I

J

K

L

M

N

O

P

Q

R

S

T

Recipe notes

All herbs are fresh, unless otherwise specified.

Parsley is fresh flat-leaf parsley.

All flour is white all-purpose flour, unless otherwise specified.

All sugar is white superfine sugar, unless otherwise specified.

Eggs are large size, butter is sweet (unsalted), and milk is whole, unless otherwise specified.

Cooking times and temperatures are for guidance only, as individual ovens vary. If using a fan oven, follow the manufacturer's instructions to adjust the oven temperatures as necessary.

Exercise caution when following recipes involving any potentially hazardous activity, including the use of high temperatures, open flames and when deep frying. In particular, when deep frying, add food carefully to avoid splashing, wear long sleeves and never leave the pan unattended.

Some recipes include raw or very lightly cooked eggs, fish or meat. These should be avoided by the elderly, infants, pregnant women, convalescents and anyone with an impaired immune system.

All spoon measurements are level unless otherwise stated. Australian standard tablespoons are 20 ml. Australian readers are advised to use 3 teaspoons in place of 1 tablespoon when measuring small quantities. 1 teaspoon = 5 ml, 1 tablespoon = 15 ml.

Phaidon Press Inc
180 Varick Street
New York, NY 10014

www.phaidon.com

ISBN: 9 780 7148 6253 8
(US edition)

A CIP catalogue for this book is available from the British Library.

Commissioning Editor: Emilia Terragni
Project Editors: Meredith Erickson and Laura Gladwin
Production Controller: Marina Asenjo

Designed by Julia Hasting
Photography by Francesc Guillamet and Maribel Ruiz de Erenchun

Printed in Italy

The Publisher would like to thank Ferran Adrià for his commitment and enthusiasm; Marc Cuspinera, Josep Maria Pinto and the entire staff at elBulli for all their hard work and assistance; and Hans Stofregen and Sophie Hodgkin for their contributions to the book.